an introduction to
OLÒ IRISh

Mediaeval Studies
The Annmary Brown Memorial
Box 1905
Brown University
Providence, RI   02912

an introduction to
OLD IRISH

R.P.M. & W.P. Lehmann

© 1975 by The Modern Language Association of America

Library of Congress Catalog Card No. 74-31960
ISBN 0-87352-288-5
Published by The Modern Language Association of America
10 Astor Place, New York, New York 10003

Paperback printing 1991

Designed by Scott Chelius

To Louis L. Hammerich

PREfACE

This handbook was produced with the aim of providing students with an introduction to Old Irish literature as well as to the language. One of the notable Old Irish stories is used as the basic text. Examples of poems, and of the glosses, supplement it. All are thoroughly annotated. The grammatical information provided in these annotations is summarized in grammatical sections dealing with specific constructions and forms. The first fifty of these sections are descriptive; many of the same matters are discussed in the second fifty sections from a historical point of view. A final glossary includes references to all words occurring in the texts. The apparatus was accordingly designed to permit a relatively easy approach to a very difficult language.

The language is difficult in part because of its syntactic structure. Students accustomed to the principal languages of modern Europe, or to the Classical languages, are unprepared for the constructions of a language in which the verb is the initial element in the clause. To meet this problem, syntax is discussed from the first, in accordance with the findings of contemporary linguistics. Morphological problems are also treated, as in handbooks of the past. This book contains an introduction to Old Irish phonology, with transcriptions of the initial texts so that students may learn to pronounce Old Irish.

An introductory handbook can only point the way toward mastery of a language and the literature surviving in it. We have tried to direct students toward skills which are essential for such mastery, by providing comments on the culture that produced Old Irish literature, by providing an introduction to paleography with facsimiles of manuscripts and comments on them, by giving notes on metrics, and the like. The included bibliographical information points out means of access to a more thorough control of the tools needed to understand the language, the literature, and the culture in which this remarkable literature flourished.

The handbook has been used in preliminary form in R. P. M. Lehmann's Old Irish course at the University of Texas. It has benefited from comments by David

Clement, Charles Dunn, William H. Heist, and Robert M. Lumiansky. Moreover, we would like to give special credit to James McCloskey for suggestions on the textual analyses and the grammatical sections, and for his careful production of the final glossary. Besides expressing our deep gratitude to these scholars, we would also like to thank the Departments of English and Linguistics, and the Linguistics Research Center at the University of Texas for the assistance necessary in the preparation of such a handbook. We are also grateful to the Dublin Institute for Advanced Studies for permission to use the Thurneysen text of the *Scéla Mucce Meic Dathó*, to the Irish Academy for providing and authorizing publication of the facsimiles, and to David Greene for permitting use of his texts of some of the included poems. We would also like to thank the American Council of Learned Societies and the National Science Foundation for grants which supported some of the work underlying this handbook.

We also express our appreciation to the Committee on Research Activities of the Modern Language Association for sponsoring this handbook, the first in a projected series. The series aims to produce handbooks that will provide ready access to important languages and literatures of the past. Preparation of this handbook has required a great deal of work. This work will best be repaid if further handbooks are prepared which will provide ready access to the important languages and literatures that lie at the basis of our own language, literature, and culture.

R. P. M. Lehmann / W. P. Lehmann
The University of Texas at Austin

contents

CONTENTS

CHAPTER III
SECTION 2

CHAPTER IV
SECTION 3a

CHAPTER V
SECTION 3b

CHAPTER VI
SECTION 4

CONTENTS

CONTENTS

CONTENTS

CONTENTS

LYRIC POEMS

CHAPTER XIX

CHAPTER XX

ABBREVIATIONS

abs.	absolute	G.	Grammar
acc./A	accusative	gem.	geminates
act.	active	gen./G	genitive
adj.	adjective	ger.	gerund
adv.	adverb	Gl.	Gloss
affirm.	affirmative	impers.	impersonal
art.	article	impf.	imperfect
attrib.	attributive	impv.	imperative
bf.	before	ind.	indicative
comp.	comparative	indecl.	indeclinable
	(forms of adj. and	indef.	indefinite
	adv.)	inf.	infinitive
compd.	compound	inst.	instrumental
condit.	conditional	interj.	interjection
conj.	conjunct	interrog.	interrogative
cons.	construct	intrans.	intransitive
cop.	copula	len.	lenites
dat./D	dative	lit.	literally
def.	definite	LL	Book of Leinster
dem.	demonstrative	m.	masculine (gen-
deut.	deuterotonic		der)
dim.	diminutive	Ml.	Milan
du.	dual	MS	manuscript
emph.	emphatic	MSS	manuscripts
esp.	especially	neg.	negative
f.	feminine (gender)	nom./N	nominative
fr.	from	nonpalat.	nonpalatal
fut.	future	NP	noun phrase

ABBREVIATIONS

nt.	neuter (gender)	vb.	verb
num.	numeral, number	vn.	verbal noun
obj.	object	voc./V	vocative
orig.	originally	VSO	Verb-Subject-Object
P.	Poem		
palat.	palatal	w.	with
pass.	passive	Wb.	Würzburg
perf.	perfective, perfect	1	first (person)
pers.	personal	2	second (person)
pl.	plural	3	third (person)
poss.	possessive		
pp.	past participle	*for languages:*	
pred.	predicate	Eng.	English
prep.	preposition	Fr.	French
pres.	present	Gk.	Greek
pret.	preterite	Goth.	Gothic
pron.	pronoun	IE	Indo-European
proto.	prototonic	Lat.	Latin
ptc.	particle	Lith.	Lithuanian
refl.	reflexive	MIr.	Middle Irish
rel.	relative	NIr.	New Irish
sent.	sentence	OCS	Old Church Slavic
SG.	Saint Gall	OE	Old English
sg.	singular	OHG	Old High German
SMMD	*Scéla Mucce Meic Dathó*	OIr.	Old Irish
		PIE	Proto-Indo-European
sub.	subject		
subj.	subjunctive	Skt.	Sanskrit
subst.	substantive	Sp.	Spanish

sYMBOLS

·   dot before a letter indicates that stress falls on the following syllable

˙   dot over a letter indicates lenition (see II.G.10)

´   long vowels are so marked in the manuscript

‾   long vowels with superposed macron are so indicated by editors; in the glossary the acute is commonly used

˘   over letters in transcriptions indicates palatalized variants (see IV. G.20); capital letters in transcriptions indicate unlenited elements

l   raised *l* after a word means the element lenites the following phoneme (see II.G.10)

n   raised *n* after a letter means the element nasalizes the following element (see III.G.15)

g   raised *g* after a word means the element geminates the following element (see v. G.25)

*   indicates a nonattested, usually a reconstructed form

SCÉLA MUCCE
MEIC ÓATHÓ

THE STORY OF MAC ÓATHÓ'S PIG

chapter I

READING AND TEXTUAL ANALYSIS, Section 1a

In this chapter and the following chapters through XVIII a complete Old Irish story will be given, the *Scéla Mucce Meic Dathó* (SMMD). This story dates from the Irish heroic age, which may have been around the beginning of our era. The account of the feast with its boasts and ordeals is similar to Latin descriptions of life among the Gauls; an excerpt from one of these descriptions is given in XII.G.56 (Ch. XII, Grammar 56; all further grammar references follow this form). The style is simple. The story includes only the incidents central to the feast and its quarrels, omitting details to the point that essential features of the heroic culture are obscure, such as the hall in which the feasts were held. The keepers of a *Bruiden* or hostel often seem to be magical persons (*Dá Derga*). The *dá* may be from *Día* 'a god.' *Dá Derga* seems to be the otherworld, perhaps the land of the dead. As noted in the final glossary, place names in Ireland today reflect the legendary *Bruidens* with the element *-breen*. The Old Irish stories accordingly illustrate the Celtic imagination with their combination of the mythical and the real.

Each word is glossed in the final glossary. But to provide an introduction to Old Irish prose texts, an analysis of each sentence and its words will also be presented for this and the next four lessons.

1. Boí rí amrae for Laignib, Mac Dathó a ainm.
2. Boí cú occo.
3. Im·díched in cú Laigniu huili.
4. Ailbe ainm in chon, ocus ba lán Hériu dia airdircus in chon.
5. Do·eth ō Ailill ocus ō Meidb do chungid in chon.
6. Immalle dano tāncatar ocus techta Ulad ocus Conchobair do chungid in chon chētna.
7. Ro·ferad fāilte friu huili, ocus ructha cuci-sium isin mbrudin.

Phonetic transcription

1. boí Ří awræ for lajñiv, mac daθó a aiňm̃.
2. boí kú ogo.

3

3. im·díxeð iN kú lajňu uĺi.
4. aiĺve aiňm̌ iN xon, ogus ba lán éřu ǧia aiřdircus iN xon.
5. do·eθ ó ailiĹ ogus ó veiðv do xuŋiǧ iN xon.
6. ima·Ĺe da·no táŋgadar ogus ťexta ulað ogus konxowař do xuŋiǧ iN xon x̌édna.
7. ro·ferað fáiĹťe fřu uĺi, ogus rugθa kuǧišuṽ išiN mruðiň.

---

1. boí   3 sg. pret. of the substantive vb. '(there) was'
   rí   m. nom. 'king'
   amrae   m. nom. adj. 'famous'
   for   prep. w. dat. and acc. 'over, above, on'
   Laignib   dat. pl. of *Lagin* (pl.) '(men of) Leinster'; raised dots have been added to the text to indicate lenition; see II.G.10; this is the practice of later MSS; earlier only *s* and *f* were so indicated
   Mac   m. nom. 'son'
   Dathó   proper name; said to be from *Dá* 'num. 2' and *Thó* 'deaf (ones)'; but see also the final glossary
   a   poss. pron. m. and nt. 'his, its'
   ainm   nt. nom. 'name'
2. boí   see sent. 1
   cú   m. nom. 'hound' (may also be feminine)
   occo   prep. *oc* 'at, by' followed by dat. of pers. pron. 'him'—normal idiom for indicating possession; here 'in the possession of him' = Eng. 'he had'
3. im·diched   *im-* 'about' followed by pret. 3 sg. of *téit* 'goes' = 'he went about'; now thought to be impf. of *im·dích (imm·di·fich)* 'protects'
   in(cú)   def. art. 'the'; nom. of *cú*
   Laigriu   acc. pl. 'Leinster'
   h-uili   acc. pl. of *uile* 'all' (*h-* is merely graphic and has no phonetic value)
4. Ailbe   proper name
   ainm   nom. as in sent. 1; note lack of cop.
   in chon   gen. sg. of *cú* 'dog'; lenited form of *c* after gen. sg. m. of def. art. *in*
   ocus   'and'
   ba   3 sg. pret. conj. 'is'; conj. is defined in I.G.4
   lán   nom. sg. 'full'
   Hériu   f. *Ériu* 'Ireland' (*H* is merely graphic)
   dia   prep. *di* 'of, from' plus poss. pron. 3 sg. 'his' anticipates the following genitival phrase *in chon*—an extremely common construction
   airdircus   m. dat. sg. 'fame'
   (in chon)   gen. sg. of *cú* w. def. art.
5. do·eth   3 sg. pret. pass. of *do·tét* 'comes'; impers. = 'there (was) a coming'
   ō   prep. w. dat. 'from'
   Ailill   dat. sg. proper name; king of Connaught, husband of Medb
   (ocus ō) Meidb   dat. sg.
   do   prep. w. dat. 'to'; construction comparable w. Eng. inf.
   chungid   vn. dat. sg. of *con·daig* 'asks'; lenition of *cungid* by prep. *do* = 'seeking'; lenition is discussed in II.G.10
   in chon   gen. sg. (regular case for the obj. of a vn.)

4

6. immalle   'at the same time' (a prepositional phrase; the stress is on the final syllable)
   dano   'then, indeed' (stress on the final syllable)
   táncatar   3 pl. pret. of *do·icc* 'comes' = 'they came'
   (ocus) techta   nom. pl. 'messengers'
   Ulad   gen. of *Ulaid* 'Ulstermen, Ulster'
   (ocus) Conchobair   gen. of *Conchobor,* king of Ulster
   do chungid in chon   see sent. 5
   chētna   gen. sg. m. of *cétna* 'same'; lenition of *chon* by the gen. sg. art. and of *chētna*
      by the gen. sg. *chon*
7. ro·ferad   3 sg. pret. pass. of *feraid*; basic meaning is 'pours' but regularly used w. *fáilte* in
      the sense 'was made'; *ro-* is a prefix marking perf. aspect
   fáilte   nom. sg. f. 'welcome'; an abstract noun from the adj. *faillid* 'happy'
   friu   prep. *fri* w. acc. 'opposite, to, with' accompanied by 3 pl. pers. pron. = 'to them'
   huili   acc. pl. 'all'
   (ocus) ructha   3 pl. pret. pass. of *berid* 'bears' = 'were taken'
   cuci-sium   *co*^g prep. w. acc. 'to, till' plus 3 sg. pers. pron. 'to him,' followed by emph.
      sium
   isin   prep. *i* w. art., acc. 'in, into (the)'
   mbrudin   f. acc. 'banquet hall, hostel'; *m-* after *isin* by nasalization. Nasalization is dis-
      cussed briefly in I.G.5.3 and more fully in III.G.15

TRANSLATION

(1) There was a famous king of the Leinstermen; Mac Dathó [was] his name.
(2) He had a hound.   (3) The hound protected all Leinster.   (4) Ailbe
[was the] name of the hound, and Ireland was full of the fame of the hound.
(5) There was a coming from Ailill and from Medb to ask for the hound.
(6) At the same time messengers also came from Ulster (lit. the Ulstermen) and
Conchobar to ask for the same hound.   (7) A welcome was prepared for all
of them, and they were taken to him into the hostel.

GRAMMAR

1. Characteristic features of a Verb-Subject-Object language

Verb-initial position.   In Old Irish, verbs stand initially in sentences, preceding
subjects and objects. Moreover, nominal as well as verbal predicates stand initially. This sentence order, often labeled VSO for Verb-Subject-Object, brings about
characteristic features of syntax and morphology, and apparently also phonology. These features have nothing to do with genealogical relationship, but rather
are determined in accordance with language type. Arabic, Classical Hebrew, and
many other languages belong to the VSO type. Some scholars have proposed
that the Insular Celtic languages adopted the VSO order from peoples who inhabited Britain before the invasion by the Celts; some have even suggested that
these peoples spoke an Afro-Asiatic language—in the former terminology, a
Hamito-Semitic language. However interesting such views may be, they are pure-
ly speculative, in view of the current state of information on the language and

ethnological characteristics of the predecessors of the Celts in Britain. Our chief concern—the understanding of the structure of Old Irish—can be assisted by an understanding of characteristics of VSO languages.

The third sentence of the text is an example of a simple sentence of the VSO type:

> Im·dīched in cú Laigniu huili
> defended the dog Leinster entire
> 'The dog defended all Leinster.'

The subject *cú* follows the verb *im·dīched* and in turn is followed by the object *Laigniu*. Other sentences containing verbs, such as the first two, also have the verb in initial position, i.e., *boí*. Nominal sentences, such as the fourth, will be discussed in a subsequent chapter, but they too have the predicate in initial position as is *Ailbe* in this sentence.

2. Nominal modifiers: relatives, adjectives, genitives

In VSO languages descriptive nominal modifiers are placed after the noun they modify. Such modifiers are relative constructions, descriptive adjectives, and genitives. The position of these three groups of modifiers can be understood from a generative point of view.

2.1. Relative constructions. From a generative view relative clauses are derived from sentences which are embedded in other sentences having an equivalent noun phrase (NP). After such embedding one of the NP's is deleted, often to be replaced by a relative marker. The relative marker is by no means necessary, as in English sentences in which the second NP is the object in its clause, e.g.,

> That was the dog [which] they wanted.

Although the relative construction was poorly developed in Old Irish, when it is found, relative markers are normally omitted, as in other VSO languages. The relative clause then directly follows its antecedent, as in the following example from II.1b.8 (Ch. II, Sec. 1b, sent. 8; all references to SMMD will follow this form):

> bruden ro·boī i nHērinn
> hostels it was in Erin
> 'hostels which were in Erin'

Old Irish has a special form of the relative verb in the present tense; it will be dealt with below, as in x.G.46. For other references see index.

2.2. Descriptive adjectives can be viewed as reduced forms of relative clauses in which the verb was the copula, as in the following derivation:

> They wanted the dog. The dog is inexpensive to groom.
> They wanted the dog which is inexpensive to groom.
> They wanted the dog inexpensive to groom.

6

In VSO languages all descriptive adjectives, not only those accompanied by a complement, regularly follow their antecedent, as in the following example from the sentence cited above: *Laigniu huili* 'Leinster entire' = 'all Leinster.'

2.3. Descriptive genitives are derived in the same way as are descriptive adjectives, and accordingly they follow the same order, as in the following derivation:

> They wanted the dog. It was the dog of their neighbor.
> They wanted the dog which was of their neighbor.
> They wanted the dog of their neighbor.

All genitives in VSO languages like Old Irish follow their nouns, as in II.1b.8 *bruden Da-Derg* 'hall of Da-derga' and I.1a.4 *ainm in chon* 'name of the dog.' (Different MSS read *Daderg* and *Daderga*.)

2.4. Marked constructions. The strict word order of Old Irish sentences assists greatly in their interpretation. We must note, however, that order may be used in language in characteristically deviant ways, for special effect. For example, in English, objects when emphasized may be placed at the beginning of a sentence, as in:

> That we took care of yesterday.

Such patterns are known as *marked*. Like English, Old Irish also departs from its normal order to convey special meanings, such as emphasis. We will discuss marked patterns subsequently.

3. Noun inflection: *o*-stem nouns

Like nouns in other Indo-European languages, Old Irish nouns are inflected for case, gender, and number. Grammars identify nominal classes by the stem-vowel nouns had in Proto-Indo-European. This stem-vowel has been lost, with only residual traces, in Old Irish; but to provide comparability with the standard scholarly grammars, the traditional designations will be used here.

Old Irish has five cases in the singular and plural: nominative, vocative, accusative, genitive, and dative; in the dual one form is used for the nominative and accusative, another for the genitive, another for the dative. It has three genders: masculine, feminine, and neuter. Masculine and neuter nouns may be inflected as *o*-stems. Examples of *o*-stem masculines are *fer* 'man' and *mac* 'son,' of an *o*-stem neuter, *scél* 'story.' In the first ten chapters the Old Irish forms will be given; in the second ten chapters accounts of their earlier shapes and origins will be given.

		M.	M.	Nt.
Sg.	N	fer	mac(c)	scél
	V	a fir	a mhic	
	A	fer	mac	scél
	G	fir	mic	scéuil
	D	fiur	macc	scéul

Pl.	N	fir	mic	scél scéla
	V	firu	maccu	
	A	firu	maccu	scél scéla
	G	fer	mac	scél
	D	fer(a)ib	mac(a)ib	scél(a)ib
Du.	NAG	fer	mac	scél
	D	fer(a)ib	mac(a)ib	scél(a)ib

4. Verb inflection: present indicative, absolute and conjunct of *berid*

Old Irish verbs are inflected for three persons in the singular and plural; in addition, the present has relative forms, as noted in I.G.2. Moreover, the Irish verb has a set of forms used alone and another set used after prefixes. The second set differs considerably from the first, which is called the absolute; the second is called the conjunct. The following are the forms of *berid* 'he bears'; the raised dot indicating an unstressed particle precedes.

		Absolute	Conjunct
Sg.	1	biru	·biur
	2	biri	·bir
	3	berid -ith	·beir
	rel.	beres(s)	
Pl.	1	berm(a)i	·beram
	rel.	berm(a)e	
	2	beirthe	·berid -ith
	3	ber(a)it	·berat
	rel.	berd(a)e bert(a)e	

5. Phonological system of Old Irish

The orthographic system for Old Irish was based on the Latin alphabet, which was poor in symbols for fricatives. This alphabet was adopted in a prehistoric period, and the characteristics of the phonological system have been determined largely by inferences based on Modern Irish. The usual value of symbols is indicated in the table below; orthographic representations are given in angled brackets. The symbols ⟨p t c⟩, single or doubled, were used to indicate voiceless and voiced stops [p t k b d g]. Followed by ⟨h⟩, they indicated voiceless fricatives. The voiced fricatives were indicated by ⟨b d g⟩. The symbol ⟨m⟩ was used both for the labial nasal and for the voiced nasalized fricatives [ṽ] [w̃]. Further information on the pronunciation of Old Irish will be given in subsequent lessons; the pronunciation may also be determined from the broad phonetic transcription of the text in this lesson. Note that initially ⟨b d g⟩ represent voiced stops unless preceded by a leniting element.

As marked in the transcribed text, consonants may be palatal or nonpalatal, that is, neutral or velar; palatals are marked with ˘ in the transcription. (See also I.G.5.3; ⟨e⟩ may indicate a preceding palatal and a following nonpalatal.)

8

Capital *N L R* indicate they are unlenited, that is, are much like English [n l r].

5.1. The system of Old Irish consonants.

		Labial			Dental		Palato-velar	
Stops	Voiceless	p			t		k ⟨c⟩	
	Voiced	b ⟨p⟩			d ⟨t⟩		g ⟨c⟩	
Fricatives	Voiceless	f ⟨ph⟩			θ ⟨th⟩	s	χ ⟨ch⟩	
	Voiced	v ⟨b⟩			ð ⟨d⟩		γ ⟨g⟩	
Nasals		m	ṽ	w̃	n		ŋ ⟨n⟩	
Liquids					r	l		
							h ⟨sh⟩	

/p/ occurred only in borrowings. The symbol ⟨h⟩ often indicated a hiatus, though [h] was a morphophonemic variant of /s/ and was prefixed to vowels (see v.G.25).

5.2. The system of Old Irish vowels. The Old Irish vowel system consisted of five vowels, short and long, and of eight diphthongs. To distinguish diphthongs ending in [i] from sequences of long vowels followed by the symbol ⟨i⟩ indicating palatalization, the three diphthongs ending in [i] are marked with an acute accent on the ⟨i⟩; in other diphthongs, the first element is marked with an acute accent.

Short vowels			Long vowels		Diphthongs			
i		u	í	ú	íu	ía		úa uí
	e	o	é	ó	éu (éo)		oí (óe)	
	a			á		áu	aí (áe)	

5.3. Sandhi variation. The consonants undergo various kinds of modification depending on their context; such modifications are known as sandhi variations, often based on the influence of phonological elements in earlier forms of the language. Thus nasalization of following elements is brought about by the numeral adjectives *secht* '7,' *ocht* '8,' *noí* '9,' *deich* '10,' which formerly ended in nasals, as may be illustrated by the Latin cognates *septem, novem, decem,* and assumed for '8.' Because of such modifications, some lexical elements may be listed in approximations of underlying forms, such as *secht[n]* or *secht n* and so on.

The three types of modification have been given special names in Irish grammar: lenition, also called aspiration; nasalization, also called eclipsis; palatalization, resulting in slender (palatal) or broad (neutral or velar) variants of the phonemes. These and the phenomenon labeled gemination will be discussed in subsequent chapters. For the present it may be noted that consonants are assumed to have palatal and neutral or velar variants: palatal variants in the neighborhood of long and short *i* and *e*, velar variants in the neighborhood of *u* and *o*, neutral variants in the neighborhood of *a*. These variants may be indicated by vowel symbols, but are not indicated in the consonants themselves, e.g., *feraib*

9

or, rarely, *ferib.* Because of the uses of vowel symbols both for vowel phonemes and for allophonic variants of phonemes, Old Irish presents great difficulties in interpreting the actual spellings.

5.4. Accentuation. Simple words have a strong stress accent on the first syllable, for example, substantives and verbs in absolute form. Compound verb forms have the accent on the element after the first preverb, whether this is the verbal element as in *im·dīched* or a further preverb as in *as·in-gaib* 'exceeds.' Articles, many pronouns, and prepositions are proclitic or enclitic. Details will be discussed in subsequent chapters.

chapter II

READING AND TEXTUAL ANALYSIS, Section 1b

The *Scéla Mucce Meic Dathó* has been excellently edited by Rudolf Thurneysen; like many other editions of Old Irish texts his is included in the Mediaeval and Modern Irish Series of the Dublin Institute for Advanced Studies. Thurneysen's edition was first published in 1951 and subsequently reprinted. His text is followed throughout including the numbering of the sections.

This selection is the concluding part of Section 1. It narrates the reception of the guests invited by Mac Dathó.

8. Is ⟨s⟩í sin in chōiceḋ bruḋen ro·ḃoī i nHērinn isind aimsir sin, ocus bruḋen Da-Ḋerg i crích Ċūalann ocus bruḋen Forgaill Manaich ocus bruḋen Me[i]c Da-Rēo i mBrēfni ocus bruḋen Da-Choca i n-īarthur Miḋi.

9. Secht ndoruis isin bruiḋin ocus secht sliḡeda trethe ocus secht tellaiḡe indi ocus secht cori.

10. Daṁ ocus tinne in cach ċoiri.

11. In fer no·t⟨h⟩ēḡeḋ iarsint ṡliḡi do·bereḋ in n-aēl isin ċoiri, ocus a·taibreḋ din chētgabāil, iss eḋ no·itheḋ.

12. Mani·tucaḋ immurḡu ní din chéttaḋall ni·bered a n-aill.

Phonetic transcription

8. iš ší šiñ iN xóḡeḋ wruḋen ro·woí i néřiŇ išiNd aṁšiř šiŇ, ogus wruḋen dá·ḋerᵊg igríx xúalaN ogus wruḋen forɣaL̄ wanax ogus wruḋen ṁek ða réo i mrevñi ogus wruḋen dá·xoga i níarᵗur v̄iḋi.

9. šext noruš išiN wruḋiñ ogus šext šlijeða ťřeθe ogus šext deLaje iNdi ogus šext goři.

10. daw̄ ogus tiŇe iŋ gax xoři.

11. In fer no·θéjeḋ iaršint hliji do·beřeḋ iN n-aél išiN xoři, ogus a·daivřeḋ ḋiñ xéd gawál̄, iš eḋ no·iθeḋ.

12. mañi·tugað i·murɣu ñí ðin xéddaðaL ñi·veřeð a·naĽ. *Also* ñi·beřeð
    (if no leniting infix anticipating obj.).

---

 8. is   cop., 3 sg. '(it) is'
    ⟨s⟩í   dem. pron. f. 'she, it'; the angled brackets indicate that s is not in the MSS
    sin   dem. 'aforementioned, that'
    in   art., nom. f., followed by lenition
    chōiced   lenited form of *cōiced* nom. f. 'fifth,' meaning here 'one of the five'
    bruden   nom. f.; see I.1a.7
    ro·boí   3 sg. pret. of *-tá, atá* 'was'; in rel. use
    i   prep. w. dat. and acc. 'in'; adds *n* before following vowel by nasalization, and *m* be-
         fore labial consonants; see *(i)mBrēfni*
    nHērinn   dat. sg. f. of *Hériu* 'Ireland'
    isind   prep. *i*, plus art.; also *isin*, as in I.1a.7
    aimsir   dat. sg. f. of *aimser* 'time'
    sin   'that'
    (ocus bruden) Da-Derg   gen. sg. = Bohernabreena, County Dublin
    (i) crích   dat. sg. f. 'district; boundary'
    Cūalann   gen. sg. of *Cúalu*, a district of Wicklow
    (ocus bruden) Forgaill   gen. sg. of *Forgall*, County Dublin
    Manaich   gen. sg. of *Manach*
    (ocus bruden) Me[i]c   gen. sg. of *mac* 'son'
    Da-Rēo   master of a hostel
    (i) mBrēfni   dat. sg. of *Brēfne*, a district in the northwest
    (ocus bruden) Da-Choca   gen. sg. of *Da-Choca*
    (i) n-ỉarthur   dat. sg. nt. of *ỉarthar* 'western part'
    Midi   gen. sg. of *Mide* 'County Meath'
 9. secht   'seven'; note following *n*
    ndoruis   nom. pl. m. of *dorus* 'door'; a late form; in Classical OIr. *dorus* was a nt. *u*-
         stem, w. nom. pl. *doirsea*
    isin bruidin   see I.1a.7; dat. sg. f. of *bruden*
    (ocus secht) sligeda   nom. pl. f. of *slige* 'road, way'; another late form; Classical OIr.
         nom. pl. was *sligi*
    trethe   prep. *tri, tre* 'through,' w. 3 sg. f. pers. pron. 'she, it'
    (ocus secht) tellaige   nom. pl. nt. 'hearth' (*t* pronounced [d]; see transcription; nasal-
         ized by *secht*; see III.G.15)
    indi   prep. *i* 'in,' w. 3 sg. f. pers. pron. 'she, it'
    (ocus secht) cori   nom. pl. f. of *core, coire* 'cauldron'
10. dam   nom. sg. m. 'ox, cattle'
    (ocus) tinne   nom. sg. m. 'pork, salted or bacon'
    in   prep. w. dat. (usually *i*, but before *cach* often *in*)
    cach (coiri)   dat. sg. f. of *cach, cech* 'each'
11. in (fer)   def. art. used in sense of 'every'
    no·t(h)ēged   impf. 3 sg. rel. of *téit, -tét* 'goes (to, off)'; lenition (here indicated by ⟨h⟩);
         no- a prefixed ptc. to indicate rel. use
    iarsint   prep. *iar* 'along, according to, after' w. dat. sg. art.; *-t* present because of the
         following *s-*

s̄ligi   dat. sg. f. of *slige*; lenition of *s* (= [h]) and of *f* (silent) are indicated by superposed dot (˙) 'road, way'

do·bered   impf. 3 sg. of *do·beir* 'puts, gives, takes, brings'

(in) n-aēl   acc. sg. m. of *aēl* 'flesh-fork'

(isin) coiri   dat. sg. f. of *core, coiri*

(ocus) a·taibred   impf. subj. 3 sg. of *do·bered* prefixed by a^n 'all that, whatever' nom.
  sg. nt. of art.; see Thurneysen G.298 (Rudolph Thurneysen, *A Grammar of Old Irish*,
  Dublin: Institute for Advanced Studies, 1946, p. 298; all further references follow
  this form)

din   prep. *di* w. dat. 'from, of, off,' w. art.

chētgabāil   dat. sg. f. of vn. of *gaibid* 'takes, seizes, obtains' prefixed by *cēt-* 'first'

iss   cop. 3 sg.

ed   'it'

no·ithed   impf. 3 sg. of *ithid* 'eats'

12. mani·tucad   impf. 3 sg. of *do·uc(c)*, a suppletive stem of *do·beir* 'gets, takes, brings,
  gives, puts'; w. prefixed *ma, mā* 'if' and neg. *ni, nī* 'not'

immurgu   'however, but' (written *im̃* in the MSS)

nī   nt. of *nech* 'thing, person'

din   prep. *di* 'from, of, off,' w. sg. art.

chēttadall   *tadall* vn. dat. sg. nt. of *do·aidlea* 'attempts, visits, hits,' w. prefix *cēt-* 'first'

ni·bered   3 sg. impf. of *berid* 'obtains, bears,' w. neg.

a   nt. of *in* 'the'

n-aill   nt. of *aile* 'second, other'

TRANSLATION

(8) That is one of the five hostels which were in Ireland at that time—as well
as the hostel of Da Derga in the district of Cualu, and the hostel of Forgall Manach, and the hostel of Mac DaReo in Brefne, and the hostel of Da Choca in the
western part of Meath.   (9) [There are] seven doors in the hostel, and seven
ways through it, and seven hearths, and seven cauldrons.   (10) There was an
ox and salted pork in each cauldron.   (11) Each man who came along the way
would plunge the flesh-fork into the cauldron; and whatever he got at his first
plunging, it was this he ate.   (12) If he did not get anything, however, in his
first attempt, he did not obtain a second.

GRAMMAR

6. Verbal nouns

In VSO languages, complements must follow finite verbs. This requirement has
led to the widespread use of verbal nouns. Since verbal nouns are treated syntactically as nouns, generally their objects are in the genitive. In I.1a.5 the verbal
noun of *con·daig* has an object in the genitive case, *in chon.* As a noun, *cungid*
is itself governed by the preposition *do* and is in the dative. The entire phrase
might be translated 'for seeking of the hound,' though it corresponds to an English infinitive complement: 'to seek the hound.'

Such gerund constructions are frequent in Irish English. It has also been proposed that the English gerund in *-ing* developed as a result of Insular Celtic influence. The present participle is used primarily as an adjective, for example, in German.

6.1. Verbal nouns may also be without objects, as in II.1b.11 and 12.

> din chētgabāil 'at the first taking (try)'
> din chēttadall 'at the first attempt(ing)'

6.2. When verbal nouns are governed by the preposition *do*, the subject or object of the action may be placed before the verbal noun in the nominative or accusative case.

> is bés leo-som in daim (nom.) do thúarcuin
> 'it is a custom with them that the oxen thresh'
> (lit. 'the oxen for threshing'). See Thurneysen G.445.

Uses of the verbal noun will be discussed further in IX.G.43.

7. Prepositions

Prepositional constructions are frequent in VSO languages, as the number met in the text may indicate. Among the prepositions in the first section are: (1) *for* 'of,' (5) *ó* 'from,' *do* 'for,' all of which introduce prepositional phrases comparable to those in English.

Besides such uses Old Irish prepositions are commonly followed by enclitic personal or possessive pronouns, e.g., (4) *dia < di* 'from' + *a* 'his, its' (possessive); (7) *friu < fri* 'to' + *u* 'them.' These combinations of prepositions plus personal pronouns are so frequent that they are treated as inflectional paradigms in grammars. They are generally referred to as conjugated prepositions. A full set is given here for *fri* 'to':

Sg.	1	frium(m)	'to me'
	2	frit(t), friut(t)	'to you'
	3 m. nt.	fris(s)	'to him/it'
	3 f.	frie	'to her'
Pl.	1	frinn	'to us'
	2	frib	'to you'
	3	friu	'to them'

These affixed forms of personal pronouns should be noted; they are also found with other prepositions, though the actual forms may be modified when so affixed.

8. Inflection of *ā*-stems

The *ā*-stems are feminine. They have *-e* in the genitive singular, *-a* in the nominative vocative accusative plural, and *-(a)ib* in the dative plural and dual. The final consonant is palatal in the accusative and dative singular, and neutral in the

14

nominative and accusative plural. Examples are *túath* 'people' (3), *bruden* 'hall,' *ben* 'woman, wife' (3), which is notable for assimilation of *b-* to following contiguous *n*.

Sg.	NV	túath	bruden	ben
	A	túaith	bruidin	mnaí
	G	túa(i)the	bruidne	mná
	D	túaith	bruidin	mnaí
Pl.	NVA	túatha	bruidnea	mná
	G	túath	bru(i)den	ban
	D	túath(a)ib	bruidnib	mnáib
Du.	NA	túaith	bru(i)din	mnaí
	G	túath	bru(i)den	ban
	D	túath(a)ib	bruidnib	mnáib

9. Verb inflection: copula and substantive verb

Old Irish has distinct forms for the copula 'be, =' and for the substantive verb 'be, exist.' The third singular present of the copula occurred in II.1b.8, 11 *is*; the third singular preterite of the substantive verb in I.1a.1 *boí*. Forms of both verbs are derived from several IE roots: *es-* 'be,' *bhew-* 'become,' and *(s)tā-* 'stand,' but the two verbs must be sharply distinguished because of their differing uses. Each will be treated further below, as in VII.G.33 and 34, in XII.G.59, and in XIV.G.69.

The present indicative forms of the copula are listed below; since the negative conjunct forms are frequent, and vary from the normal conjunct forms, they too are listed here.

		Absolute	Conjunct	Conjunct negative		
Sg.	1	am	-da	ni-ta	-da^l	[lenites]
	2	at (it)	-da	ni-ta	-da^l	[len.]
	3	is	-d, -t, --	ní		
	rel.	as^l				
Pl.	1	ammi(n)	-dan	ni-tam	-tan^l	[len.]
	2	adib (idib)	-dad	ni-tad	-dad^l	[len.]
	3	it	-dat	ni-tat	-dat	
	rel.	ata (at)^l [len.]				

10. Lenition

Lenition, also called aspiration in some handbooks, refers to a laxer articulation in the production of consonants. It is caused by preceding vowels (some of which have disappeared). Lenition occurs between vowels in words, and also initially, when a word stands after another that formerly ended in a vowel. Forms causing lenition are indicated by a raised ^{l} after the form, as in II.G.9.

Lenited stops become fricatives; thus /p t k b d g/ > [f θ χ ƀ ð γ].

Lenited *p t c* are written ⟨ph th ch⟩; lenited *b d g* have no special indications

15

in the older texts, but here a dot above the letters indicates lenition of the voiced stops and *m* as is the practice of later scribes. Lenited *f* is lost, and occasionally omitted in writing; *s* becomes [h], though when from *sp* or *sv* it becomes [f].

Lenited *n l r* are laxer than are their unlenited forms. Like *b d g* they have no special indications. Lenited *m* was a nasalized [$\tilde{v}$] or [$\tilde{w}$].

10.1. Nominal inflections which brought about lenition in the following words, notably adjectives and genitives, are the nominative singular feminine, the nominative plural masculine, the genitive singular masculine and neuter, the dative singular of all genders, as in i.1a.6 [χon x̣édna].

The article and other limiting modifiers such as *cach* 'each,' *uile* 'all' lenite the initial consonants of nouns in the same case forms given in the preceding paragraph, as in [*iN* χ*on*].

Lenition is also found after the vocative particle *a*, after the conjunctions *ocus* 'and' and *no* 'or,' and after other words which will be noted when they appear in this text.

chɑpτεR III

READING AND TEXTUAL ANALYSIS, Section 2

In the second section the messengers from Connaught and Ulster come before
Mac Dathó and announce the gifts they are willing to give for the hound.

1. Ructha trá na techta ina imḋai cuci-siuṁ do airiuc thuile dōiḃ r̄iasíu
   do·ḃerthae a mbiad dōiḃ.
2. Ro·r̄äiḋset a n-athesca.
3. 'Do chungiḋ in chon do·dechammar-ni' ol techta Connacht '.i. ó Ailill
   ocus ó Ṁeiḋḃ; ocus do·bértar tri fichit cét lilgach hi cétóir ocus ċarpat
   ocus da ech bas dech la Connachta, ocus a chommaín cinn ḃliaḋna
   cenmothā sin.'
4. 'Dia chungiḋ dano do·dechammar-ni ó Chonchoḃur' ol techta Ulaḋ; 'ocus
   ni messa Conchoḃar do charait ocus dano do thaḃairt sét ocus indile
   ocus do·bērthar a chomméit cétna a tūaith, ocus ḃiaiḋ deġcaratraḋ de.'

Phonetic transcription

1. rugθa trá na ťexta ina imᵭai kuǧi-šuw̃ do air̃ug θuiľe dóiv r̃iasíu
   do·verθæ a ṁiaᵭ dóiv.
2. ro·ráiᵭšed a n-aθeska.
3. 'do xuŋiᵭ in xon do·ᵭexaMar-ñi' oL ťexta koNaxt, 'eᵭ·ón ó aL̃iL̃ ogus
   ó ṽeᵭv; ogus do·bérdar ťr̃i ñ̃ixiᵭ ǩéd L̃ilgax i gédór̃ ogus xarpad ogus da
   ex bas ᵭex la koNaxta, ogus a xoMíñ ǩiṄ ṽl̃iaᵭna ǧenmoθá šín.'
4. 'dia xuŋiᵭ da·no do ᵭexaMar-ñi ó xonxowur' ol ťexta ulaᵭ; 'ogus ñi
   ṁesa konxowar do xaraᵭ ogus da·no do θawair̃ť šéd ogus iñ̃diľe, ogus
   do bérθar a xoMéiᵭ ǩédna a dúaθ, ogus viaᵭ ᵭeɣkaradraᵭ de.'

---

1. ructha   3 pl. pret. pass. of *berid* 'carries' = 'were brought'; see I.1a.7
   trá   'then'

na techta   art. pl. nom.; see I.1a.6

ina   prep. *i* 'in, to' w. poss. pron. 3 sg.

imdai   acc. sg. f. of *imda* 'couch'

cuci-sium   prep. *co* 'to, up to' w. affixed pers. pron. 3 m. + emphasizing suffix

do   prep. 'to, for'

airiuc   dat. sg. nt. of *airec* 'finding, obtaining'; vn. of *ar·icc* 'finds, obtains'

thuile   gen. sg. f. of *tol* 'wish'; lenited by preceding dat. sg.; see II.G.10.1—*airec tuile* is a
stereotyped phrase meaning 'to be entertained'

dóib   *do* + pers. pron. 3 pl.

ríasíu   conj. w. perf. subj. 'before'

do·berthae   past subj. pass. of *do·beir* 'gives, brings, puts'

a mbiad (dóib)   nt. sg. nom. acc. art. *a n-*, from *in*, + *biad* nt. sg. nom. = 'food'

2. ro·ráidset   3 pl. *ro*-perf. of *ráidid* 'talks' = 'they said'

a n-athesca   acc. pl. nt. of *athesc* 'report'

3. do chungid in chon   see I.1a.6

do·dechammar-ni   perf. 1 pl. of *do·tét* 'comes' = 'we have come'

ol   'says, said' without inflection

techta Connacht   see I.1a.6 + gen. pl. of *Connachta* 'Connaught'

.i.   abbreviation for Lat. *id est*, Ir. *ed-ón* 'to wit, that is'; often corresponds to colon
and does not need to be translated

ó Ailill ocus ó Meidb   see I.1a.5

(ocus) do·bértar   fut. pass. 3 pl. of *do·beir* 'will be given'

tri fichit   'three' + nom. pl. of *fiche* 'a score'

cét   gen. pl. nt. 'hundred'

lilgach   gen. pl. f. 'milch-cow'

hi cétóir   *i* 'at' + *cét-* 'first' + *úar* 'hour, time' = 'at once'

(ocus) carpat   acc. sg. m. 'chariot'

(ocus) da   'two'

ech   nom. du. of *ech* 'horse'

bas   pres. subj. rel. of *is* 'is'; '(which) will be'

dech la (Connachta)   'best' + *la* prep. 'in the opinion of'

(ocus) (a) chommaín   f. nom. sg. of *commaín* 'equivalent'

cinn   nt. dat. sg. of *cenn* 'end, head' = 'at the end of'

bliadna   f. gen. sg. of *blíadain* 'year'; *b-* lenited by preceding dat. sg.

cenmothá   prep. w. acc. 'besides'

sin   acc. sg. 'that, this'; see II.1b.8

4. dia   *do* + poss. pron. 3 sg. 'for its'

(chungid) dano   see I.1a.6; 'also'

do·dechammar-ni ó Chonchobur   see sent. 3

ol techta Ulad   see I.1a.6; gen. pl. of *Ulaid* 'Ulster'

(ocus) ni   'not'

messa   'worse'

(Conchobar do) charait   dat. sg. m. of *cara* 'friend'

(ocus dano do) thabairt   dat. of *tabairt*, vn. of *do·beir* 'gives'

sét   gen. pl. m. 'valuables'

(ocus) indile   gen. pl. f. 'cattle'

(ocus) do·bérthar   fut. pass. 3 sg. of *do·beir* 'will be given'

(a) chomméit   nom. sg. f. 'equal quantity'

(cétna) a túaith   prep. w. dat. + nasalization (see III.G.15) 'from'; *túaith* 'north' (ocus) biaid   fut. 3 sg. of *·tá* 'is'

degcaratrad   *deg-* 'good' + *caratrad* nom. sg. nt. 'friendship'

de   prep. w. dat. 'of, from, in consequence of' + pers. pron. 3 sg. 'that'

GRAMMAR

11. Prepositional patterns

In II.G.7 we noted that prepositions are frequently used in Old Irish. The first sentence of Section 2 gives excellent examples of such uses.

11.1. Here *ina* is the preposition *i* followed by a possessive pronoun. This is the unstressed possessive pronoun, which has the following form:

1 sg.	mo, mu, m	Cause lenition
2 sg.	do, du, t	Cause lenition
1 pl.	ar^n	Causes nasalization
2 pl.	far^n, for^n	Cause nasalization

In the third person *a* is used, but it influences the following initial element differently, as follows:

3 sg. m. nt.	a	Causes lenition
3 sg. f.	a	Causes gemination
3 pl.	a	Causes nasalization

11.2. Here *do* is followed by a verbal noun. This in turn is followed by a genitive and by a prepositional compound consisting of *do* and the third plural personal pronoun. The entire sequence might be translated literally: 'for obtaining of wish for them'; it is usually interpreted as a stereotyped phrase meaning 'to entertain, to show hospitality toward.' As this analysis may illustrate, prepositions are thus used with verbal nouns to indicate complements of preceding verbs, and also with affixed pronouns to indicate the role of persons involved in the action expressed by verbal nouns.

A similar construction with *do* is found at the beginnings of sentences 3 and 4; the complement is initial to indicate marking. See I.G.2.4.

12. Noun inflection: *i-* and *u*-stems

Nouns of the *i*-stem declension may be masculine, feminine, or neuter; only masculines and neuters are found in *u*-stems. The two inflections have influenced each other: the genitives singular and dual of *i*-stems have been influenced by *u*-stems; the genitive plural of *u*-stems by *i*-stems.

A feminine noun of *i*-stems, *suil* 'eye,' is given here; masculines are inflected in the same way; neuters differ only in having *-e* in the nominative vocative accusative plural. The final consonant in the N V A D Sg. and N A Du. has palatal quality.

A neuter noun of *u*-stems, *dorus* 'door,' is given here; masculines differ only in the nominative plural, where they have *-e* or *-a* or *-i* preceded by a neutral consonant, and in the vocative and accusative, where they have -*u*. As indicated in the textual analysis for II.1b.9, *dorus* has masculine forms in late texts. The final consonant in the N V A D Sg. and N A Du. has *u*-quality.

		i-stems	*u*-stems
Sg.	N	súil	dorus
	V	súil	dorus
	A	súil	dorus
	G	súlo, súla	doirseo, doirsea
	D	súil	dorus
Pl.	N	sú(i)li	dorus, doirsea
	V	sú(i)li	doirsea
	A	sú(i)li	dorus, doirsea
	G	sú(i)le	doirse
	D	sú(i)lib	doirsib
Du.	NVA	súil	dorus
	G	súlo, súla	doirseo, doirsea
	D	sú(i)lib	doirsib

13. The verb system

Inflectional categories and their uses. Verbs are inflected in Old Irish for voice, tense, mood, number, and person. Moreover, as we have noted in Chapter I, some of these inflections may be absolute and conjunct; further, special relative forms exist. The conjunct inflection is used after prepositions, *ro*, *no*, interrogative and negative particles, and conjunctions. See I.G.4.

There are two voices, active and passive. Active verbs may have either active or deponent inflection, that is, an inflection based on the PIE middle. (The middle voice indicated that an action was carried out with reference or benefit to the subject; e.g., Sanskrit *yajate* 'he sacrifices [for his own benefit].')

There are five tenses: present, imperfect, preterite, future, and secondary future. The present tense indicates present action. The imperfect tense indicates repeated or customary action in the past. The preterite tense indicates simple past action. The future tense indicates future action. The secondary future indicates potential action, either in the past or future. The perfect (usually accompanied by a preverb) expresses completed action.

The indicative mood indicates declarative statements. The subjunctive mood indicates uncertainty, and in subordinate clauses, volition or expectation. The imperative mood indicates commands.

There are three persons in the singular and plural.

Special relative forms are found in the absolute active third singular, first and third plural of indicative and subjunctive present, preterite, and future of simple verbs, as included in the paradigms given below. As indicated in I.G.2, relative forms are used to introduce relative clauses.

The verbs inflected in these various categories are either strong or weak. Strong verbs are primary, not derived from nouns or adjectives. Most weak verbs are denominative. They have a stem ending either in *a*-quality or *i*-quality. The *a*-verbs correspond to Latin first conjugation verbs in *-āre*.

The forms of verbs are based on five different stems:

(1) The present stem is used in the present and imperfect indicative and in the imperative.
(2) The subjunctive stem is used in the present and past subjunctive.
(3) The future stem is used in the future and secondary future.
(4) The active preterite stem is used in the preterite indicative, active and deponent.
(5) The passive preterite is used in the passive preterite indicative.

The forms made from each of these stems will be given in this chapter and subsequent chapters. Since not all forms of any verb are attested, it is customary to use as paradigms two of the most widely attested weak verbs: *móraid* 'magnifies' for verbs of *a*-quality, and *lécid* 'leaves' for verbs of *i*-quality. For strong verbs *berid* 'bears' is used, for the deponents *suidigidir* 'places.'

14. Verb inflection: forms made from the present stem

PRESENT INDICATIVE, ABSOLUTE

		Weak		Strong	Deponent
		a-quality	*i*-quality	(see I.G.4)	
Sg.	1	móru / mór(a)im(m)	léiciu / lécim(m)	biru	suidigur
	2	mór(a)i	léci	biri	suidigther
	3	mór(a)id	lécid	berid -ith	suidigidir
	rel.	móras(s)	léces(s)	beres(s)	suidigedar
Pl.	1	mórm(a)i	léicmi	berm(a)i	suidigmir
	rel.	mórm(a)e	léicme	berm(a)e	suidigmer
	2	mórth(a)e	léicthe	beirthe	suidigthe
	3	mór(a)it	lécit	ber(a)it	suidigitir
	rel.	mórd(a)e, móraite	léicde, lécite	berd(a)e, bert(a)e	suidigetar, -eddar

PRESENT INDICATIVE, CONJUNCT

Sg.	1	·móru / ·mór(a)im(m)	·léiciu / ·lécim(m)	·biur	·suidigur
	2	·mór(a)i	·léci	·bir	·suidigther
	3	·móra	·léci	·beir	·suidigedar
Pl.	1	·móram	·lécem	·beram	·suidigmer
	2	·mór(a)id	·lécid	·berid -ith	·suidigid -ith
	3	·mórat	·lécet	·berat	·suidigetar, -eddar

IMPERFECT INDICATIVE, ALWAYS CONJUNCT

Sg.	1	·mór(a)in(n)	·lécin(n)	·berin(n)	·suidigin(n)
	2	·mórtha	·léicthea		·suidigthea
	3	·mórad	·léced	·bered	·suidiged -eth

Pl.	1	·mórm(a)is	·léicmis	·beirmis	·suidigmis
	2	·mórth(a)e	·léicthe		·suidigthe
	3	·mórt(a)is	·léictis	·beirtis	·suidigtis -ddis

IMPERATIVE, ABSOLUTE AND CONJUNCT

Sg.	1			biur	
	2	mór	léic	beir	suidigthe
	3	mórad -ath	léced -eth	bered -eth	suidiged -eth
Pl.	1	móram	lécem	beram	suidigem
	2	mór(a)id	lécid -ith	berid -ith	suidigid -ith
	3	mórat	lécet	berat	suidigetar

15. Nasalization (eclipsis)

Words with original final nasal may alter the initial element of the following word. Therefore, the process is now generally known as nasalization. Since the result, however, may differ from expected effects of nasalization, the process is often known especially in reference to modern Irish as eclipsis.

By nasalization the following modifications take place:

p t k ⟨c⟩	become voiced: [b d g]
b d g	are preceded by the homorganic nasals [mb nd ŋg] and later become [m n ŋ]
f	becomes voiced: [ƀ]
s r l m n	are unchanged, but when preceded by a proclitic vowel they are geminated (see v.G.25)
vowels	are preceded by [n]

In the writing system nasalization is indicated regularly only for vowels, and /b d g/, which are written *mb nd ng*, and /f/, which is often written *b* [ƀ w v].

15.1. Nasalization is found after the accusative singular and the genitive plural of all nouns and the neuter nominative accusative singular of all inflected words, with the following exceptions:

(1) Dependent genitives or prepositions with suffixed personal pronoun may or may not take nasalization.

(2) Unstressed syllables do not nasalize.

(3) Between two consonants nasalization may not occur.

(4) The following neuters do not cause nasalization: *alaill* 'another,' *aill* 'second,' *na* 'any,' *ní* 'anything,' *ced, cid* 'what,' *ed* 'it,' infixed neuter personal pronoun third singular.

15.2. Nasalization is also found after the following numeral forms: after *secht* '7,' *ocht* '8,' *noí* '9,' *deich* '10'; after genitives of *coíc* '5,' *sé* '6'; after the neuter dual forms and the dative in all genders of *da* '2.'

15.3. Nasalization is also found after various particles, conjunctions, and prepositions:

(1) after the relative particle *(s)a*

22

(2) after the interrogative particle *in*

(3) after the conjunctions *a* 'when,' *ara* 'so that,' *co, con* 'so that,' *dia* 'if,' *ó ua* 'since'

(4) after the prepositions *co* 'with,' *i* 'in,' *iar* 'after,' *re, ría* 'before'

(5) after the infixed personal pronoun of the third singular masculine, and often after the infixed personal pronoun *s* of the third singular feminine and third plural

15.4. In some relative clauses the initial element of the verb is nasalized. Nasalization also takes place after absolute relative forms of the copula.

15.5. Examples:

(1) III.2.1 a mbiad: *a* here is neuter nominative singular; III.G.15.1

(2) II.1b.9 Secht ndoruis: III.G.15.2

(3) II.1b.10 in cach: *i* is the preposition; III.G.15.3(4)

        cach = NIr. *gach*, i.e., *c* = unlenited *g*;

        therefore *in cach* = [iŋ gax]

chapter IV

READING AND TEXTUAL ANALYSIS, Section 3a

The third section indicates how Mac Dathó reacted to the dilemma of having two seekers of the hound. This section includes the only poem of the story, a dialogue between 'the man' and 'the woman,' Mac Dathó's wife. Such verse is commonly interjected in the prose of Old Irish story, and in Old Norse saga, possibly through imitation of Irish.

The stanza pattern is *deibide*, the cut stanza. Each line has seven syllables. The final stressed syllable of the first line rhymes with an unstressed final syllable of the second; this pattern is repeated in the third and fourth lines. Alliteration is optional, but often introduced, as in the last line of the third stanza: *mnā maith main mug*. The first stanza is in a more archaic pattern, rhyming only in the second and fourth lines; but lines 1 and 2 have a common seven-syllable pattern ending in three syllables: / x x. The *deibide* meter of the remaining stanzas is that common in Irish story. In its rhymes consonants are arranged in sets, such as voiced fricatives and liquids, as in stanza 2, *-aig*: *-ail*; or resonants, as in stanza 3, *-elar*: *-enar*.

1. Ro·lá diḋiu i socht innī Mac Dathó co·rrabe tri thráth cen diġ cen
   biaḋ, acht 'co immorchor ón taíḃ co araile.
2. Is and dixit a ḃen: 'Is fota in troscuḋ i·taí.
3. Atá biaḋ lat cenco·n-essara.
4. Ciḋ no·taí?'
5. Nicos·n-ārlastar.
6. Is and dixit in ḃen:
7. Tucaḋ turḃaiḋ chotulta   do Mac Dathó co-a thech,
   boíthi nī no·chomairleḋ   cenco·labraḋar fri nech.
8. As·⟨s⟩oí, do·soī ūaim do ḟraiġ   in ferg fēne co londgail;
   a ḃen treḃar, dos·beir moḋ   bith dia cēiliu cen chotluḋ.
9. [In fer:] As·bert Cremthann Nia Nāir: ni·tardda do rúin do ṁnāiḃ.
   rūn ṁnā nī maith con·celar   main ar ṁuġ ni·aithenar.

24

Phonetic transcription

Notice especially where nonpalatal consonants precede high front vowels. This does not apply to Lat. [diksit].

1. Ro·lá diðu i soxt iŇi mak daθó go·Rave tři θráθ gen ǒij gen viað, axt
   go iMorxor ón tív go ar·aĭe.
2. iš aNd diksit a ven: 'iš foda in troskuð i·dᵊí.
3. a·tá ƀiað lat gengo·nessara.
4. ǧið no·tᵊí?'
5. nigos·náRLasdar.
6. iš aNd diksit in ven:
7. tugaθ turwiǒ xodulda   do wak daθó goa θ̆ex,
   boíθi ňí no·xow̃iřleð   gengo·Lawrað ar fř̃i ňex.
8. as·sí, do·sí uaṁ do raγ̃   in ferᵊg fēňe go LoNgiĺ;
   a ven třewar, dos·ƀeř moð   ƀiθ ǯia ǩéĭu gen xodluð.
9. ás·bert krew̃θaN Ňia Nář: ňi·taRda do ruň do wᵊnáiv.
   Rún w̃ná Ní maθ̆ gon·ǧelar   mᵊíň ar w̃uγ ňi·aθ̆enar.

---

1. ro·lá   3 sg. *ro*-pret. of *fo-ceird* 'puts'; here impers. 'it put'
   didiu 'then'
   i socht   *i* + acc. sg. m. 'silence'
   inní Mac Dathó   art. acc. sg. m. + *i* (= *é* 'he'); w. proper names 'the (aforementioned)'
   co·rrabe   *co n-* conj. 'until; and as a result' + *ro·boí*, as in II.1b.8; note effect of initial
        accent on *robói*
   tri thráth   *tri* + *tráth* 'canonical hour,' then 'day' as here
   cen dig   prep. w. acc., leniting; 'without' acc. sg. f. of *deug* 'drink'
   cen biad   see III.2.1
   acht   'but, except'
   'co immorchor   *oc* prep. w. dat. 'at' + poss. pron. 3 sg. m. = 'at his'; dat. sg. m. 'turning
        round, tossing'; vn. of *imm·es·cuirethar* 'moves around'
   ón   *ó* = prep. w. dat. 'from' + art.
   taíb   dat. sg. m. 'side'
   co araile   prep. w. acc. 'to' + acc. sg. nt. 'other'
2. is   3 sg. of cop. 'it is'
   and   prep. *i* + 3 sg. pron. 'in it'; as here, 'then, there'
   dixit   Lat. 3 sg. perf. of *dicō* = 'said'
   a ben   3 sg. m. poss. pron. 'his' leniting + *ben* nom. sg. f. 'woman, wife'
   is fota   3 sg. cop. + *fota* 'long'
   in troscud   nòm. sg. m. of art. + *troscud* 'fasting'
   i·taí   2 sg. pres. of *-tá* 'you are,' following *i* 'in' (+ rel. = 'in which'); [t] nasalized by
        prep. *iⁿ*
3. atá biad   3 sg. '(there) is' + noun
   lat   prep. w. acc. *la* 'with' + 2 sg. pers. pron. 'beside you' = 'you have'
   cenco·n-essara   *cen* 'without'; *co* conj. 'that'; 2 sg. pres. subj. of *ithid* 'he eats'

25

4. cid 'what [is it]'
   no·taí rel. ptc. no- + 2 sg. pres. atí, i·taí 'you are'; 'What is it that you are?' = 'What is it that ails you?'
5. nicos·n-árlastar nicon- 'not' + infixed 3 sg. f. pers. pron. 'her' + ro-pret. 3 sg. of ad·glá-dathar 'speaks to'
6. is and dixit in ben see sent. 2
7. tucad 3 sg. perf. pass. of do·beir 'brings, puts' = 'is brought'; do·ucc is used to supply perf. forms of do·beir
   turbaid nom. sg. f. 'disturbance, prevention'
   chotulta gen. sg. m. of vn. cotlud 'sleeping,' from con·tuili 'sleeps' (note loss of syllable between t and l when stress falls on prefix in vn.)
   do Mac Dathó prep. 'to'
   co-a thech prep. 'to' + m. poss. pron. 'his' + tech acc. sg. nt. 'house'
   boíthi 3 sg. pret. boí of -tá + pers. pron. 3 sg. 'there was for him' = 'he would have'
   (ní) no-chomairled see II.1b.12; 3 sg. past subj. rel. of con·airlethar 'he is deliberating'; a late form
   cenco·labradar cenco·n- 'though not'; 3 sg. pres. of labraithir 'speaks'
   fri nech prep. w. acc. 'to, with'; acc. sg. m. of nech 'anyone'
8. as·soí 3 sg. pres. 'he turns away'
   do·soi 3 sg. pres. 'he turns toward'
   ūaim ó prep. w. dat. 'from' w. 1 sg. pers. pron.
   do fraig do w. dat. sg. f. 'wall'
   in ferg art. w. nom. sg. m. 'anger'
   fēne gen. sg. f. of fían 'band of warriors'; the two words make up a kenning meaning 'hero' from 'band of warriors'
   co londgail co w. dat. sg. f. of gal 'valor,' preceded by adj. lond 'angry'; prefix provid-ing an unstressed syllable as required in deibide meter
   (a ben)trebar sent. 2 + adj. 'careful, prudent'
   dos·beir mod 3 sg. pres. ind. do·beir w. infixed pers. pron. f. 'she bestows attention on it'
   bith f. vn. of -tá, proleptic infixed pron. -s- in dos·ber
   dia cēiliu do w. 3 sg. poss. pron. + dat. sg. m. of céle 'other, companion'
   cen chotlud cen + nt. vn. cotlud, as in sent. 7
9. as·bert Cremthann Nia Nāir 3 sg. pret. of as·beir 'said' + name of a legendary ruler of Ireland
   ni·tardda neg. + 2 sg. ro-subj. of do·beir 'gives'
   do rúin 2 sg. pron. 'your' + acc. sg. of rún 'secret'
   do mnāib prep. w. dat. pl. f. of ben; see II.G.8
   rūn mnā nom. sg. + gen. sg.; /m/ of mnā lenited by preceding f. ā-stem
   ní maith neg. + adv. 'well'
   con·celar 3 sg. pres. pass. of con·ceil 'hides, conceals'; 'a woman's secret is not well concealed'
   main nom. sg. f. 'treasure'
   ar mug prep. w. dat. and acc. 'for' + acc. or dat. sg. m. of mug 'slave'
   ni·aithenar neg. + 3 sg. pres. pass. of ad·fen 'it is given (in recompense), requited, re-paid'; w. ar 'to, for'

The translation of text in this chapter follows in Chapter v, p. 33.

GRAMMAR

16. Introduction of sentences by forms of the copula

Chapter IV, Section 3a provides an illustration of a sentence type common in Old Irish. The first clause indicates an element that seems to be subordinate to the second clause, though it may be emphasized. By the pattern of such sentences, an adverbial element is emphasized, and the main verb is appended to it; moreover, the VSO order is maintained. An SVO language, like English, achieves the same emphasis by placing the adverb initially in the sentence: 'then his wife said to him.'

The quotation in IV.3a.2 also emphasizes the element after *is*. In such sentences it is more difficult to indicate the emphasis on a word like *fota*. From a literal translation 'it is long, the fasting in which you are' one may need to introduce adverbs, such as: 'You certainly are making a long fast.'

17. Noun inflection: consonantal stems (dentals, velars, -*s*)

Subclasses of consonant stems are determined by the final consonants, which generally are lost in the nominative singular; some can be determined from the oblique cases. Forms will be given here for a dental stem, a velar, and an *s*-stem; since the *s* is lost in Old Irish, *s*-stems must be determined from related forms in other IE dialects. The vocative singular has the same form as the nominative. Since consonant stems may belong to any of the genders, the gender of forms listed here is given.

		Dentals	Velars	*s*-stems
		M.	M.	Nt.
Sg.	NV	car(a)e 'friend'	rí 'king'	teg, tech 'house'
	A	car(a)it	ríg	teg, tech
	G	carat	ríg	taige
	D	car(a)it	ríg	taig, tig
Pl.	N	car(a)it	ríg	tige, taige
	AV	cairtea	ríga	tige, taige
	G	carat	ríg	tige, taige
	D	cairtib	ríg(a)ib	tigib
Du.	NVA	carait	ríg	teg
	G	carat	ríg	taige
	D	cairtib	ríg(a)ib	tigib

18. Personal pronouns

Few personal pronouns are found under stress. Most pronominal forms are clitics. These are of various kinds and forms.

18.1. One set of clitics may be added to all pronouns, and also verbs, as in the form *do·dechammar-ni* of III.2.3; *ni* simply emphasizes the first plural of the verb. These clitics are referred to as emphasizing particles, though some scholars are unhappy with the terminology because the particles themselves are unstressed. The initial *s* is never lenited, but after vowels it may be geminated. The forms are:

1 sg.	se, sa	1 pl.	ni, nai
2 sg.	siu, so, su	2 pl.	si
3 sg. m.	som, sem, sium	3 pl. m.	
f.	si	f.	like sg. of m.
nt.	som, sem	nt.	

18.2. Stressed personal pronouns, also with emphasizing particles.

1 sg.	mé	'I'	emph.	me(i)sse, mese
2 sg.	tú	'you'		tussu, tusu
3 sg. m.	(h)é	'he'		(h)é-som/-sium, (h)é-side
f.	sí	'she'		sissi, si-ede
nt.	(h)ed	'it'		
1 pl.	sní	'we'		snisni, sníni, sisni, sinni
2 pl.	sí	'you'		sissi, sib
3 pl.	(h)é	'they'		hé-ssom

These forms are used as predicate nominatives after the copula.

18.3. Infixed personal pronouns. When used with verbs except as predicate nominatives, personal pronouns are unstressed. They are affixes to preverbs, and accordingly are said to be infixed.

They may be direct objects. They may also be indirect objects of the verb 'be.' Or they may indicate the subject of passives which have impersonal force.

There are three classes of infixed personal pronouns, distinguished by their uses after certain elements.

Class I forms are used after all particles, such as the negative *ni*, and after preverbs which originally ended in a vowel: *ar, di, do* (pretonic for *to*), *fo, im(m)*, *no, ro*. The original vowel of the second syllable of *ar* and *imm* is maintained before pronouns beginning with consonants, e.g., *aro/u-, immu-*. The *o*, of *do*, *fo, no, ro*, is lost before *-a*, yielding *d-a·*, etc. After *ni a* is lost, yielding *ní* 'not it, not him.'

Class II forms are used after preverbs ending originally in consonants: *ad-*, *aith-, com-, ess-, etar-, for-, frith-, in-*. Class II forms have initial unlenited *d*, often written *t*. The preverbs *ad-, aith-, ess-, oss-, ni-* combine with the initial *d* to become the homophone *at-*; *com-* and *frith-* become *cot-, frit-*.

Class III forms are used after the relative *(s)aⁿ* combined with a preverb, after *iⁿ* 'in which,' after the conjunctions *araⁿ* 'in order that,' *conⁿ, coⁿ* 'so that,' *diaⁿ* 'if when,' and after the interrogative *in*. It is also used with relative verbs.

The effect of pronouns on following elements is indicated by superposed *l* (lenition) and *n* (nasalization).

28

		I	II	III
Sg.	1	m(m)^l	dom^l, dum^l, dam(m)^l tom^l, tum^l, tam(m)^l	dom^l, dum^l, dam(m)^l
	2	t^l	tot^l, tat^l, t^l	dat^l, dit^l
	3 m.	a^n, -^{n}	t^n (ta^n)	(i)d^n, (did^n), -^{n}, da^n
	f.	s^n, s	ta, da	da
	nt.	a^l, -^{l}	t^l	da
Pl.	1	n(n)	ton, tan(n), don	din, don, dun, dan(n)
	2	b(f)	tob, tab, dob, dub	dob, dub, (dib), dab
	3	s^n, s	ta, da	da

When infixed pronouns are used with simple verbs the particle *no-* is placed before them, as in *no·mbertaigedar* of VI.4.1.

18.4. Relative constructions. Old Irish has no special relative pronouns, using infixed and suffixed pronouns to refer to the subject of the clause.

19. Verb inflection: forms made from the subjunctive stem

As noted in III.G.13, the subjunctive is used to indicate volition and expectation, or also uncertainty. It is found more frequently in subordinate than in principal clauses.

There are two subjunctive formations, an *a*-subjunctive characterized by an original long *ā* added to the verbal stem, and an *s*-subjunctive. The *s*-subjunctive is formed only from strong verbs with stems ending in dental or velar stop or fricative, or in *nn*. Only forms of the *a*-subjunctive will be listed here, in the same format as that used in III.G.14.

PRESENT SUBJUNCTIVE, ABSOLUTE

		Weak		Strong	Deponent
		a-quality	*i*-quality		
Sg.	1	móra	lécea	bera	*suidiger
	2	mór(a)e	léce	ber(a)e	suidigther
	3	mór(a)id ·(a)ith	lécid ·ith	ber(a)id ·(a)ith	suidigidir
	rel.	móras(s)	léces(s)	beras(s)	suidigedar
Pl.	1	mórm(a)i ·(a)immi	léicmi	berm(a)i	suidigedar
	rel.	mórm(a)e	léicmi	berm(a)e	suidigmer
	2	mórth(a)e	léicthe	berth(a)e	suidigthe
	3	mór(a)it	lécit	ber(a)it	suidigitir
	rel.	mórd(a)e ·t(a)e, mór(a)ite	lé(i)cde ·te, lécite	berd(a)e, bert(a)e	suidigetar

PRESENT SUBJUNCTIVE, CONJUNCT

Sg.	1	·mór	·léic	·ber	·suidiger
	2	·mór(a)e	·léce	·ber(a)e	·suidigther
	3	·móra	·lécea	·bera	·suidigedar

29

Pl.	1	·móram		·lécem	·beram		·suidigmer	
	2	·mór(a)id	-aith	·lécid -ith	·ber(a)id	-(a)ith	·suidigid -ith	
	3	·mórat		·lécet	·berat		·suidigetar	

PAST SUBJUNCTIVE

Sg.	1	·ber(a)in(n)	Pl.	1	·berm(a)is
	2	·bertha		2	·berth(a)e
	3	·berad -ath		3	·bert(a)is

The forms of the past subjunctive are identical with those of the imperfect indicative, except that in strong verbs the neutral quality of the final consonant of the stem is often indicated. Only forms of the strong verb are accordingly given here.

20. Palatalization

As noted in I.G.5.3 all consonants in Old Irish may have two distinct qualities:
(1) neutral quality, often called broad
(2) palatal or *i*-quality, often called slender
These qualities were determined by adjoining vowels, especially following vowels that had disappeared. The modification is often referred to as infection. It can be compared with *i*- and *u*-umlaut (or mutation) in Germanic languages.

A consonant so affected had a secondary articulation comparable to that of back vowels (*o*, *u*) and the central vowel (*a*), or that of front vowels (*e*, *i*). In modern Irish there is a similar contrast between neutral (broad) and palatal (slender) quality.

As a secondary characteristic the quality was not indicated in the consonants, but it is often specified by the use of "glide-vowels." Thus the nominative of 'name' *ainm* includes an *i* to indicate the palatal quality of the following consonants: [aiṅṁ], as indicated in the transcription for Chapter I. Similarly, the *u* in -*biur*, I.G.4, simply indicates *u*-quality of the following consonant [bir^u]. If, however, as in *firu*, the accusative plural of *fir*, a back vowel follows the consonant, no "glide-vowel" is written.

For the present, palatalized consonants can be best learned from the transcriptions. Subsequently, the original forms of words will be given, to indicate which consonants are palatal. The original endings of the singular *o*-stem inflection will be given here to illustrate the basis for the final quality of the forms of *fer*, *mac*, and *scél*.

N	fer^a	mac^a	-os	scél^a	-om
V	a fir^i	a mhic^i	-e		
A	fer^a	mac^a	-om	scél^a	-om
G	fir^i	mic^i	-i	scéuil^i	-i
D	fiur^u	macc^u	-ōi	scéul^u	-ōi

chapter V

READING AND TEXTUAL ANALYSIS, Section 3b

The poem in section 3a is concluded here. As indicated, it continues as a dialogue between 'the man' and 'the woman.'

10. [In ben:] Cid fri mnaī at·bertha-so
    ní na⟨d⟩·tét do menma-so,
    manid·epled ní airi,
    tēti menma neich aili.

11. [In fer:] Cú Mes-Roīda meic Dathó,
    do·foeth mór fer find fria rath,
    ba olc lathe etha dó;
    bid līa turim a chath.

12. Manip do Chonchobor berthair,
    nicon·faicēbat a slūaig
    is derb bid mogda in gním,
    bas mó do būaib na do thír.

13. Mad do Ailill ⟨beith⟩ éra
    dodon·béra mac Māgach,
    silis Fālmag darsin túaith,
    atan·ebla i luim lúaith.

14. [In ben:] Tāthut airle lim-sa fris
    tabair dōib-sium dib līnaib,
    ní olc fri īarmairt n-indi,
    cumma cīa·thōetsat imbi.

15. [In fer:] In chomairle at·biri-siu,
    Ailbe, do·ro⟨f⟩oīd Dīa,
    is ⟨s⟩í ním·déni cutal.
    nicon·fes cīa ō·tucad.

---

10. cid   interrog. 'what?, what is (it)?' or *cia* 'although' + past subj. of cop. 'although it be to a woman that you might say it'
    fri mnaī   prep. as in sent. 7, + acc. of *ben* as in sent. 8
    at·bertha-so   past. subj. 2 sg. of *as·beir* w. infixed nt. obj. pron. Class II leniting and 2 sg. emph. ptc. 'you might tell'
    manid·epled   conj. 'if' + neg. *ni* + past subj. 3 sg. of *at·baill* 'perishes, is lost' w. infixed 3 sg. nt. pers. pron. Class III after *mani*
    ní airi   nt. of *nech* 'anything'; *ar* + pers. pron. 3 sg. nt. 'on account of that'
    ní na⟨d⟩·tét   'anything' + 'that not' + pres. 3 sg. 'go to'; w.*menma* = 'comprehend'
    do menma-so   poss. adj. 'your' + m. sg. nom. 'mind' + emph. ptc. for *do*
    tēti menma   *tēt* + affixed 3 sg. pers. pron. + m. sg. nom.
    neich aili   gen. sg. m. of *nech* 'someone' + gen. sg. of *aile* 'other'

31

11. cú Mes-Roïda meic Dathó   *Mes-Roïda* 'fosterling of the Great Wood' is a name for *Mac Dathó*, in the gen. + gen. of *mac*

ba olc   I.1a.4 + adj. 'evil'

lathe   nom. sg. nt. 'day'

etha   pret. pass. rel. of *téit* 'he was come (for)'

dó   *do* + 3 sg. m. pers. pron. 'for it'

do·foeth   3 sg. fut. of *do·fuit* 'will fall'

mór fer find   nom. sg. nt. 'great number' + gen. pl. of *fer* + adj. 'fair'

fria rath   *rath* 'grace'; acc. after *fri* + 3 sg. poss. pron. 'for his sake, because of him'

bid   3 sg. fut. of *is* 'will be'

lïa   comp. of *il* 'more'

turim   dat. sg. f. 'enumeration' = '(more) than can be counted'; vn. of *do·rími*; OIr. expresses standard of comparison w. the dat.

a chath   nom. sg. m. of *cath* 'fighting, battle' w. lenited *c* after poss. adj. *a¹* 'his' = 'for it'

12. manip   see sent. 10; *mani* + cop. pres. subj. 3 sg. 'if it be not to Conchobar that it is given'

do Chonchobor   note lenition after *do*

berthair   3 sg. pres. subj. pass. of *berid* = 'it is borne (given)'

is derb   cop. + adj. 'sure, clear'

bid mogda   3 sg. fut. of *is* + adj. 'churlish, mean'

in gním   nom. sg. m. 'act,' following art.; this phrase is sub. used w. pred. adj. *mogda*

nicon·faicēbat   see IV.3a.5 'not' followed by 3 pl. fut. of *fo·ácaib* 'they will . . . leave behind'

a šlūaig   nom. pl. m. of *slúag* 'troop' following 3 sg. poss. pron.; note lenition of *s*

bas   fut. rel. of *is*

mó do būaib   comp. of *mór* = 'more' + dat. pl. of *bó* 'cow, cattle' after prep. 'of'

na do thír   for *iná*, reduced form of *indaas* 'than' + dat. sg. nt. of *tír* 'land' after prep.

13. mad   *má, ma* 'if' w. 3 sg. pres. subj. of *is* 'if it is'

do Ailill   prep. + dat.

beith   3 sg. subj. pres. of *tá* 'is'

éra   nom. sg. nt. 'refusal'; vn. of *éraid*

silis   3 sg. fut. of *sligid* 'cuts down'

Fálmag   acc. sg. of poetic name of Ireland

darsin   prep. *tar* 'across, throughout' + f. sg. art.

túaith   acc. sg. f. of *túath* 'people'; note differing idiom fr. Eng., where *tar* would govern *Fálmag*

dodon·béra   3 sg. fut. of *do·beir* 'carries' + infixed 1 pl. pers. pron.—an unusual class of infix, perhaps to gain a syllable

mac Māgach   a hero of Connaught, named in Sec. 16; Ailill or his brother Cet

atan·ebla   3 sg. fut. of *ad·aig* 'drives to, reduced' w. infixed 1 pl. pers. pron.

i luim   prep. + acc. sg. f. of *lom* 'bare'

lúaith   acc. sg. f. 'ashes'

14. táthut   3 sg. abs. *táith of *tá* + suffixed 2 sg. pers. pron. 'is to you' = 'you have'

airle   acc. sg. f. 'advice'

lim-sa fris   prep. *la* 'with' w. affixed 1 sg. pers. pron.; see II.G.7 on *fris* 'about it'

ní olc fri iarmairt   neg.; sent. 11 + prep. + acc. sg. f. 'consequence'

n-indi   *i* + affixed dat. sg. f. pers. pron.

tabair   2 sg. impv. of *do·beir* 'gives'

dóib-sium   *do* + affixed 3 pl. pers. pron., w. emph. 3 pl. ptc.
dib línaib   dat. of *dá* 'two' + dat. du. of *lín* 'number' = 'both'
cumma   adj. 'equal, indifferent'; here pred. adj. w. cop. omitted
cia·thóetsat   interrog. 'who, how' + 3 pl. fut. of *do·fuit* 'falls'; see sent. 11
imbi   prep. *im* 'around, about' w. 3 sg. m./nt. affixed pers. pron.
15. in chomairle   nom. sg. f. def. art. leniting following *c*; cf. *airle* of sent. 14 'advice'
at·biri-siu   2 sg. ind. pres. of *as·beir* 'says' + 3 sg. infix + emph. 2 sg. ptc.
is ⟨s⟩í ním·déni   *is sí*; see II.1b.8; neg. 3 sg. pres. of *do·gni* 'makes' w. infixed 1 sg. pers. pron.
cutal   adj. 'empty, weak; humble'
Ailbe   see I.1a.4
do·ro⟨f⟩oid   3 sg. *ro*-pret. of *do·foidi* 'sends (to one)' w. 3 sg. m. infixed pers. pron.
Dia   nom. sg. m. 'God,' here disyllabic; this line is obscure, possibly 'Ailbe, God sent him'
nicon·fes   neg. + pass. of *ro·fitir* 'is known'
cia   interrog. 'who'; w. the following prep. *ó* as antecedent of the rel. clause
ó·tucad   pret. pass. of *do·beir* 'brings,' prefixed by prep. *ó* 'from,' here used to indicate agent w. rel.; note lack of rel. marker which is commonly omitted; the poem ends w. same word as that beginning it = 'It is not known by whom he was taken'

TRANSLATION

(The poem beginning in IV.3a.7 and concluding here is translated below.)

7.   Disturbance of sleep was brought
to Mac Dathó and his house;
he had something that he was considering;
he does not speak to anyone.

8.   He turns away, he turns from me to the wall,
the warrior of the bands with valor;
his prudent wife, she gives it attention
that her mate is without sleep.

9. [Man:]   "Crimthann Nia Náir said:
'Do not give your secret to women.
The secret of a woman is not well concealed;
treasure is not paid to a slave.' "

10. [Woman:]   "What would you say to a woman
if something were not lost on that account?
A thing that you do not understand,
someone else may understand."

11. [Man:]   "The hound of Mes-Roida, son of Dathó,
evil was the day when he was come for:
many fair men will fall for his sake;
more than can be counted will be the fighting for him.

12.   "Unless he is given to Conchobar,
it is certain the deed will be mean;
his army will not leave behind
more of cattle than of land.

13.   "If it be refused Ailill
he will strike Ireland throughout her tribes;
the son of Magach will take us;
we will be reduced to bare ashes."

14. [Woman:] "I have advice for you about it,
not evil the sequel of it:
give it to the two of them
no matter who will fall because of it."

15. [Man:] "The advice that you speak,
it is that does not make me humble:
Ailbe, God sends him,
it is not known by whom he was taken."

GRAMMAR

21. Syntactic patterns with infixed pronouns, suffixed personal pronouns, and possessive pronouns

Chapter III, Grammar 14 has given the forms of the personal pronouns and of the infixed pronouns. As noted there, stressed forms of personal pronouns are rare. Since they were generally unstressed, pronouns were severely reduced in form. Like other reduced forms of pronouns they are of crucial importance in interpreting sentences, and accordingly their functions must be noted as well as their forms.

21.1. Infixed pronouns. When personal pronouns are used with verbs, they are placed after preverbs and thus said to be infixed. An example is *ním·déni* of sentence 15 above. Here the first singular infixed pronoun is placed after the negative *ní,* which is preposed before the third singular present of *do·gni* 'makes,' here in its prototonic form *-déni,* because of the negative. As in other such verb forms, the infixed pronoun is object of the verb. The composite form accordingly means: 'does not make me.' Such infixed pronouns may be understood by comparison with French patterns like *je t'aime* 'I love you.' If, like Antoine Meillet, *The Comparative Method in Historical Linguistics,* trans. G. B. Ford, Jr. (Paris: Champion, 1967, pp. 38–39), one regards *je, tu, il* as 'pure grammatical signs' rather than pronouns the parallelism is very close; object pronouns like Fr. *te* and OIr. *m* are 'infixed' after grammatical signs like *je* and *no, ní.*

Other verb forms in which the infixed pronouns are objects are found in v.3b.13, both with first plural pronouns: *ad·ebla* is the third singular future of *ad·aig, do·béra* the third singular future of *do·beir.* In each the infixed first person pronoun is object, as the analysis indicates. Such objects may be the sole

34

direct object. They may also be used proleptically, that is, when the object is expressed subsequently, as in v.3b.10 *at·bertha·so* and in the third gloss of Chapter VI *d·a-gníu-sa*. This is the first singular present of *do·gni* 'makes,' in its deuterotonic form; *a* the neuter infixed pronoun anticipates the subsequent object *sin* 'that.'

21.2. Suffixed personal pronouns. Suffixed pronouns are added when words, either verbs or prepositions, are stressed. Like infixed pronouns they may be objects. Apart from their position, suffixed pronouns do not differ from infixed pronouns when used with verbs. A simple verb, like *beirid* in the absolute (i.e., no negative, question particle, or other prefix forcing a conjunct form), may in the third singular only suffix or infix a direct object. The infix is attached to a meaningless particle, *no* or *nu*, that forces a conjunct form of the verb, e.g., *nom-beir* 'he carries me.'

With the substantive verb the object indicates possession, as in v.3b.14: *tā-thut*, where -*ut* is second singular. The form means: 'there exists for you = you have.' These forms are rare and their occurrence is highly restricted. They occur only in early materials.

Suffixed pronouns are used frequently after prepositions. As noted in the grammar, II.G.7, the combinations are often referred to as conjugated prepositions. Syntactically, they correspond to sequences of phrases plus pronouns. In II.G.7, forms with the preposition *fri* 'against' were listed. Other prepositions accompanied by personal pronouns are given in VIII.G.38; those governing the dative (38.a), the accusative (38.b), and both the accusative and the dative (38.c).

Forms of the conjugated preposition *do* 'to' (for other conjugated prepositions see Thurneysen G.272–76):

		Simple forms	Emphatic forms
Sg.	1	dom, dam	dom-sa, dam-sa
	2	duit, dait, deit, dit	duit-siu, de(i)t-siu
	3 m. nt.	dó, dáu	dos(som)
	f.	dí	disi, dissi
Pl.	1	dún(n)	dún-ni, dún-nai
	2	dúib	dúib-si
	3	do(a)ib, duaib	doïb-som, doaib-sem, dóib-sem

Conjugated prepositions may govern either the accusative or the dative, and often show a difference of meaning depending on the case governed: *ar* 'for, on account of,' *i* 'in, into,' *for* 'on.'

21.3. Possessive pronouns. These are old genitives of personal pronouns, which are not further inflected. They are unstressed and are placed before nouns, either as simple words, as in v.3b.12 *a slúaig* 'his troop' or after prepositions, as in III.2.4 *dia* 'for its.'

The forms of the unstressed possessive were given in III.G.11.1. Syntactically, these possessives may have all the uses of genitives. Thus in III.2.4 *Dia chungid* 'for its asking' the possessive is an objective genitive, and the phrase means 'to request it, to ask for it.'

22. Noun inflection: consonantal stems (-*n*, -*r*)

There are two subclasses of *n*-stems, those with lenited -*n* and those with unlenited -*n*; all neuters belong to the second subclass. Examples of nouns with lenited -*n* are *toimtiu* feminine 'opinion,' which has no plural or dual, and *cú* masculine 'hound'; examples of nouns with unlenited -*n* are *Ériu* feminine 'Ireland' and *ainm* neuter 'name.'

The *r*-stems comprise only masculine and feminine kinship nouns; forms of *ath(a)ir* masculine 'father' are given here, but since its vocative plural is not attested, that form of *bráth(a)ir* 'brother' is given.

	n-stems				*r*-stems
	lenited -*n*		unlenited -*n*		
Sg. N/V	toimtiu	cú	Ériu	ainm	ath(a)ir
A	toimtin	coin	Érin(n)	ainm	ath(a)ir
G	toimten	con	Éren(n)	anm(a)e	athar
D	toimte, -in	coin	Ére, Érin(n)	anm(a)im(m), ainm	ath(a)ir
Pl. N		coin		anman(n)	a(i)thir
V					bráithre
A		cona		anman(n)	aithr(e)a
G		con		anman(n)	aithr(a)e
D		con(a)ib		anman(na)ib	aithr(a)ib
Du. NA		coin		ainm	
G		con			athar
D		con(a)ib		anman(na)ib	athr(a)ib

23. Determiners: the article, demonstratives, and emphatic particles

23.1. The definite article. The article is used before nouns to indicate definiteness; since a following genitive or a possessive pronoun conveys such a meaning, nouns with such elements do not have the article. That is to say, a definite noun phrase has no more than one marker of definiteness. Thus, in i.1a.3 the article is used with *cú*: *in cú* 'the dog' but not in i.1a.4 with *ainm*: *ainm in chon* '(the) name of the dog.' But the article is mandatory before a noun followed by a restrictive relative, as in xiii.Gl.7 (Ch. xiii, Gloss 7; references to glosses will follow this form): *isin núall do-n-gniat* 'in the cry that they made.' The article is also used with demonstratives, as in ii.1b.8: *isind aimsir sin* 'at that time.' Other less frequent uses will be discussed when they occur.

Forms of the article are:

	M.	Nt.	F.
Sg. N	in, int (before vowels)	a^n	ind^l, int (before ṡ)
A	in^n, -sin^n	a^n, -sa^n	in^n, -sin^n
G	in(d)^l, int (before ṡ)		inna^g, na^g
D	-(s)in(d)^l, -(s)int (before ṡ)		

	M.	Nt. F.
Pl. N	in(d)^l, int (before ṡ)	inna^g, na^g
A		inna^g, na^g, -sna^g
G		inna^n, na^n
D		-(s)naib

23.2. Demonstrative pronouns. One demonstrative is formed by adding to the · article a deictic particle *í(hí)*; the particle is stressed. Particles referring to place may also be used with nouns preceded by the article: *so, sa* (with unlenited *s*) and after palatals, *se, seo, sea*, e.g., *in lebor·so* 'this book.' Such forms may be nominal as well as adjectival, e.g., *int-i-siu* 'this one.'

23.3. Emphasizing particles may be used with personal pronouns, possessive adjectives, and verbs. They are placed after stressed forms, eg., v. 3b.15 *at·biri-siu* 'you say' + second singular particle. Nonpalatal (broad) and palatal (slender) forms exist.

		Nonpalatal	Palatal
Sg.	1	-sa	-se (-sea)
	2	-su, -so	-siu
	3 m.	-som (-sum, -sam)	-sem, -sium
	f.	-si	-si
	nt.	-som (-sum, -sam), són, ón	-sem, -sium
Pl.	1	-ni, -nai	-ni
	2	-si	-si
	3	-som	-sem, -sium

24. Verb forms made from the preterite stem

Only forms of the indicative are made. Since the preterite indicating completed action is preceded by *ro*, the conjunct is the most common form; the absolute will not be listed here. Forms with *ro* indicate completed action, or perfective force. The *ro* preterite is thus referred to as a perfect form; the perfect contrasts with narrative forms, which lack *ro-*.

The preterite has three inflections: an *s*-preterite, which all weak verbs take; a *t*-preterite, formed by verbs in *-l*, *-r*, and some in *-m*, *-g*; a suffixless preterite made by other strong verbs.

		Weak		Strong (*t*-pret.)	Deponent
Sg.	1	·mórus	·léicius	·biurt	·suidigsiur
	2	·mór(a)is	·lécis	·birt	·suidigser
	3	·mór	·léic	·bert	·suidigestar
Pl.	1	·mórsam	·léicsem	·bertam(m)ar	·suidigsemmar
	2	·mórs(a)id	·léicsid	·bert(a)id	·suidigsid
	3	·mórsat	·léicset	·ber(ta)tar	·suidigsetar

The forms given for *·bert* are stressed. Enclitic forms are as follows:

Sg. 1	as·ru-burt	Pl. 1	·ru-bartm(m)ar
2	·ru-b(a)irt		·ru-bartid
3	·ru-bart	3	·ru-bartatar

The suffixless preterite forms have various methods of formation, generally
· with reduplication. The resultant forms are highly complex. As example, the
preterite of -ic(c) (do-ic, tic 'comes,' ro-ic, ric 'reaches') will be given here.

Sg. 1	·ánac	Pl. 1	·áncammar
2	·ánac	2	·anc(a)id
3	·an(a)ic	3	·áncatar

25. Gemination

When consonants are doubled after certain words, the process is known as gemination. The process is graphic, indicating that the consonants concerned are not
lenited; that is to say, the words bringing about gemination do not cause lenition. They do, however, prefix h to vowels. Though differing in these ways from
phonological processes like palatalization, nasalization, and lenition, the traditional term is maintained here to characterize the effects of some words on following elements.

By late Old Irish gemination was not generally observed; geminated consonants are indicated only when the two words are written as one, as in *cuccum-
sa* 'to me' from *co* 'to, till' and the first singular suffixed pronoun (XVI.16.3);
but other forms made with *co* are not geminated, e.g., *cucum* 'to me' XII.12.11.

Gemination was brought about after *inna, na*, the genitive singular feminine,
and the nominative plural feminine and neuter, and the accusative plural of the
article, as indicated by the raised postposed *g* in v.G.23.1; also after the possessive pronoun feminine *a*, and the infixed personal pronouns third singular feminine and third plural *da, ta, a*. It is also brought about after the third singular
preterite and modal *ba* from *is* 'is,' except in relative constructions, and after *nī*
'is not'; sentence 11 of Section 3b above would be read [ba holk], and sentence
14 [ni holk] (both are written *holc* in some manuscripts, including the Book of
Leinster). (When *h* is written in Irish, it is usually silent. Only later was it used
for the sound.) Moreover, various uninflected words bring about gemination: *a*
'out of,' *co, cu* 'to,' *fri* 'against,' *la* 'with'; and, in pretonic position, prepositions
ending in a vowel, *ro, no*, the interrogatives *cia, ce, co*, and the negatives *nī* and
na before verbs, except when followed by infixed pronouns or in relative constructions. Other geminating elements will be noted as they occur.

Gemination is the last of the phonological phenomena to be discussed. Like
lenition, nasalization, and palatalization it will be referred to below, especially
when unusual forms with it occur.

25.1. Gemination and delinition. The consonants *l r n* are unlenited before
t d s l r n and after *s l n r*; before and after other consonants they are lenited.
The lack of lenition, or delinition, after *s l r n* is related to the process involved
in gemination.

38

Since such lenited and unlenited sounds are often not indicated in writing, information must frequently be based on the pronunciation in modern dialects. Thus *chomairle* 'counsel' v.3b.15 has unlenited *l*; the form *comairlle* is found in the glosses.

The unlenited form may also be spread through a paradigm. The nominative *lín* 'number,' as in *línaib* v.3b.14, has a variant *línn*, based on the accusative, in which the two *n*'s are regular. For further details see Thurneysen G.75–76.

chapter vi

READING AND TEXTUAL ANALYSIS, Section 4

1. Īar sin at·racht sūas ocus no·mbertaigedar.
2. 'Bad maith dūn' olse 'ocus dona hōegedaib dod⟨o⟩n·āncatar.'
3. Anait sidi leis trí laa ocus tēora aidchi.
4. Ocus tēit leo for leth (.i. la techta Connacht prius).
5. 'Ro·bá-sa trā' olse 'i n-imsnim mōr ocus cuntabairt mōir co·nderglē .i. do·ratus⟨s⟩a in coin do Ailill ocus do Meidb.
6. Ocus tecat ar chenn in chon co sochruid ocus co hūallach, ocus ros·bía lind ocus biad ocus ascada, ocus bērtait in coin, ocus is fochen dóib.'
7. Buidig sidi dano.
8. Luid īar sin co Ulad.
9. 'Do·ratus⟨s⟩a trá' olse 'asmo chuntabairt in coin do Chonchobur.
10. Ocus bad uallach tīastar ara chenn .i. formna mathe Ulad.
11. Bērtait ascada uili ocus ros·bia fáilte.'

---

1. īar sin   prep. *iar*[n] 'after' w. dem.; adv. 'then'
   at·racht   3 sg. pret. of *at·raig* = 'he rose'
   sūas   adv. 'up'
   no·mbertaigedar   3 sg. pres. conj. of *bertaigidir* 'shakes' w. infixed pers. pron. 3 sg. m. = 'exults, makes a flourish'
2. bad   2 pl. impv. of *is* (leniting)
   maith dūn   adj. (see IV.3a.9) and *do* + pers. pron. 1 pl. = 'be good to us, entertain us, show us hospitality'
   ol   without inflection 'says, said' w. *se* 'he'
   dona hōegedaib   *do* + art. pl. (*na h-*) + *óegi* dat. pl. m. 'guests'
   dodon·āncatar   cf. *táncatar*, I.1a.6, w. infixed pers. pron. 1 pl., rel.; see Thurneysen G.258 and V.G.24

40

3. anait   3 pl. pres. of *anaid* 'stay'

    sidi   pl. unstressed form of *suide* 'that, this, aforementioned'

    leis   prep. *la*^h 'with' w. 3 sg. pers. pron.

    laa   acc. pl. nt. of *laa* 'day'; for forms of numerals, see VI.G.28

    aidchi   acc. pl. f. of *adaig* 'night'

4. téit   see V.3b.10; 3 sg. pres.

    leo   prep. *la*^g w. 3 pl. pers. pron. (raised ^g signifies gemination; see V.G.25)

    for leth   prep. + acc. sg. nt. 'side'

    la techta Connacht prius   see I.1a.6, w. Lat. *prius* = 'first'; probably originally a gloss to explain *leo*

5. ro·bá-sa   *ro*-pret. 1 sg. of *is* w. emph. pron.; see v.G.23.3

    trá . . . imsním   see III.2.1; dat. sg. m. 'anxiety'

    mōr, móir   see VI.G.27 for adj. inflection

    cuntabairt   dat. sg. f. of *cuntabart* 'doubt'

    co·nderglé   3 sg. *ro*-pret. of *di·glé* 'becomes clear,' following *con-* 'until'

    do·ratus-sa   1 sg. *ro*-pret. of *do·beir* + emph. pron.; lit. 'I have given,' though used modally; see glossary under *do·beir*

6. tecat   3 pl. impv. of *do·ic* 'comes'

    ar chenn   acc. sg. nt. of *cenn* 'head'; w. *ar* = 'to meet'

    co sochruid . . . hūallach   adverbial 'magnificently . . . proudly'; note use of *co* w. adj. to form adv.

    ros·bía   3 sg. fut. of *tá*, w. *ro*- to support infixed 3 pl. pers. pron.

    lind   nom. sg. nt. 'drink, ale'

    ascada   nom. pl. f. of *ascaid* 'present'; vn. of *ad·saig*

    bērtait   3 pl. fut. of *berid*, w. petrified affixed pers. pron. 3 sg. nt.; contrast unaffixed *bérait*

    fochen   stress on *e* 'welcome'

7. buidig   nom. pl. m. of *buidech* 'satisfied or thankful'

8. luid   3 sg. pret. of *téit*

9. do·ratus   1 sg. *ro*-pret. of *do·beir* = 'I have given'

    asmo   *a* + 1 sg. poss. pron. 'out of, from'

10. bad uallach   impv. 3 sg. of *is*; see sent. 6; lit. 'let it be proud(ly) that it may be gone to fetch it'

    tiastar   pass. subj. rel. of *téit* 'goes'

    formna mathe   nom. pl. 'bands'; gen. pl. of *maith* 'noblemen'

GLOSSES

Stories like SMMD were transmitted orally for long periods and recorded finally in various manuscripts; accordingly, the language is frequently modified by comparison with Middle Irish. The best contemporary sources for Old Irish are glosses. Most of those that have been preserved were written down in monasteries on the Continent, at Würzburg, Milan, and Turin among other places. For an understanding of Old Irish grammar these are highly important because of their antiquity. See XVII.G.81 for further details.

In this and subsequent lessons selected glosses will be given. They are identified in accordance with the conventional references to the manuscripts. Wb. = Würzburg; Ml.= Milan; Tur. = Turin; SG. = Saint Gall.

1. Wb. 12ᶜ 29.   nī ar formut friḃ-si as-biur-sa in so.

   ní   neg. cop.
   ar   'on account of' (prep. w. dat. or acc.)
   formut   dat. sg. nt. 'envy' (vn. of *for-moinethar*)
   frib-si   'to' (2 pl.)
   as·biur-sa   1 sg. pres. ind. deut. *as·beir* 'says'; the nonrel. is found here because it does not follow a nom. or an acc.; if the cop. is used in such sentences to bring forward a noun in the nom. or acc., the main vb. takes a rel. form
   'It is not because of envy toward you that I say this.'

2. Wb. 24ª 38.   nī epur a n-anman sund.

   -epur 1 sg. proto. pres. ind. of *as·beir*
   a n-anman nt. pl. acc. *ainm* 'name'
   sund 'here'
   'I do not say their names here.'

3. Wb. 14ᵈ 26.   is i persin Ċrist d-a-gníu-sa sin.

   d-a-gníu-sa 1 sg. deut. pres. ind. of *do·gní* 'does'; infixed pron. nt. *a* anticipates obj. *sin* 'that'
   'It is in the person of Christ that I do that.'

GRAMMAR

26. Noun inflection: *io-* and *iā*-stems

The various vocalic and consonantal inflections characterized by a single vowel (*o*, *ā*, *i*, *u*) or a single consonant (dentals, velars, *s*, *n*, *r*) have been given in the preceding chapters. Here stems with *i* or *i̯* before the vowels *o* and *ā* are given. They differ from the simple inflections in that the vowel of the final syllable has not been lost. The paradigms given here may be compared with those in I.G.3 and II.G.8. To illustrate *io*-stem masculines, forms of *céle* 'companion' are given; and *cride* 'heart' for *io*-stem neuters. To illustrate *iā*-stem feminines, forms will be given for *soilse* 'light,' and for *blíad(a)in* 'year,' in which the final consonant in the NV Sg. and the NA Du. has palatal quality; these represent two subclasses of the *iā*-stems.

		io-stems			*iā*-stems
		M.	Nt.	F.	F.
Sg.	N	céle	cride	soilse	blíad(a)in
	V	céli	cride	soilse	blíad(a)in
	A	céle	cride	soilsi	blíadn(a)i
	G	céli	cridi	soilse	blíadn(a)e
	D	céliu	cridiu	soilsi	blíadn(a)i, blíad(a)in

Pl.	N	céli	cride	soilsi	blíadn(a)i
	V	céliu	cride	*soilsi	*blíadn(a)i
	A	céliu	cride	soilsi	blíadn(a)i
	G	céle	cride	soilse	blíadn(a)e
	D	célib	cridib	soilsib	blíadn(a)ib
Du.	NA	céle	cride	soilsi	blíad(a)in
	G	céle	cride	soilse	*blíadn(a)e
	D	célib	cridib	soilsib	*blíadn(a)ib

27. Adjectives and adverbs

Adjectives are in general inflected like nouns. There are five classes. A full paradigm is given only for *becc* 'small,' an -*o* and -*ā* stem. Inflections of the -*io* and -*ia* stems, e.g., *uile* 'all'; *i*-stems, e.g., *maith* 'good'; *u*-stems, e.g., *dub* 'black,' and consonant stems may be noted in Thurneysen G.225–28.

The forms of *becc* are as follows:

		M.	F.	Nt.
Sg.	N	becc	becc	becc
	V	bicc	becc	becc
	A	becc	bicc	becc
	G	bicc	bicce	bicc
	D	biucc	bicc	biucc

		M.	F. Nt.
Pl.	N	bicc	becca
	V	biccu	becca
	A	biccu, becca	becca
	G	becc	becc
	D	becc(a)ib	becc(a)ib

27.1. Position of adjectives, and their inflection. Predicate nominatives are inflected and agree with their subject in gender. As noted in I.G.2, attributive adjectives follow their nouns; they agree with them in gender, number, and case. Limiting adjectives, however, generally precede their nouns: *cach* 'each,' *nach* 'any,' *uile* in the sense of 'all,' the cardinal and ordinal numerals.

27.2. Adverbs. Adjectives may become adverbs by having the article *in* before the dative. In late Old Irish, adverbs may also be made with *co*, as in sentence 6 of this chapter.

28. The numerals

The cardinal numerals are as follows:

1	óen	5	cóic[l]	9	noi[n]
2	da	6	se[g]	10	deich[n]
3	tri	7	secht[n]	20	fiche
4	ceth(a)ir	8	ocht[n]	30	tricho

40	cethorcho	70	sechtmogo	100	cét
50	coíca	80	ochtmogo	1000	míle
60	sesca (see also *tri fichit cét* III.2.3)	90	nocha		

28.1. Syntactic uses of the cardinals, and their forms. The cardinals from 1 to 10 are adjectival; the remaining are nominal. *cóic* and *sé* nasalize before genitive plurals.

The cardinal for 1 is used chiefly in composition.

The cardinals for 2, 3, and 4 are inflected.

2

	M.	F.	Nt.
NA	da^l, dá^l	di^l, dí^l	da^n, dá^n
G	da^l, dá^l	da^l, dá^l	da^n, dá^n
D	(all genders) dib^n, deib^n		

3 and 4

	M. Nt.	F.	M. Nt.	F.
N	tri	teoir, teuir, téora	ceth(a)ir	cethéoir, cethéora
A	tri	téora	cethri	cethéora
G	tri	téora		cethéora
D	trib	téoraib	*cethrib	cethéoraib

To make cardinals between 10 and 100, the digit is given, followed by the genitive of the 'ten' in question, e.g., *a ocht deac* '18,' *a ocht coícat* '58.' The noun is inserted before the *deac* or *coícat* as in *na dá apstal déc* 'the twelve apostles.'

28.2. The ordinals are as follows:

1st	cétnae	6th	se(i)ssed
2nd	tán(a)ise; aile	7th	sechtmad
3rd	tris	8th	ochtmad
4th	cethramad	9th	nómad
5th	cóiced	10th	dechmad

29. Verb inflection: forms made from the future stem

There are two principal classes: the *f*-future, in general used for weak verbs; the *a*-future and *s*-future, which are originally reduplicated forms of the subjunctive stem. Here only forms of the *f*-future will be given.

		FUTURE			
		Absolute		Conjunct	
		Active	Deponent	Active	Deponent
Sg.	1	léicfea	suidigfer	·léiciub	·suidigfer
	2	léicfe	suidigfider	·léicfe	·suidigfider
	3	léicfid/th	suidigfithir	·léicfea	·suidigfedar
	rel.	léicfes(s)	suidigfedar		

44

Pl.	1	léicfimmi	*suidigfimmer	·léicfem	* ·suidigfemmar
	rel.	léicfimme	*suidigfemmar		
	2	léicfithe	*suidigfide	* ·léicfid	* ·suidigfid
	3	léicfit	*suidigfitir	·léicfet	·suidigfetar
	rel.	léicfite	*suidigfetar		

29.1. The secondary future. The secondary future is also called the conditional. It is used in a modal sense to indicate potentiality, and also to indicate that an action would occur when regarded from a specific past time.

The forms of *lécid* provide the pattern also for deponents.

Sg.	1	·léicfin(n)	Pl.	1	·léicfimmis
	2	·léicfeda		2	* ·léicfide/the
	3	·léicfed/th		3	·léicfitis

30. The Old Irish spelling system

The forms encountered up to now in the texts and the grammars illustrate the difficulties faced by the devisers of a spelling system for Old Irish based on the Latin alphabet.

30.1. Symbols for fricatives. The Latin alphabet contained only the fricative symbols *f s h*; on the basis of Greek borrowings, however, the compound symbols *ph th ch* were used for fricatives. Irish scribes maintained these uses. There were, however, no symbols for voiced fricatives; accordingly, the Irish scribes simply used the symbols for voiced stops. The following symbols were then used for fricatives:

	Voiceless	Voiced
Labial	f, ph [f]	b [v] [w]
Nasal labial		m [ṽ] [w̃]
Interdental	th [θ]	d [ð]
Dental and alveolar	s [s]	--
Palatal and velar	ch [χ]	g [γ]

30.2. Symbols for stops. Inasmuch as *b d g* were used to indicate voiced fricatives, *p t c* were commonly used to indicate voiced stops, especially in medial and final position, that is, where lenition (yielding fricatives) is most common. The voiceless velar stop may be written *cc*, and the voiceless dental *tt*; but the voiceless labial stop is rarely written *pp*. The phonetic values of single *p t c* are then as follows:

   (1) initially *p t c* represent voiceless stops

   (2) medially and finally they may represent voiceless or voiced stops; between vowels they represent voiced stops, especially in weakly stressed words, such as *ocus* [ogus] 'and'

Initially and when doubled *b d g* represent voiced stops. But after vowels they represent voiced fricatives. After consonants other than *m n l* they may represent either voiced stops or fricatives.

30.3. Symbols for vowels, for palatal or neutral quality of the consonants, and for diphthongs. The manuscripts may or may not distinguish long vowels from short vowels. When they do, an acute accent mark is placed over longs. Editors of Old Irish texts consistently mark long vowels with acute accents, distinguishing between long *í é á ó ú* and short *i e a o u*. Some editors, like Thurneysen in his edition of this text, indicate long vowels not marked by manuscript scribes with a macron, e.g., I.1a.5 *ō*. Grammars and dictionaries generally use acute accents for all long vowels.

In unstressed syllables, vowel symbols are chosen to indicate the quality of the neighboring consonants as well as that of the vowels. The following chart indicates the basis of their use.

Vowels in unstressed syllables may be written as follows:	
between palatal consonants	i
between neutral consonants	a
between velar consonants	u
between palatal and neutral consonants	e
between neutral and palatal consonants	(a) i
between velar and palatal consonants	(u) i
between palatal and velar consonants	iu
between velar and neutral consonants	$\begin{Bmatrix} o \\ u \end{Bmatrix}$
between neutral and velar consonants	$\begin{Bmatrix} o \\ u \end{Bmatrix}$

Vowel symbols are also used to indicate the quality of neighboring consonants in stressed syllables, as in I.1a.1 *Laignib* [lajñiv]. In this way *i*, either before or after other vowel symbols, may simply indicate palatal quality of the neighboring consonant; also *a* is fronted.

The symbol *e* indicates that the preceding consonant is palatal, the following one neutral, as in *ben* = [b̆en]. In *berid* (frequently written *beirid*) the quality of the following consonant is indicated by the *i* after the *e*.

The symbols *a* and *u* are used to indicate that the neighboring consonant is neutral. Thus, in the *a*-subjunctive one gets *beraid* in contrast with the indicative *berid*; the *a* merely indicates the neutral quality of the *r*.

Since the vowel system also contains diphthongs, sequences of vowels may be ambiguous. To indicate the diphthongs, editors generally place acute accent marks over one symbol of a diphthong, as follows: *aí, oí, uí; áe, óe, áu, éo, íu, ía, úa* (*ia* and *ua* are always true diphthongs, whether marked or not; i.e., the two elements are not used merely to distinguish the quality of the neighboring consonants).

If a consonant is palatal and the neighboring vowel front, as in *rí*, or if the consonant is neutral and the neighboring vowel low or back, as in *lán* and *cú*, simple consonant and vowel symbols are used.

30.4. Symbols for resonants.   The symbols *l r m n* are used to indicate the resonants. These may be palatal or neutral, lenited or unlenited, as discussed in the preceding paragraph and in II.G.10 and IV.G.20.

30.5. The symbol h.   The letter *h* did not represent a sound in Old Irish. It was used with short words consisting only of vowel symbols, e.g., *hó* beside *ó* 'from.' It was also used before *ui, ua*, possibly to prevent Latin-like pronunciations [vi], as in *huile* 'all.' On the other hand, [h] was pronounced before vowels following forms that produced gemination, such as *ba*; thus, *ba olc* in v.3b.11 is pronounced [ba holc].

30.6. Other symbols.   The Latin letters *k q y z* were rarely used. The symbol *x* represents [xs], or [ks].

30.7.   The precise origins of the spelling conventions for Old Irish present many problems. It has been proposed that some conventions, especially those for the stops *t/d* and so on, were taken over from British scribes.

chapter VII

READING AND TEXTUAL ANALYSIS, Section 5

In this section the arrival of the men of Connaught (the people from the West) and the men of Ulster (from the East) is reported. Ulster, Connaught, and Mac Dathó's Leinster, the area around Dublin, make up three of the five provinces, or *cóiced*'s, lit. 'fifths,' of Ireland; the other two are Munster and Meath. The guests are welcomed and preparations are made for a feast with the killing of the pig.

1. I n-ōenló immurġu ro·dālsat-soṁ etir aníar ocus anair.
2. Niro·follaiġed lēo-soṁ dano.
3. Táncatar dā cōiced Hērenn i n-ōenló co·mbátar i ndoruss ḃruiḋne Meic Dathó.
4. Do·luiḋ-seom fessin ara cenn ocus feraiḋ fāilti friu.
5. 'Ni⟨ḃ⟩·farc⟨h⟩elsaṁ, a ócu', olse; 'ar apaiḋe is mochen dūiḃ.
6. Taī̇t issin less!'
7. Lotar īaruṁ uili isin mbruiḋin, leth in tiġe dano la Connachta ocus in leth aile la Ulto.
8. Nibo ḃec in tech dano, secht ndoruiss ind ocus coíca imḋaḋ itir cech dā dorus.
9. Niptar aiġthi carat im ḟleiḋ immurġu bátar isin taiġ.
10. Sochaiḋe díḃ ro·fūachtnaiġ fri araili⟨u⟩.
11. Trī chét bliaḋan rīa ngein Chrī̇st ro·boī̇ in cocaḋ etorro.
12. Marbthair dōiḃ dano in ṁucc Ṁeic Dathó.
13. Trī fichit gaṁnach oca ḃiathaḋ siḋe co cenn secht mbliaḋan.
14. Tri neiṁ immurġu no·ḃíata co·ralta ár fer n-Ērenn impe.

---

1. i n-ōenló   *oín-*, *óen-* 'one, single' + dat. sg. of *laa*, *lá* 'day' = 'on the same day'
   immurgu   see II.1b.12

ro·dálsat-som   3 pl. *ro-s*-pret. of *dálaid* 'appoints, makes a tryst'; see V.G.23.3 for *som*

etir . . . ocus   'both . . . and, as well as ' (see sent. 8 below)

an-iar   'from the west'

an-air   'from the east'

2. niro-follaiged   *ro*-pret. pass. sg. of *follaigidir* 'neglects,' preceded by neg. ptc.

   léo-   see VI.4.4; prep. *la*- + acc. w. 3 pl. suffixed pron. *la* expresses agent in pass. constructions

3. táncatar   see I.1a.6

   co·mbátar   3 pl. pret. rel. of *tá* 'is'; cf. *co·rrabe* in IV.3a.1

   i ndoruss   'in front of'; lit. 'at the doors' (acc. pl.); words for 'door' are commonly in the pl., as in Lat. *forēs*, OE *duru*, from an acc. pl.

4. do·luid-seom   3 sg. pret. of *do·tét* 'comes'

   fessin   'self'

   ara cenn   see III.2.3 *cinn; ara—ar* 'for' + *a*^{n} 3 pl. poss. pron.; 'to meet them'

   feraid fáilti   see I.1a.7

5. nib·farchelsam   1 pl. *ro*-pret. of *fo·cíallathar*, w. neg. ptc. and infixed 2 pl. pers. pron.; 'we did not provide for you'

   ócu   voc. pl. m., w. *a*, of *óc* 'warrior, young man'

   ar apaide   'nevertheless, but'

   mochen   (stress on *e*) 'welcome'; see *fochen* VI.4.6

6. tait   2 pl. impv. of *do·tét* 'comes'

   less   acc. sg. m. of *les* 'the enclosed space around a building'; see V.G.23.1 for def. art. after *i*

7. lotar   3 pl. pret. of *téit*; see sent. 4 above

   iarum   prep. *íar*^{n} 'after, according to' w. affixed nt. sg. pers. pron. = 'afterwards, then'

   leth   acc. sg. nt. 'half'

   tige   gen. sg. nt. of *tech* 'house'; dat. sg. *taig* in sent. 9

   la   prep. w. acc. 'with, by'

   aile   nom. sg. nt.; see II.1b.12; late form

8. bec   'small'; after neg. 3 sg. pret. of *is*

   ind   use of pers. pron. w. *i*^{n} corresponding to *in tech*

   coíca   see VI.G.28

   imdad   gen. pl. of *imda* after *coíca*; see III.2.1

   itir   prep. w. acc. 'between' (same word as in sent. 1 above)

   cech   du. acc. w. *dá* 'each two, each pair'

9. niptar   3 pl. pret. of *is* 'be' w. neg.

   aigthi   nom. pl. f. of *agad* 'face'

   carat   gen. pl. m. of *cara*; see III.2.4 *c(h)arait*

   fleid   acc. sg. f. of *fled* 'banquet'; note lenition after prep. *im* 'round, at'

   bátar   see sent. 3 above

   i-sin   prep. *i*^{n} + art. (dat. sg. leniting)

10. sochaide   nom. sg. f. 'large number'

    dib   3 pl. affixed pers. pron. w. *di* 'of'

    ro·fúachtnaig   3 sg. rel. *ro*-pret. of *fúachtnaigid* 'trespasses, injures'; note the construction of the sentence, w. a rel. vb. following a pred. nom. sentence: '[it was (there was) one group of them] which had feuded against the other'

    fri arailiu   acc. pl.; see IV.3a.1

11. tri chét   see VI.G.28

bliadan   gen. pl. f.; see III.2.3 and VI.G.26

ría n-   prep. w. dat. 'before'

gein   dat. sg. nt. 'birth'

ro·boí   subst. vb. is not rel. form because preposed element is not sub. or obj.

cocad   nom. sg. m. 'war'; for def. art. see sent. 9

etorro   prep. *itir*, as in sent. 8 above, w. affixed pers. pron. 3 pl.

12. marbthair   pres. pass. of *marbaid* 'kills, slaughters'; *do* expresses indirect obj. 'for them'

mucc   nom. sg. f. 'pig'; gen. *mucce*, as in title; dat. *muic*; nom. pl. *mucca*

13. (trí fichit) gamnach   see III.2.3; gen. pl. f. 'milch-cow'

oca   prep. w. dat. 'at, near' w. f. sg. pers. pron.

bíathad   vn. dat. sg. from *bíathaid* 'feeds, nourishes'; note impf. pass in sent. 14

side   unstressed form of *suide* 'aforementioned' after poss. pron. *oca*

co cenn   prep. w. acc. = 'until the end'

14. tri   prep. w. acc. 'through'

neim   acc. sg. nt. 'poison, venom'

no·bíata   see sent. 13; prefix *no-* always w. impf.

co·ralta   past subj. pass. of *fo·ceird* 'puts, performs' = 'might be carried out'

ár   nom. sg. nt. 'slaughter, massacre'

impe   prep. *im* 'about' w. 3 sg. f. pers. pron. 'about it, because of it'

GLOSSES

4. Wb. 21ᶜ19.   is oc precept soscéli attó.

oc   prep. 'at' (this construction w. the vn. forms a progressive aspect)

precept   vn. of *pridchid* 'preaches'

soscéli   'gospel' *so*—a prefix contrasting w. *do*—meaning 'good' vs. 'bad,' 'favorable' vs. 'unfavorable,' etc.; *scél* = 'story' (The composition is like Eng.: good + spell = gospel; both formed on *euangelion*)

attó   1 sg. pres. ind. of subst. vb. 'I am'

'It is preaching the gospel that I am.'

5. Wb. 27ᶜ22.   is airi am cimbid-se hóre no pridchim in rúin sin.

airi   3 sg. nt. of *ar* 'for' = 'therefore, on account of that'

am   1 sg. pres. ind. abs. of cop.; note not rel. form; see sent. 11 above and VI.Gl.1

cimbid   m. 'captive, prisoner'—*se* emph. 1 sg.

hóre   'because' (causes nasalization)

no pridchim   1 sg. pres. of *pridchid* 'preaches'; the rel. marker *no* is prefixed to simple verbs used relatively in the pres. and fut. ind. and the pres. subj. which have no special rel. form

rúin   acc. of *rún* 'secret, mystery'

'It is for this that I am a prisoner, because I preach that mystery.'

6. Wb. 32ª21.   at féchem dom.

at   2 sg. pres. cop.

féchem   m. 'debtor'

dom   prep. *do* + 1 sg. pron.; this construction has the force of 'one of my'
'You are a debtor of mine.'

GRAMMAR

31. Comparative constructions

As a VSO language, Old Irish has comparative constructions of the pattern: Adjective Pivot Standard. An example is v.3b.11: *bid līa turim* 'it will be more than enumeration.' The pivot may be indicated by the dative of the standard, as in *turim*, or by *inda* or *ol* 'than,' as in x.10.3: *Is ferr . . . indaī-siu* 'he is better than you.'

Comparatives may also be used predicatively, as in III.2.4: *ni messa Conchobar* 'not inferior is Conchobar.'

The comparative is formed for regular adjectives by adding *-iu*, *-u*, with palatalization of the preceding consonant: *sen* 'old,' *siniu* 'older.'

The superlative is formed by adding *-em*, *-am*, or *-imem*: *cóem* 'handsome,' *cóimiu* 'handsomer,' *cóemem* 'handsomest'; *úasal* 'high, noble,' *úaisliu* 'nobler,' *úaislimem* 'noblest.'

Some of the most common adjectives are irregular, as in the other Indo-European languages. The following are among the most common:

Positive	Comparative	Superlative
bec 'little'	laigiu, lugu	lugam, lugimem
il 'much'	lía	--
maith 'good'	ferr	dech, deg
már, mór 'great'	máo, máa, má, mó	máam
olc 'bad'	messa, messu	messam

Old Irish also has an equative, with suffix *-ithir*, *-idir*: *léir* 'eager, diligent,' *lérithir* 'as eager, as diligent.' Irregular forms are *lir* 'as many,' *móir* 'as great.' With the equative the standard is in the accusative.

32. Interrogatives

Questions not introduced by an interrogative pronoun have initial *in*, *inn* (nasalizing), as in XV.15.8: *in fīr?* 'Is it just?' An affirmative answer is generally presupposed, as also in XII.12.3: *Inn é so Muinremor?* 'Is not that Muinremor?'

The interrogative pronouns are *cía* 'who' and *cid*, *ced* 'what,' as in XIII.13.3 *Cīa so?* 'Who is this?'; IV.3a.4: *Cid no-taí?* 'What ails you?' There is also a predicative genitive: *coich*, *cuich* 'whose?' It may be used for *cía* 'who' as in XIV.14.3: *Cuich so?* 'Who(se) is this?'

Weakly stressed interrogatives are *ce*, *ci*, *cía*, used for all genders and numbers. They are also combined with following words, as with *indas* 'manner,' as in IX.7.4: *Cindas fír lib?* 'What-manner true in-your-opinion' = 'What do you think?' Compare *Cīa indas* in VIII.6.8. *Cindas* may then be equivalent to 'how,' as in VIII.6.7: *Cindas rainnfither in mucc?* 'How should the pig be divided?'

33. The substantive verb and the copula

As noted in II.G.9, Old Irish has a substantive verb 'be' as well as the copula. The substantive verb indicates presence or existence; the copula simply equates the subject and the predicate. Compare: IV.3a.3: *Atá biad lat* 'There is food beside you' = 'Food is present next to you' (subst. vb.); IV.3a.2 *Is fota in troscud* 'Is long the fasting' = '[Your] fasting is long.'

The substantive verb is often used with a dative to indicate possession, as in V.3b.14: *Táthut airle lim-sa fris* 'exists-for-you advice with-me about-it' = 'I have advice for you about it.'

Like forms of the verb 'be' in English, both the substantive verb and the copula are based on several roots. Moreover, they are frequently unstressed and accordingly have a variety of forms. Paradigms will be given here and in VII.G.34, though the forms and their uses are best learned by noting their occurrences in texts.

33.1. Forms of the substantive verb: ·tá, atá. The most common form is *atá, attá < *ad·tá; *ad* was dropped after a conjunct particle. Absolute forms of the present are found only after comparatives and *ol-*, as in IX.7.3 *oldás* 'than is'; X.10.3 *indaí-siu* 'than you are.'

33.2. Present indicative conjunct.

Sg.	1	·táu ·tó	Pl.	1	·taam
	2	·taí		2	·taïd
	3	·tá		3	·taat
Pass.		·táthar			

The form *fil* is used rather than *atá*, as in XVI.16.8 *nad·fil*. This is the usual relative form and the usual conjunct form except after an infixed dative pronoun or after a relative governed by a preposition: IV.3a.2 *i·taí* 'in which you are'; VIII.6.8 *i-taat* 'in which they are.' *Fil* is impersonal and the pronoun subject is infixed.

33.3. The substantive verb also has a consuetudinal present, meaning 'is usually, is generally.'

			Absolute	Conjunct
Sg.	1		bíuu	·bíu
	2			·bí
	3		biid, biith	·bí, enclit. ·ru-b(a)i
	rel.		bís	
Pl.	1		bímmi	·biam
	rel.		bímme	
	3		biit, bíit	·biat, enclit. ·ru-bat
	rel.		bíte	
Pass. Sg.	3		bíthir	·bíther, enclit. rubthar
	rel.		bíther	

52

33.4. *Imperative.*

	Sg.	2	bí		Pl.	biid
		3	bíth, bíd			

33.5. *Subjunctive.*

		Present Subjunctive		Past Subjunctive
		Absolute	Conjunct	
Sg.	1	beu, beo	·béo	·beinn
	2		·bée	·betha
	3	beith, beid	·bé, enclit. ·roi-b	·beth, ·bed, enclit. ·ro-bad
	rel.	bes(s)		
Pl.	1	be(i)mmi	·bem, enclit. ·ro-bam	·bemmis
	2	be(i)the	·beith, enclit. ·ro-bith	·bethe
	3	beit	·bet, enclit. ·ro-bat	·betis, enclit. ·roibtis
	rel.	bete		
Pass. Sg.	3	bethir	·bether	
	rel.	bether		

33.6. *Future.*

		Absolute	Conjunct
Sg.	1	bia	
	2	bie	
	3	bieid, bied	·bia, ·bía
	rel.	bias	
Pl.	1	be(i)mmi	·biam
	2	bethe	·bieid, ·bied
	3	bieit, biet, bíet	·biat
	rel.	be(i)te	

33.7. *Preterite.*

		Conjunct			
Sg.	1	·bá, enclit. ·roba, ·raba	Pl.	1	·bámmar
	2	·bá		2	·baid
	3	·boí, ·baí, enclit. ·rob(a)e, ·rab(a)e		3	·bátar

33.8. *Verbal noun.*

buith, buid, bith, as in IV.3a.8

34. Forms of the copula

Forms of the present indicative absolute, conjunct, and conjunct negative were given in II.G.9. Other forms are as follows:

53

34.1. Imperative.

	Sg.					Pl.	1	ban
		2	ba				2	bad, bed
		3	bad, bed				3	bat

34.2. Subjunctive.

		Present		Past	
		Absolute	Conjunct	Absolute	Conjunct
Sg.	1	ba	-ba		-bin, -benn
	2	ba	-ba		-ptha
	3	ba	-b, -p	bid	-bad, -pad
	rel.	bes, bas		bed, bad	
Pl.	1		-ban	bemmis	-bemmis
	2	bede	-bad		
	3		-bat, -pat	betis, bitis	-bdis, -ptis
	rel.	bete, beta, bata			

With the conjunctions *cía* 'although' and *mǎ* 'if,' *ma-ni* 'if not,' the present subjunctive forms are:

	Sg.	3	cid, cith, ced, ceith	Pl.	3	cit
			mad			mat
			manip			

The past subjunctive forms are:

	Sg.	3	cid	Pl.	3	citis, cetis
			mad			matis

34.3. Future.

		Absolute	Conjunct
Sg.	1	be	
	2	be, ba	-be, -pa
	3	bid, bith	-be, -pe, -ba, -pa
	rel.	bes, bas	
Pl.	1	bemmi, bimmi, bami	
	2		-beth
	3	bit	-bat, -pat
	rel.	beta	

34.4. Preterite and imperfect indicative passive.

		Absolute	Conjunct
Sg.	1	basa	-bsa, -psa, -sa
	2	basa	-sa
	3/rel.	ba	-bo, -po, -bu, -pu

54

Pl.	1		-bommar, -bum(mar)
	3	batir, batar	-btar, -ptar
	rel.	batar	

In the first and second singular the emphasizing particle -sa has been added to the forms. Conjunct first singular forms are: with ni, nipsa; with ro, ropsa; with ni and ro, nirbsa.

35. The passive

The passive has one form for all persons but the third plural, which has a special form. When the first and second persons are used, infixed pronouns indicate the subject. Forms of car(a)id 'loves' illustrate these for the present and perfect. For the use of no and nu see v.G.21.2.

		Present		Perfect	
Sg.	1	no-m·charthar	'I am loved'	ro-m·charad	'I was loved'
	2	no-t·charthar	'you are loved'	ro-t·charad	'you were loved'
	3	carth(a)ir, ·carthar	'he, she, it is loved'	ro·carad	'he, she, it was loved'
Pl.	1	no-n·carthar	'we are loved'	ro-n·carad	'we were loved'
	2	no-b·carthar	'you are loved'	ro-b·carad	'you were loved'
	3	cart(a)ir, ·cartar	'they are loved'	ro·cartha	'they were loved'

35.1. Passive present indicative forms for the verbs given in III.G.14 are as follows:

	Absolute			
Sg. 3	mórth(a)ir	léicthir	ber(a)ir	suidigthir
rel.	mórthar	léicther	berar	sudigther
Pl. 3	mór(a)itir, mórt(a)ir	léictir, lécitir	bert(a)ir	suidigtir
rel.	móratar, mórtar	léicter, lécetar	bertar	suidigter

	Conjunct			
General form	·mórthar	·léicther	·berar	·suidigther
Pl. 3	·móratar, ·mórtar	·lécetar, ·léicter	·bertar	·suidigter

35.2. Imperative passive.

General form	mórthar	léicther	berar, ta-barr	suidigther
Pl. 3	mórtar	léicter	bertar	suidigter

35.3. Subjunctive passive.

	Absolute			
Sg. 3	mórth(a)ir	léicthir	berth(a)ir	suidigthir
rel.	mórthar	léicther	berthar	suidigther
Pl. 3	mórt(a)ir, mór(a)itir	léictir, lécitir	bert(a)ir	suidigtir
rel.	mórtar, móratar	léicter, lécetar	bertar	suidigter

General form	Conjunct			
General form	·mórthar	·léicther	·berthar	·suidigther
Pl. 3	·mórtar, ·moratar	·léicter, ·lécetar	·bertar	·suidigter

Other passive forms will be discussed in the notes as they occur.

chapter VIII

READING AND TEXTUAL ANALYSIS, Section 6

With Section 6 the central part of the story begins: an exchange between heroes of Ulster and heroes of Connaught concerning the most eminent warrior. He would have the honor of dividing the pig and taking for himself the best portion. Such exchanges preceding combat are characteristic features of heroic story. Among the best known is that between the suitors and Odysseus in Books xx and xxi of the *Odyssey*. Others are that between the sons of Njall and their besiegers before the burning, and that between Hildebrand and Hadubrand in the Old High German *Hildebrandslied*. Dramatic exchanges may not lead to battle, as in the *Beowulf* or in Book VIII of the *Odyssey*. In SMMD there is little question concerning the outcome. The exchanges, dominated by the Connaught warrior Cet from IX.8 through XIV.14, lead to a confrontation between Cet and Conall in XV.15 and the battle between Connaught and Ulster in XVIII.18. Section 6 provides the setting for the exchanges and eventual battle.

1. Tucaḋ dóiḃ ῑaruṁ in ṁucc ocus ċethorcha daṁ dia tarsnu cenmothā a mbiaḋ archenae.
2. Mac Dathó fessin ocond ḟert⟨h⟩iġsecht.
3. 'Mochen dúiḃ' olse.
4. 'Ni daḃar saṁail riss sin; ataat aiġe ocus ṁucca la Laiġniu, a testa de-sin mairfithir dúiḃ i mbárach.'
5. 'Is maith in ṁucc' ol Conchobar.
6. 'Is maith immurġu' ol Ailill.
7. 'Cindas rainnfither in ṁucc, a Chonchoḃuir?' ol Ailill.
8. 'Cῑa indas' ol Bricne mac Carḃaiḋ anúas ane asind imḋai, 'bale i·taat láith ġaile fer n-Ērenn sund, acht a-rrann ar choṁraṁaiḃ?
9. Ocus do·rat cách díḃ builli dar sróin a chēili riaṁ.'
10. 'Dēntar!' ol Ailill.
11. 'Is maith' ol Conchoḃar; 'atát gillai dún is·taiġ im·rul⟨l⟩atar in cocrích.'

1. tucad   3 sg. perf. pass. of *do·beir* = 'was brought'
   cethorcha   see VI.G.28, followed by gen. pl. of *dam*
   dia tarsnu   meaning unclear; according to Thurneysen 1935:61, from the adj. *tarsna* 'transverse' and *do* 'to, for' w. 3 sg. poss. pron. = 'to it transversely, across it' (f. like *mucc*)
   (cenmothá a mbiad) archenae   'besides'; see the earlier occurrence of *cenmothá* in III.2.3
2. fessin   VII.5.4
   ocond   prep. *oc* 'at' w. art.
   ferthigsecht   dat. sg. f. 'stewardship'; the sentence is pred. nominal, w. the prepositional phrase as pred.
3. mochen   as in VII.5.5
   dúib   *do* + 2 pl. pron.
4. dabar   prep. *di* 'of, from' + 2 pl. poss. pron.
   samail   dat. sg. f. 'likeness'
   riss   prep. *fri(ri)* + 3 sg. nt. pers. pron., followed by *sin* 'the aforementioned, that'; like 2, a nominal sentence, though in the neg.; according to Thurneysen 1935:26 the sentence means: 'That is not by reason of your equality to it' = 'This quantity of meat is not offered to you as though it were equal to your title . . . you shall get more tomorrow'
   ataat   3 pl. pres. of *atá*; see VII.G.33.2
   aige   nom. pl. nt. of *ag* 'cattle'
   (a) testa   rel. 'what' + (*do-es-tá-*) 'is lacking'
   de-sin   prep. *di* 'from' + 3 sg. pers. pron. 'from it' + dem. 'there, then'
   mairfithir   pass. fut. of *marbaid*; see VII.5.12
   dúib   prep. *do* 'for' + 2 pl. affixed pron.
   i mbárach   'tomorrow'
5. maith   IV.3a.9
7. cindas   from *cía, cid* 'who, what' + *indas* 'manner' = 'how'
   rainnfither   fut. pass. rel. of *rannaid* 'divides, carves'; note the rel., which indicates that *cindas* is to be interpreted as a pred. nom. sentence: 'what (is the) manner'; this pattern is found in the echo question of Bricne in sent. 8, which sets off the exchange
8. Bricne   appears in other MSS as *Bricriu* (cn- develops into cr-) and e (palat. consonant + vowel + nonpalat. off-glide is phonetic equivalent of *-iu*; note early *Deirdriu* later *Deirdre*)
   anúas ane   'from above' + a ptc. used after adverbs of place
   asind imdai   *a^g* prep. 'out of' + art., followed by dat. sg. f. of *imda* 'couch'
   bale i n-   'there where'; *bale* m. 'place'; same word as *Baile Atha Clíath* 'the place of the ford of the sticks/hurdles/wattles,' the Irish name for Dublin
   láith gaile   nom. pl. m. of *láth* + gen. sg. f. of *gal* 'fight' = 'warriors'
   sund   'here'; see VI.Gl.2
   a-rrann   gen., obj. f. of vn. of *rannaid*; see sent. 7
   chomramaib   dat. pl. m. of *comram* 'contest'; *ar* 'by means of'
9. do·rat   ro-pret. 3 sg. of *do·beir*
   builli   acc. sg. f. 'blow'
   sróin   acc. sg. f. 'nose'
   céili   gen. sg. m. of *céle* 'companion, other'; see IV.3a.8
   riam   adv. from prep. *ría* 'before'

10. dēntar   impv. pass. of *do·gní* 'does'
11. gillai   nom. pl. m. of *gille* 'young man, warrior'
    dún   *do* + 1 pl. pers. pron.; used w. *·tá* to indicate possession
    is·taig   dat. sg. nt. of *tech* after prep. *i*
    im·rullatar   3 pl. *ro*-pret. of *im·tét* 'goes around' from **im-ro·lod·atar*
    cocrích   acc. sg. f. 'borderland'

GLOSSES

7. Wb. 5^{b}28.   is inse nduit. ní tú no-d n-ail acht is hé no-t ail.

    inse (anse)   'difficult'
    nduit   *do* + 2 sg.
    ail   3 sg. conj. pres. ind. of *ailid* 'nourishes, supports'
    no-d   *no* used to infix pron. for class of infix; see Thurneysen G.260–61;
       -d^n: see Strachan (p. 26), 3 sg. m. type C infix, and n. 1
    no-t   w. 2 sg. infix
    'It is difficult for you. It is not you that nourishes it, but it is it that nourishes you.'

8. Ml. 51^{c}g.   isin nūall do-n-gniat hō ru maith for a nāimtea remib.

    isin   i + art. *issind^l*, *issin^n*
    nūall   nt. 'cry'
    do-n-gniat   3 pl. pres. ind. deut. nasalizing rel. clause where antecedent is
       obj. of the vb. of the rel. clause; see Thurneysen G.317
    hō   *ó, ua* 'after, when' w. perf.
    ru maith   3 sg. pres. w. *ro*- as equivalent of perf. (*maidid* w. *for* + the de-
       feated *re^n* + the victor)
    nāimtea   acc. pl. of *namae* 'enemy'
    remib   3 pl. 'before them'
    'In the cry that they made when they defeated the enemy' lit. 'when it
    broke before them on the enemy.'

9. Wb. 12^{c}22.   ro·cluinethar cách in fogur & nícon fitir cid as·beir.

    ro·cluinethar   3 sg. pres. ind. deponent 'hears'
    fogur   m. 'sound'
    nícon   'not' in independent negation; like *ro·cluinethar*, *ro·fitir* drops the
       ro- when it has another preverb; see Thurneysen G.351; *nícon* lenites,
       yielding *fitir*
    fitir   'know' (pret. form w. pres. or pret. meaning cognate w. OE *witan*) de-
       ponent
    cid   nt. of *cía* 'who, what'
    as·beir   lenited *b*; see Thurneysen G.314
    'Everyone hears the sound and does not know what it says.'

59

GRAMMAR

36. Simple declarative sentences

The grammar sections of Chapters VIII to X will summarize the common syntactic patterns, using illustrations from SMMD.

Simple sentences may be verbal or nominal. In both patterns the verbal or predicate element is placed in initial position.

36.1. Verbal sentences.

a. Verbal sentences may consist only of a verb.

   IV.3a.8 As·soí 'he turns away'

b. The verb may be accompanied by a subject.

   III.2.3 do·bértar tri fichit cét lilgach 'three score hundred cows will be given'

c. The verb may be accompanied by a subject and an object; the order is then VSO.

   I.1a.3 Im·díched in cú Laigniu huili 'the hound protected all Leinster'

   In such sentences the subject may be expressed only in the verb.

   III. 2.2 Ro·rāidset a n-athesca 'they stated their reports'

   Such patterns are expected in imperatives.

   VII.5.6 Taĩt issin less! 'come into the enclosure'

In any patterns adverbial expressions are placed after the basic elements, as in III.2.3 where *hi cétóir* 'at once' follows *lilgach*.

36.2. Nominal sentences.

a. Nominal sentences may consist of two nominal phrases. Of these the first is the predicate.

   I.1a.1 Mac Dathó a ainm 'his name [was] Mac Dathó'

   Either constituent may have modifiers.

b. Either nominal element may be a prepositional phrase and the predicate may also be an adverb.

   II.1b.10 Dam ocus tinne in cach coiri 'beef and pork [was] in each cauldron'

c. Nominal sentences may consist only of predicate nouns; this pattern is found especially when a relative construction follows.

   VII.5.10 Sochaide díb // ro·fūachtnaig ... '[there was] a large number of them // which was feuding'

d. Nominal sentences may have an adjective in the predicate; it may be accompanied by the copula.

   I.1a.4 ba lán Hériu . . . 'Ireland was full . . .'

Compare the position of the adjective in predicative use with that as attributive in *bói rí amrae* 'there was a famous king.'

As with verbal sentences, adverbial expressions are placed after the basic elements.

37. Prepositional expressions

Old Irish makes great use of prepositions, especially with accompanying possessive and personal pronouns. As indicated in II.G.7, prepositions are so closely associated with such pronouns that they are often treated as inflections. Further paradigms will be given in VIII.G.38. Here some of the relationships expressed by prepositional constructions are summarized.

    a. Prepositions may be used with personal pronouns following the copula and an adjective.

    VIII.Gl.7 is inse nduit 'for you it is difficult'

    Doit, a form consisting of *do* 'to, for' plus the second singular personal pronoun *-it*, functions semantically like the subject, or topic, in a nominal sentence. Similarly, in

    III.2.4 biaid degcaratrad de 'from it will be friendship'

    de, a form made from the preposition *di* 'from' plus the third singular personal pronoun, is related by the future of *·tá* to the predicate noun.

    b. The substantive verb used with suffixed forms of *oc* indicates possession.

    I.1a.2 Boí cú occo 'was a hound at him' = 'he had a hound'

    In passive constructions the agent may also be indicated by a preposition with affixed pronoun.

    VII.5.2 Niro·follaiged léo 'it was not neglected by them'

    c. A sequence of prepositional expressions may be found in sentences.

    v.3b.14 Táthut airle lim-sa fris 'I have advice for you about it'

    In this clause the first two words express the sentence: 'you have advice.' These are followed by two prepositional expressions: 'with me myself' and 'about it.' The prepositional expressions may be related to the basic clause as indicated in the translation given above. Such constructions are often difficult, as in VIII.6.1 and 4. Yet they allow very compact means of expression, as in

    VIII.6.4 a testa de-sin mairfithir dúib 'what is lacking from it there will be slaughtered for you'

    For the interpretation of such sequences a knowledge of the "inflected forms" of prepositions is highly important.

38. Further prepositions with personal pronouns

In II.G.7, the forms of the preposition *fri* followed by personal pronouns are listed. Here further prepositions are given, with affixed personal pronouns in one of their possible forms; it is assumed that others exhibiting variation can be recognized, as between *o* and *u*, or *e* and *i*.

a. Prepositions governing the dative.

		di 'from'	do 'to'	oc 'at'	ó(úa) 'from, by'
Sg.	1	dím(-sa)	dom	ocum, ocom	úaim
	2	dít	duit	ocut	úait
	3 m. nt.	de	dó	occo	úad
	f.	dí	dí	occi	úadi
Pl.	1	dín	dún	ocunn	úain
	2	díb	dúib	occaib	úaib
	3	díb	dóib	occaib	úadib

b. Prepositions governing the accusative (see II.G.7 for forms of *fri* 'against').

		la 'with'	tri, tre 'through'	tar, dar 'over, beyond'
Sg.	1	lem	trium	thorum, thorom
	2	lat	triut-su	torut-su
	3 m. nt.	leiss	triit	tarais
	f.	lee	tree	tairse
Pl.	1	linn	triun-ni	torunn
	2	lib	triib	toraib
	3	leu, léo	triib	tairsiu

c. Prepositions governing both the accusative and the dative.

		at 'for, on account of'	for 'on'	i 'in, into'
Sg.	1	airium	form	indium
	2	airiut	fort	indiut
	3 m. nt.	D airiu	for	and
		A airi	foir	ind
	f.	airre	D fuiri	indi
			A forrae	inte
Pl.	1	erunn	fornn	indiunn
	2	airib	fuirib	indib
	3	airriu	D foraib	indib
			A forru	intiu

d. As indicated in the first form given here, *dím-sa*, the personal pronoun may be followed by emphasizing particles; these are given in IV.G.18.1.

e. Prepositions may also be followed by forms of the article; these are listed in V.G.23.1. For *do*, the following forms are found in SMMD:

Sg. dond, don   Pl. dona h-

As these illustrate, the initial vowel of the article is lost; the same reduction of the article is found with *di* and *ó ua*.

After prepositions which originally ended in a consonant, the article is found in the form *sin*, often with doubled *s*. These prepositions are *a* 'out of,' *co* 'with,' *fri* 'against,' *i* 'in,' *iar* 'after,' *la* 'with,' *re* 'before,' *tar* 'across,' and *tri, tre* 'through.' Forms found with *i* are:

acc. sg. m. f.	issin, isin	acc. pl.	isna
dat. sg.	isind, issin	dat. pl.	isnaib

f. Prepositions may also be followed by forms of the possessive pronoun, as noted in v.G.21.3. For *do*, the forms are:

Sg.	1	dom	Pl.	1	di-ar^n
	2	dot		2	dobar
	3	dia, día		3	dia

The possessive pronouns are based on the unstressed forms, as given in III.G.11.1.

g. In expressions consisting of copula + adjective + *la*, the object of *la* indicates a person, and the copula may be translated 'seems,' or the entire sentence may be paraphrased as below:

is inse let 'it seems difficult to you,' i.e., 'you think it difficult'

Contrast such expressions with that in VIII.Gl.7:

is inse nduit 'it is difficult for you'

39. Forms made from the present stem

As indicated in III.G.13, the Irish verb has five stems, and forms are made directly from these, not necessarily from one root. Moreover, because of phonological variations the stems made from one verbal root may vary considerably, especially if the verb is strong.

Three inflections are made from the present stem: the present indicative, the imperfect, and the imperative; see III.G.14.

The present indicative is normally used to indicate present time, as in VI.Gl.2:

nī epur a n-anman sund 'I do not say their names here'

In this sentence a simple action is indicated. The present may also be used to indicate continuous or repeated action, as does the present indicative of *do·gní* in VI.Gl.3:

is i persin Críst d-a-gníu-sa sin 'It is in the person of Christ that I do that'

The present indicative is also used as a historical present, that is, to indicate greater vividness for actions of the past, as in VI.4.4 *Ocus tēit leo for leth* 'and he (i.e., the messenger group) goes to this side.' (In SMMD most of the verbs are in the imperfect or preterite, since the incident is reported as an event of the past; present indicatives occurring so far are historical presents—see also VI.4.3.)

The imperfect indicates repeated or customary action, in contrast with the preterite which indicates a single action in the past; it is often translatable as 'used to.' Examples of imperfect forms are found in II.1b.11 and 12 *no·thēged* 'who came (again and again),' *do·bered* 'he would put/thrust,' and in the other verb forms of these sentences, as identified in the textual analysis of the passage. Such imperfects may be contrasted with preterites in the same section, such as *ro·boi* 'which used to be/was' in II.1b.8, as well as with the preterites in the earlier sentences: I.1a.1 *boí* 'there was,' I.1a.3 *im·díched* 'he protected,' I.1a.6 *táncatar* 'they came.'

The imperative is used to indicate commands or necessary action, as in the third person: VII.5.6 *Taít issin less!* 'Come into the enclosure'; VI.4.6 *Ocus tecat ar chenn in chon* 'And let them come to meet the hound.'

A summary of the uses of other verb forms will be given in the two following chapters.

40. Substantives: nouns and pronouns; uses of the cases

Substantives are inflected for three genders and three numbers; these categories indicate congruence or agreement. Substantives are also inflected for five cases: nominative, vocative, accusative, genitive, and dative. A brief statement on their principal uses is given here.

    a. The nominative is used as the case of the subject and the predicate noun, as in the examples in VIII.G.36. It is also used in an absolute sense, especially before sentences; its relationship is then often indicated by a pronoun: v.3b.11 *Cú Mes-Roida meic Dathó, ba olc lathe etha dó* 'The hound of Mes-Roida of Mac Dathó evil was the day they sent for it.' Such nominative forms are also found after coordinating conjunctions when following an inflected preposition.

    b. The vocative is the case of address; it is always preceded by the leniting particle *a*.

    c. The accusative is used to indicate the object of verbs, also with verbs of going and coming (cf. Lat. *Romam íre* 'go to Rome').

        It is also used after certain prepositions; see VIII.G.38.c.

        It is also used to indicate time, usually duration: IV.3a.1 *co·rrabe tri thráth . . .* 'and as a result he was for three days . . .'

        It is also used to indicate the standard after the equative.

    d. The genitive is used descriptively, or to specify more precisely another noun: IV.3a.7 *turbaid chotulta* 'prevention of sleeping'; IV.3a.8 *in ferg fēne* 'the warrior of a band.' In both of these phrases the following genitive describes or specifies the preceding noun.

        The genitive is also used to indicate the object, or the subject, of a verbal noun; this construction contrasts sharply with the use of the accusative pronoun, or the simple noun after gerunds in English. The English constructions 'for killing it, for killing the pig' may be compared with the verbal noun plus genitive in XVI.17.5 *do rainn na-mmucce* lit. 'for dividing of the pig.'

Other uses of the genitives, as after adjectives and predicatively, are readily interpreted.

e. The dative is used after certain prepositions; see VIII.G.38. These uses correspond to many constructions with the dative in other Indo-European languages, as in VI.4.6 *is fochen dóib* 'welcome (is) to you.'

The dative is also used to indicate the standard in comparative constructions, as in V.3b.11 *bid līa turim* 'it will be more than enumeration/can be counted.'

The dative is also used in adverbial patterns, as noted in VI.G.27.2.

chapter IX

READING AND TEXTUAL ANALYSIS, Sections 7 and 8

In the first of the two sections included here the challenges and boasting are general. By Section 8 one man, Cet, has won out, and the subsequent exchanges are between him and individual warriors of Ulster.

Section 7

1. 'Ricfaither a les do ġille innocht, a Chonchoḃuir,' ol Senlāech Araḋ a Crūachnaiḃ Con-Alaḋ anı́ar; 'ba menic rota Lūachra Deḋaḋ lim-sa foa tóin, menic ag mēith dı́ḃ d'⟨f⟩ācḃāil acum-sa.'
2. 'Ba méthiu a n-ag fo·rācḃais-⟨s⟩iu ocainni' ol Muinreṁur mac Gerrginn, '.i. do ḃrāthair faḋéin .i. Cruaichniu mac Rūaḋluim a Crūachnaiḃ Con-Alaḋ.'
3. 'Nibo ḟerr siḋe' ol Luġaiḋ mac Con-Ruı́ 'oldās Inloth Mōr mac Fergusa meic Lēti fo·rācḃaḋ la Echbél mac nDeḋaḋ hi Teṁair Lōchra.'
4. 'Cindas fir liḃ' ol Celtchair mac Uithec⟨h⟩air 'Conganchness mac Deḋaḋ do ṁarḃaḋ daṁ-sa ocus a chenn do ḃēim de?'

---

1. ricfaither   fut. pass. of *ro·ic* 'reaches, comes to'; impers. use
   a   3 pl. poss. pron.; anticipates gen. pl. *do gille*
   les   acc. sg. m. 'need' = 'you will need'
   menic   'often'
   rota   'reddish, dirty water'
   lim-sa   *la* + suffixed 1 sg. pron.; equivalent to agent in pass. constructions
   foa tóin   *fo* + 3 pl. poss. pron. 'under' + *tón* dat. sg. f. 'buttock' = 'often I had the dirty water of Lúachair Dedad under their arses'
   ag mēith   *ag* sg. of *aige* VIII.6.4 + adj. 'fat'; comp. *méthiu* in sent. 2

66

fácbáil   dat. sg. f. of vn. *fácbál*, fr. *fo·ácaib* 'leaves (behind)'; governed by prep. *do(d')*
'to, for'; in such constructions *do* relates the vn. w. its obj., here *ag.*; the vn. phrase
functions as sub. of the matrix sentence

acum-sa   prep. *oc* 'with' w. 1 sg. pers. pron.; cf. the prep. w. 1 pl. pers. pron. in sent. 2 =
'[it was] often that they left one of their fat calves behind with me'

2. fo·rácbais   2 sg. *ro*-pret. of *fo·ácaib*; cf. pass. in sent. 3
   fadéin   'self' = '(your) own'

3. ferr   'better'
   oldás   'than (is)'

4. fir   Thurneysen supplies macron; see glossary; better as gen. sg. of *fer* 'what kind of man
   do you think he is?'
   marbad   dat. sg. m. of vn. of *marbaid* 'kills, slaughters'
   béim   vn. dat. sg. of *benaid* 'cuts off'

Section 8

1. Imma·tarlae dóib fodēoid co·tarat int oinfer for firu Hérenn .i. Cet mac
   Māgach do Chonnachtaib·
2. Do·fūargaib side immurgu a gaisced ūas gaiscedaib int sluaig ocus ro·gab
   scin inna láim ocus dessid ocon muicc.
3. 'Fogabar do feraib Hērenn trá' olse 'oinfer tairisme comrama frim-sa, no
   lécud na-mmucce do rainn dam!'

---

1. imma·tarlae   *imma* 'mutually' + 3 sg. *ro*-pret. (*do·ro·lā-*) of *do-cuirethar* 'places'; meaning unclear; -*tarlae* usually = 'it happened'; here probably w. *imma*· 'they came together'; w. *dóib* 'they grappled with one another'
   fodēoid   'at last, finally'
   co·tarat   *co* conj. 'until, that' + 3 sg. *ro*-pret. of *do·beir* 'brings, puts' + *for* = 'defeats';
   int oinfer is sub.—'one man defeats the men of Ireland'

2. do·fūargaib   3 sg. *ro*-pret. of *do-ocaib* 'raises, hangs up'; the preeminent warrior could
   raise his 'armor' (*gaisced*) higher than the others
   úas   prep. 'above'
   int sluaig   gen. sg. m. of art. and *sluag* 'army'
   ro·gab   3 sg. *ro*-pret. of *gaibid* 'takes, seizes'
   scin   acc. sg. f. of *scian* 'knife'
   láim   acc. sg. f. of *lám* 'hand'
   dessid   3 sg. *ro*-pret. of *saidid* 'sits down'; < *di-en-said*, in which the prefixes are perf.,
   used instead of *ro*-

3. fogabar   impv. pass. of *fo·gaib* 'finds, gets'
   tairisme   gen. sg. m. of *tairisem* 'sustaining'; vn. of *do·arsissedar*
   comrama   gen. sg. m. of *comram* 'contest, combat'
   no lécud   'or' + vn. of *léicid* 'lets, leaves'
   rainn   dat. sg. of *rann*, vn. of *rannaid* 'divides'; see VIII.6.7; an impv. sentence: 'the let-
   ting of the dividing of the pig to me!' = 'Let me divide the pig'; see XI.11.1, XVI.17.4

GLOSSES

10. Wb. 15ᵇ 28. a mbás tïaġme-ni do-áirci bethiḋ dúib-si .i. is ar ḃethiḋ dúiḃ-si tïaġmi-ni bās.

aⁿ   sg. nt. def. art.
mbás   nt. acc. 'death'
tïagme-ni   rel. 1 pl. pres. ind. of *téit* 'goes'—note that it takes a direct obj.
do·áirci   3 sg. pres. 'effects, causes'
ar   prep. leniting 'on account of, for the sake of'
bethid   dat. *beth(a)id* 'life'
dúib-si   *do* + 2 pl. + emph.
tïagmi-ni   1 pl. pres. ind. of *téit*
bás   acc.
'The death that we die (lit. 'go') which causes life to you,' i.e., 'It is for the sake of life to you that we die.'

11. Ml. 112ᵇ 13. is deṁniu liunn a n-ad-chïam hūa śūliḃ ol-daas an ro-chluinemmar hūa chlūasaiḃ.

demniu   comp. of *demin* 'certain'
liunn   *la* 'with, by' + 1 pl. 'We think that more certain'
a   'what, that which' (sub. of *is*) nasalizes a following vowel but lenites initial of vb. (*a* = 'when' nasalizes a following vowel and nasalizes initial)
ad·chïam   1 pl. pres. of *ad·cí* 'sees'
húa, ó   prep. w. dat. 'from' also expresses agent w. pass.
oldaas   'than' compd. of subst. vb. + inflected (*an ro* [*a Ro*] = *arro*)
ro·chluinemmar   1 pl. pres. ind. (for *ch* see *ad·chïam*)
chlūasaib   dat. pl. of *clúas* f. 'ear'
'We think that more certain,' i.e., 'That is more certain to us which we see with [the] eyes than that which we hear with [the] ears.'

12. Wb. 11ᵃ 4. rethit huili & is oïnfer gaiḃes búaiḋ diiḃ inna choṁalnaḋ.

rethit   3 pl. pres. ind. of *rethid* 'runs'
oïnfer   = *oinar* 'one man'
gaibes   rel. pres. ind. (Strachan, p. 36); the initial of special rel. forms of simple verbs is not lenited in Wb.; see Thurneysen G.315
búaid   acc. sg. nt. 'victory'
diib   *di* + 3 pl. (often in partitive use)
inna   *iⁿ* + m. sg. poss. pron. (leniting)
chomalnad   m. 'fulfillment' vn. of *comalnaithir* = 'for completing it'; obj. of vn. in gen.
'All run and it is one single man of them who takes [the] victory for completing it.'

GRAMMAR

41. Compound sentences

The clauses of compound sentences are connected by means of conjunctions, but the word order of such clauses is like that of simple sentences. The relationship between two clauses is then indicated by specific conjunctions and by the inflections of verbs. Some of these relationships are indicated below.

41.1. Coordination. Clauses may be coordinated by linking them with *ocus*. Each clause is then treated as a simple sentence, as in I.1a.4 *Ailbe ainm in chon, ocus ba lán Hériu.* A disjunctive relationship is indicated by the conjunction *no, nu* 'or.'

41.2. Adversative relationship. An adversative relationship between clauses is indicated by *immurgu*, as in II.1b.12 *Mani·tucad immurgu.* As this clause illustrates, the meaning 'but' may be included in other clauses, such as the conditional clause introduced here by *ma.* An adversative relationship may also be expressed by the conjunction *acht*, as in VIII.Gl.7.

A concessive relationship is expressed by *cía, ce* 'although,' as in v.3b.10 *Cid fri mnaī.* Here *cía* has as suffix the third singular past subjunctive of *is.*

41.3. A conditional relationship is indicated by *ma* 'if,' as in v.3b.13 *Mad do Ailill.* Here *ma* has as suffix the third singular present subjunctive of *is*; the past subjunctive would have the same form, as in XVI.16.7. *Dia^n* is frequently found with the meaning 'if' as well as 'when.'

The conjunction *ma* is commonly found with the negative *ni*, in the sense 'unless,' as in v.3b.12 *Manip do Chonchobor* 'Unless (if not) to Conchobar.'

41.4. Temporal relationships are indicated by a number of conjunctions: *in tan* 'when' (see XV.15.1), *(h)ó* 'since' (see VIII.Gl.8), *co* 'until; that,' *ara* 'in order that,' and *a* (see IX.Gl.11 above). All these temporal conjunctions nasalize. As the meanings indicate, *co* may express a variety of relationships; these may be illustrated by its use in IV.3a.1 *co·rrabe* 'until he was, and as a result he was, so that he was.' For an example of *co* with the meaning 'so that' see X.9.5 *corot·aicciller* 'so that I may speak with you.' In narrative prose, *co* is often semantically empty, being little more than a sentence connective.

41.5. A causal relationship may be indicated by *ar* 'for, because,' as in XII.12.12 *Ar ba mese* 'For it was I.' As noted above, these conjunctions have no effect on the further word order of the clause. The normal order in all clauses is: Verb Subject Object, VSO.

42. The order of verbal qualifiers

In VSO languages nominal modifiers, that is, relative constructions, descriptive adjectives, and genitives are placed after nouns, as noted in I.G.1 and 2. By a similar principle verbal qualifiers are placed before verbs. Two of the verbal qualifiers are those expressing interrogation and sentence negation.

42.1. Interrogation is marked by interrogatives which generally stand initially in clauses. There is a weakly stressed interrogative pronoun *ce, ci, cia,* which is used for all genders and numbers, and a stressed *cía* 'who,' *cid, ced* 'what,' and plural *citné* 'who, what,' as in xi.11.3 *Cía and-so?* 'Who is this?' For an example of *cid*, see xvi.16.2.

When interrogative pronouns are not used, a question is introduced by the particle *in^n*, as in xii.12.3 *Inn é so Muinremor?* 'Is this Muinremor?'

42.2. Negation is marked by *ní, ni*, which is geminating; these particles always stand before the verb, as in vi.Gl.2. Before imperatives, the negative particle is *nă*, which geminates. Both particles have been extended with various suffixes, as in the forms *nicon·* 'not,' *nad·* 'that not,' *nach·* 'why not.'

The form *ní*, which geminates, can also be the negative copula; it is then placed before any element in the sentence, as in vi.Gl.1 *ní ar* 'It is not because of.'

In negative questions the negative particle follows the interrogative marker, as in Wb. 5^{a}21 *in-nád·cúalaid·si?* 'Have you not heard?'

Negatives may be followed by infixed pronouns, and then have the form *nach-, nách-*, as in Ml. 32^{d}5 *nacham·dermainte* 'forget me not.' They may also be combined with conjunctions, especially *mani·* 'if not' and *ceni* 'though not.'

43. On the uses of verbal nouns

In ii.G.6 some uses of verbal nouns were described, especially their uses as abstract nouns corresponding to infinitives in many other languages. Examples in subsequent sections of the text illustrate more of their characteristics. Although as verbal nouns their objects are in the genitive case, they may have subjects, and they may be related to other nouns by means of prepositions, notably *do*. *Do* connects a substantive with a verbal noun, governing either the substantive or the verbal noun as illustrated in the following examples.

43.1. Verbal nouns may be used like infinitives introduced by 'for . . . to.'

> x.9.3 Niba fír . . . Cet do rainn na mucce
> 'It is not just for Cet to divide the pig'

Here the subject of the verbal noun, *Cet*, is in the nominative; it is connected to the verbal noun by *do*, which governs the dative, as in the example given in ii.G.6.2. In x.9.3 the verbal noun is accompanied by a genitive, which indicates the object.

By contrast, in xi.11.1 the nominative *in mucc* is related to the infinitive by *do* and may be interpreted as object of the verbal noun.

> xi.11.1 no in mucc do rainn
> 'or the pig (is) for dividing'
> 'or I will divide the pig'

See also ix.8.3 with two verbal nouns in an independent clause.

43.2. The subject may also be connected to the verbal noun by *do*, as in the following phrase of a section added to SMMD but not included in this book.

cen airiugud dó
'without his perceiving' < 'without perceiving by him'

Here the third singular affixed personal pronoun of *dó* indicates the subject of the verb 'perceive.' For a similar relationship, see x.9.8 *dún*. The example given here also illustrates that other prepositions than *do* may govern verbal nouns.

In some uses the verbal noun, as well as the subject, may be governed by *do*, as in ix.7.4:

Cindas fir lib . . . Conganchness . . . do marbad dam-sa
'What kind of man does he seem to you . . . Conganchness for killing by me?'
'What do you think of him, my having killed Conganchness?' (see ix.8.3)

Verbal nouns in this way serve as complements and often are comparable to subordinate clause constructions in English.

44. Forms for indicating action in the past

Old Irish has three sets of forms to indicate action in the past: an imperfect made from the present stem, as indicated in iii.G.14; a preterite, as indicated in v.G.24; forms prefixed with *ro-*, labeled the perfect or perfective (in some verbs other prefixes *ad-*, *com-* have the function of *ro-*).

The imperfect indicates repeated or customary action in the past; the preterite indicates simple action in the past; the perfect indicates completed action. The perfect may then be made from present indicative, imperfect, and preterite forms; with all of them it adds the notion of completion, whether in the present, past, or future.

With the present indicative, *ro-* indicates action completed when another action takes place; see Thurneysen G.342. In SMMD it is most commonly used with the preterite, as in ix.8.2 *ro·gab*, viii.6.11 *im·rullatar*, and many others.

Forms with *ro-*, notably subjunctives, may also have modal uses, expressing possibility or capability, as in x.9.5:

corot·aicciller
'so that I may speak to you'

The conjunction *co n-* 'until, that, and' with *ro*-subjunctive forms indicates a wish, as in this example, and may be translated 'so that, in order that.' Another example is *co·ralta* in vii.5.14.

As in *corot·aicciller*, *ro-* is often followed by infixed personal pronouns: first singular *rom·*, second singular *rot·*, third singular masculine *ro·n-*, third singular feminine *ros·*, third plural *ros·* as in vi.4.6 *ros·bía*.

45. Adverbs

Adverbs of various forms may be used in the predicate, generally at the end of the clause, such as *fodēoid* in ix.8.1. Irish is remarkable, however, in having a series of symmetrical adverbs in which the initial element indicates the relationship of the second. The initial elements are:

71

t-	= rest:	t-úas 'above'	t-ís 'below'
s-	= motion toward:	s-úas 'upward'	s-ís 'downward'
an-	= motion from:	an-úas 'from above'	an-ís 'from below'

These prefixes are also used with adverbs of direction: *air* 'east,' *dess* 'south,' *íar* 'west,' and *túaid* 'north.' Moreover, a speaker is assumed to be facing the east, and accordingly *air* also means 'in front,' *dess* 'to the right,' *íar* 'behind,' and *túaid* 'to the left.' Assuming that a speaker is facing to the right of this page, these adverbs can be arranged as follows:

túaid 'north, left'
sathúaid, fathúaith 'northward'
antúaid, atúaid 'from the north'

tíar 'west, behind'		tair 'east, in front'
síar 'westward'	SPEAKER	sair 'eastward'
aníar 'from the west'		anair 'from the east'

dess 'south, right'
sadess, faces 'southward'
andess 'from the south'

The adverbs 'here' and 'there' are less symmetrical in structure, with the following sets:

here	sund, sunda	there, beyond	t-all
toward here	il-le	toward there	inn-un(n) -onn
from here	de-ṡiu	from there	an-all

chapter x

READING AND TEXTUAL ANALYSIS, Sections 9 and 10

In the two sections included here, two heroes of Ulster rise to Cet's challenge, Loegaire in Section 9, Oengus the son of Lám Gábuid in Section 10. Neither withstands his response.

Section 9

1. Ni·frith lāech a t⟨h⟩airisṁe.
2. Ros·lá i socht na h-Ulto.
3. 'At·chí sūt, a Lōeġairi,' ol Conchoḃar.
4. 'Niba fír' ol Lōeġaire 'Cet do rainn na mucce arar m-bēlaiḃ-ni.'
5. 'An biuc, a Lōeġairi, corot·aicciller!
6. Is bés dúiḃ-si far n-Ultaiḃ' ol Cet, 'cech mac ġaiḃes gaisceḋ acaiḃ, is cucainni cenn a ḃáiri.
7. Do·cūaḋais-siu dano isin cocrích.
8. Imma·tarraiḋ dún indi.
9. Fo·rācḃais in roth ocus in carpat ocus na heocho, ocus at·rulais fēin ocus ġaí triut.
10. Nis·toirchi in muicc fon indassin.'
11. Dessiḋ siḋe dano.

---

1. ni·frith   pret. pass. of *fo·gaib* 'finds,' following neg. prefix
   láech acc. sg. m. 'warrior'; for *tairisme*, see IX.8.3
2. ros·lá   *ro*-pret. 3 sg. of *fo-ceird* 'puts,' w. infixed 3 pl. pers. pron.; lit. 'it put them'–the infixed pron. anticipates the direct obj. *na h-Ulto*
   socht   acc. sg. m. 'silence'
3. at·chí   2 sg. pres. of *ad·cí* 'sees,' w. infixed 3 sg. nt. pers. pron.
   sút   'that'

73

4. niba   3 sg. fut. of *is* w. neg. prefix
   ar   prep. 'before' + *ar n-* 'our'
   bélaib   dat. pl. m. of *bél* 'lip,' pl. 'mouth'; w. *ar* = 'before, in the presence of'
5. an   2 sg. impv. of *anaid* 'stops' = 'wait!'
   biuc   adverbial dat. of *becc* 'little'
   corot·aicciller   1 sg. subj. of *ad·gládathar* 'speaks to,' w. *ro-* followed by 2 sg. pers. pron. after *co^n* 'so that'
6. bés   nom. sg. m. 'custom'
   dúib-si far n-Ultaib   'among you Ulstermen'; prep. *do* + 2 pl. suffixed pron. + emph. ptc. + 2 pl. poss. pron. + dat. pl. *Ulaid*, in appositional use after pers. pronouns in all cases; see Thurneysen G.160
   gaibes   rel. sg. pres. of *gaibid* 'receives'
   acaib   *oc* 'among, at' w. 2 pl. pers. pron.
   cucainni   *co^g* 'to, up to' w. 1 pl. pers. pron.
   cenn a báiri   *cenn* 'head, end' + gen. = 'his goal'
7. do·cūadais-siu   2 sg. *ro*-pret. of *téit* 'comes, goes' w. emph. suffix; *cocrích* VIII.6.11
8. imma·tarraid   3 sg. *ro*-pret. of *do·airret* 'meets'; used impersonally w. *imma·* 'mutually'; w. *dún* = 'we met'
9. fo·rácbais   see IX.7.2 and 3
   roth   acc. sg. m. 'wheel'
   eocho   acc. pl. of *ech* 'horse'
   at·rulais   2 sg. *ro*-pret. of *as·luí*, w. infixed nt. pers. pron.; 'you escaped'
   gaí   nom. sg. m. 'spear'
   triut   see VIII.G.38.b
10. nis·toirchi   2 sg. pres. of *do·roich* 'attains,' following neg. and 3 sg. f. (nasalizing) infixed pers. pron.
   fon indas-sin   'in that way'

Section 10

1. 'Niba fír' ol lāech find mór do·dechaid assind imdai, 'Cet do rainn na mucce arar mbélaib-ni.'
2. 'Coich and-so?' ol Cet.
3. 'Is ferr di lāech indaī-siu' ol cāch, 'Ōengus mac Lāṁe Gābaid sin di Ultaib.'
4. 'Cid dia·tā Lāṁ Ġābuid fora athair-siuṁ?' ol Cet.
5. 'Cid áṁ?'
6. 'Ro·fetar-sa' ol Cet.
7. 'Do·cūadus-sa sair fecht and.
8. Ēgthir immum.
9. Do·roich cách.
10. Do·roich dano Lám.
11. Tārlaic urchor do ġaī ṁór form-sa.
12. Dos·lēicim-se dō in ngaī cétna co·mbert a lāiṁ de, co·mboī for lár.
13. Cid do·bérad a ṁac do choṁraṁ frimsa?'
14. Téit Ōengus ina ṡuide.

1. láech find mór   *láech*, accompanied by 2 descriptive adjectives; see V.3b.11
   do·dechaid   3 sg. *ro*-pret. of *do·tét* 'comes; arises'
   assind   prep. *a* + art.; see VIII.G.38.e
   Note repetition of sequence from x.9.4
2. coich   'who (is)' VII.G.32; originally ḡen. sg. of interrog. pron. *cia*, but genitival function lost, possibly in a pattern like 'whose (son) (is) here?'
3. ferr   'better'; prep. *di* 'of' w. dat. = 'better as a warrior'
   indaí-siu   'than you are'; see VII.G.33.1
4. cid   'what' + *diatā* < *di* 'from' + *-atá-* 'is,' 'why is'; w. *for* = 'why is . . . called'
   fora   prep. *for* 'on' w. 3 sg. poss. pron.
   athair   dat. sg. m. 'father'
5. ám   'indeed'—a questioning challenge
6. ro·fetar-sa   1 sg. pres. of *ro·fitir* 'knows'
7. do·cūadus   1 sg. *ro*-pret.; cf. X.9.7
   sair   see IX.G.45
   fecht and   'once upon a time'; *fecht* is nt. and nasalizes
8. égthir   pres. pass. of *égid* 'screams' (impers.)
   immum   prep. 'around' + 1 sg. pers. pron.
9. do·roich   3 sg. pres. 'comes'; examples of historical pres. in this and next line
11. tārlaic   3 sg. *ro*-pret. of *do·áilci* 'lets down; casts' (Thurneysen supplies long mark on *ā*,
   but the vowel might be short)
   urchor   acc. sg. m. 'cast, throw'
   form   see VIII.G.38.c
12. dos·lēicim-se   1 sg. pres. of *do·lé(i)ci* 'throws, casts,' w. meaningless infixed pron.
   dó   see VIII.G.38.a
   co·mbert   3 sg. pret. of *berid* 'bears, carried off,' after conj. *co n-* (note that it is occasionally difficult to distinguish btw. consecutive and connective uses of *co n*)
   co·mboí   3 sg. pret. of *·tá* 'is'
   lár   dat. sg. nt. 'ground; floor'
13. do·bérad   3 sg. condit. of *do·beir* 'gives, brings' = 'would bring'
14. téit   3 sg. pres. 'goes; attains'
   suide   acc. sg. nt. of *suide*, vn. of *saidid* 'sits down'; note periphrastic construction here
   vs. X.9.11

GLOSSES

13. Wb. 6ᶜ7.   léic úait inna bíada milsi & tomil innahísiu do-m·meil do
   chenél.

   léic   2 sg. impv. of *lécid* 'leaves, lets go, allows'
   úait   *ó* + 2 sg.; see VIII.G.38.a
   inna   acc. pl. art.
   bíada   pl. of *bíad* nt. 'food'
   milsi   fr. *milis* 'sweet' acc. pl. 'palatable' (*l* delenited bf. *s*)
   tomil   2 sg. impv. of *do·meil* 'consume, eat, enjoy'
   innahísiu   acc. pl. of *int-í-siu* 'this'

do-m·meil   3 sg. pres. of *do·meil* in nasalizing rel. clause
do   2 sg. poss. pron. leniting
chenél   nt. *o*-stem 'race, tribe'
'Put away the sweet foods and consume these that thy race consumes.'

14. Wb. 10ᵈ23.   mad ar lóg pridcha-sa, .i. ar m'ētiuth & mo thoschith, ní-m bia fochricc dar hési mo precepte.

mad   'if it be; if it were' *ma* + pres. subj. 3 sg. cop.
ar   'for' w. dat. or acc.
lóg   nt. 'price, pay'
pridcha-sá   1 sg. pres. subj. of *pridchid* 'preaches'
mo, m'   1 sg. poss. pron.
ētiuth   'clothing'
toschith   (initial lenition by poss. pron.) 'food'
ní-m bia   3 sg. fut. of subst. vb.; infixed pron. has dat. rel. 'there will not
   be to me, I shall not have'
fochricc   f. *ā*-stem 'reward'
dar hési   *éiss* f. 'track' w. poss. pron. or gen. 'after, in place of'
'If it were for pay that I be preaching, that is, for my clothing and food, I shall not have a reward after my preaching.'

15. Tur. 110ᶜ.   ba bés leu-som do-bertís dá boc leu dochum Tempuil, ⁊ no·lēicthe indala n-aí fon díthrub co pecad in popuil ⁊ do-bertís maldachta foir, ⁊ no·oircthe didiu and ō popul tar cenn a pecthae ind aile.

bés   m. 'custom'
leu-som   *la* + 3 pl. + emph. 'with, by,' here 'among'; see VIII.G.38.b
do·bertís   3 pl. impf. of *do·beir* 'give, take, bring'; independent construction; more usual vn. or nasalizing rel. clause
dá   num. 2 leniting
boc   m. du. 'he-goat'
dochum   nominal prep. w. gen.; Thurneysen G.536 'to'
⁊   usual MS writing of *ocus*; ampersand for *et* used occasionally also
no·lēicthe   impf. pass. sg. of *léicid* 'leaves, lets go, allows'
indala   'second, one of two' *indala n-aí* 'one of the two'; Thurneysen
   G.279–80, 285; see *ind aile* 'the other'
fon   prep. 'under' + art.
díthrub   m. 'desert'; *fon díthrub* 'to the desert'
coⁿ   prep. w. dat. 'with'
pecad   m. 'sin'
popuil   m. gen. sg. 'people'
maldachta   'curses'
foir   prep. 3 sg. m. acc. 'on'; see VIII.G.38.c
no·oircthe   impf. pass. of *orcaid* 'slays'

76

didiu   'hence, therefore'
ō   expresses agent w. pass.
tar cenn   'instead of; on behalf of; for'
a   3 pl. poss. *n-*
pecthae   gen. pl. of *pecad* 'sin'; gen. w. *cenn*
'It was a custom with them (= they had a custom): they used to take two
goats with them to the Temple, and one of them used to be allowed [to
go] into the desert with [the] sin of the people and they used to curse him,
and hence the other would be killed there by the people for their sins.'

GRAMMAR

46. Relative constructions

As noted in I.G.2.1, III.G.13, and VIII.G.36.2.c, a relative clause in Old Irish
stands after its antecedent. No relative particle is used except when a preposition introduces the clause. In the third persons of many inflections, and also in
the first plural, special relative forms of verbs in the present tense may be used
when the relative is subject or object, as in:

IX.Gl.12   is oínfer gaibes búaid
'it is one man who takes the prize'

IX.Gl.10   a mbas tíagme-ni
'the death that we go/die'

Other person forms are preceded by the particle *no*:

IV.3a.4   Cid no·taí?
'What [is it] that you are/that ails you?'

46.1. Pretonic prepositions, *ro, no*, and the negative particles, as also the forms
of the copula are followed by lenition or nasalization of the following element.
    Leniting relative clauses are mandatory when the antecedent is equivalent
with the deleted subject of the relative clause:

II.1b.11   In fer no·thēged
'(every) man who went'

VII.5.10   Sochaide díb ro·fūachtnaig
'(it was) a group of them which was feuding'

46.2. Relative constructions may have a less direct relationship with their antecedent than in English. In this way they may correspond to subordinate constructions introduced by conjunctions:

v.3b.11   ba olc lathe etha dó
'was evil the day [when] it was come for him'

In this sentence the passive relative of *téit* simply is placed after 'day,' and the relationship may best be indicated by the conjunction 'when'; similarly, the pas-sive relative in VIII.6.7 *Cindas rainnfither in mucc* from *cía indas* 'what is the manner [in which] the pig will be divided?' Relative constructions must then be interpreted more broadly than in English. They may also be used in Old Irish to indicate indirect speech.

47. Periphrastic constructions indicating state

Verbs followed by nouns that are often introduced by *i* indicate entry into a state and continuation of that state. Compare the following expressions for 'sit down.'

x.10.14   Téit Ōengus ina suide
(lit. Ōengus went into his sitting)
'Ōengus went to sit down and stayed sitting there'

IX.8.2   dessid ocon muicc
'he sat down beside the pig' (simple action)

IV.3a.1   Ro·lá didiu i socht innī Mac Dathó
'Then Mac Dathó became (and stayed) silent'

IX.7.1   Ricfaither a les . . .
'You will have need . . .'

Gloss 14 (*ní-m bia fochricc dar hési* 'It will not be for a reward for me' = 'I will not have . . .') similarly indicates the achievement of a state and its continuation.

48. The future and the subjunctive

The simple future, as noted in VI.G.29, indicates future time. The secondary fu-ture, which is also called the conditional, may be used to indicate potentiality, as in x.10.13 *Cid do·bérad a mac* 'What could bring his son.' In this use it is similar to the subjunctive.

The subjunctive, however, may indicate greater uncertainty as in conditional clauses. Two subjunctives occurred in v.3b.10 *Cid fri mnaī at-bertha-so manid· epled ní airi* 'Even to a woman you may speak if nothing would be lost.' The subjunctive is common in this use in indefinite relative constructions, and in negative clauses indicating uncertainty.

49. Verbal prefixation

As noted in I.G.1, prefixation is a common process in VSO languages. Prefixa-tion has led to many changes in verb forms because of the strong initial stress accent. As a result vowels were weakened and lost; such changes will be dis-cussed in the second half of the grammar.

The difference in position of stress has led to contrasting deuterotonic and prototonic (first-syllable stressed) forms. When prefixes, often prepositions, are placed before verbs, the stress normally falls on the syllable after the prefix, as in *as·biur* 'I say' of VI.Gl.1; if the stressed syllable is the verb stem, it remains relatively unchanged in form. When, however, the stress falls on the first prefix, the stem may be considerably modified, as in *epur* 'I say' of vi.Gl.2. Such a stress position is brought about here by the preceding negative particle; the interrogative *in* and various conjunctions also require prototonic forms. The following are further examples of such variants.

Deuterotonic	Prototonic
ad·cí 'sees'	·aicci
as·beir 'says'	·epir
con·tuili 'sleeps'	·cotlai
do·beir 'gives'	·tab(a)ir
do·ic 'comes'	·tic
do·gní 'does'	·déni

SMMD includes examples of such prototonic forms, e.g., v.3b.15 *ním·déni*. Other negatives with different prefixes are found in the same section: v.3b.12 *nicon·faicēbat* (from *fo·ácaib*) and iv.3a.6 *nicos·n-ārlastar* (from *ro-ad·gládathar*). Except in greatly modified forms like the last, the verb stem can generally be determined if one notes the reduced forms of the accented prefixes, as in ·*tabair* above. The form *Nis·toirchi* of x.9.10 might then readily be related to *do·roichi*. The reductions involved provide fascinating problems in historical phonology, some of which will be taken up in the following chapters.

50. Impersonal constructions

In the last three chapters the primary sentence patterns of Old Irish have been reviewed: the VSO structure of sentences and the sentences introduced by copulas. Each of these sentence types may be extended by complements, often involving verbal nouns, and by relative constructions. Besides these syntactic characteristics, Old Irish has a fondness for impersonal constructions. Many of these involve prepositional phrases or inflections.

A simple example is the pattern used to express possession, as in i.1a.2 *Boí cú occo* 'was hound to him' = 'He had a hound.' In a subsequent sentence, an impersonal construction again puts the emphasis on the content of the verb rather than on a vaguely identified subject as must be done in the English translation: i.1a.5 *Do·eth ō Ailill* 'there was a coming from Ailill' = 'Messengers came from Ailill.'

Similar verbal expressions are found in the selections for this chapter: x.9.2 *Ros·lá i socht* 'it put in silence' = 'they fell silent'; x.9.8 *Imma·tarraid* 'was a meeting mutually' = '(we) met one another.'

Emphasis on the verbal action may be strongest in the passive constructions. A number of passive forms have occurred in the first ten sections; these illustrate that in Old Irish the passive sentence is not a modified form of an active sentence. The term "passive" can be highly misleading if interpreted in this way. An example in this chapter is x.10.8: *Ēgthir immum* 'There was screaming around me.' The persons involved are not important. The action is. Through use

79

of impersonal verbal constructions, whether active or passive, Old Irish epic prose manifests a strong verbal style, with emphasis on the action rather than on the persons involved in it. In this way it is curiously like the vigorous prose style of the historical books of the Old Testament. Modern Irish grammars label these as "autonomous forms," based on the native Irish term *saorbhriathar* 'free-verb.' In Modern Irish grammar "passives" are designated as *saorbhriathar*, that is, "autonomous" or "free" verbs.

chapter XI

Section 11 contains the challenge of Eogan mac Durthacht. He too is over-whelmed.

1. 'In comram do thairisem beus' ol Cet, 'no in mucc do rainn.'
2. 'Niba fír a-rrann duit-siu cētomus' ol lāech find mór de Ultaib.
3. 'Cīa and-so?' ol Cet.
4. 'Ēoġan mac Durthacht sin' ol cách '.i. rí Fernmaiġe.'
5. 'At·chondarc-sa riam' ol Cet.
6. 'Cairm indom·acca?' ol Ēoġan.
7. 'I ndorus do thiġe oc tabairt tānae bó hūait.
8. Ro·éġed immum-sa isin tír.
9. Tānacais-⟨s⟩iu fon égim.
10. Ro·lēcis gaī form-sa co·rrabae asmo scíath.
11. Do·llēcim-se duit-siu in ngaī cétna co·lluid tret chenn ocus co·mbert do súil asdo chiunn.
12. Atot·chiat fir Hērenn co n-oínsúil.
13. Messe thall in súil n-aili asdo chinn.'
14. Dessid side dano.

---

1. comram . . . beus nom. sg. m. w. adv. 'still'; a nominal sentence w. the prepositional phrase introduced by *do*—'the combat for sustaining still'—indicating a further challenge; the 2 clauses of the sentence are parallel; *rann*, vn. of *rannaid*, has occurred previously (see VIII.6.8)
2. duit-siu *do* w. 2 sg. affixed pers. pron., w. emphasizing enclitic w. sub. of vn.
   cētomus 'first'
   lāech nom. sg. m. 'warrior'
3. and-so 'this'

81

4. sin 'that'
5. at-chondarc-sa   1 sg. *ro*-pret. of *ad·cí* 'sees,' w. infixed 3 sg. pers. pron., followed by emphasizing enclitic

     riam   adv., derived fr. prep. *ría* 'before'
6. cairm in-   'where' (*ce + airm* = 'what place')

     indom·acca   2 sg. pret. of *ad·cí*, w. 1 sg. pron. infixed
7. oc tabairt   prep. 'at, by' w. vn. of *do·beir*

     tánae bó   gen. sg. f. of *tán, táin* 'driving off'; w. *bó* = 'cattle raid'

     húait   prep. *ó* 'from,' w. 2 sg. pers. pron.
8. ro·éged   3 sg. *ro*-pret. pass. of *égid* 'screams'; see the noun *égim* 'scream' in sent. 9 and X.10.8

     immum-sa   prep. *im* 'around' w. 1 sg. pers. pron.
9. tánacais-siu   2 sg. pret. of *do·ic* 'comes'
10. ro·lécis   2 sg. *ro*-pret. of *lé(i)cid* 'throws'

     co·rrabae   *·rabae*, 3 sg. *ro*-pret. (*ro·boí*) of *·tá* 'is,' following *co n-* 'so that'

     asmo   prep. w. dat. *a^g* 'out of' w. 1 sg. poss. pron.; see *asdo*, w. 2 sg. poss. pron. in sent. 11

     scíath   dat. sg. m. 'shield'
11. do·llécim   1 sg. pret.; see sent. 10

     co·lluid   *·luid* is 3 sg. pret. of *téit* 'goes [to]'; see sent. 10 for this and subsequent *co n-* construction

     tret   prep. w. acc. 'through,' w. 2 sg. poss. pron.

     co·mbert   3 sg. pret. of *berid* 'carries off'

     súil   acc. sg. f. 'eye'
12. atot·chiat   3 pl. pres., w. 2 sg. infixed pers. pron., of *ad·cí* 'sees'

     co n-   prep. w. dat. 'with,' followed by compd. made up of *oín-, óen-* 'one, single' and *súil*
13. messe   'I'

     thall   3 sg. pret. rel. of *do alla* 'takes off'; note the use of the rel. of vb. after a sub. which in its more explicit use would be preceded by the cop.

     n-aili   note nasalization of adj. after acc. sg.
14. See X.9.11

GLOSSES

16. Ml. 107ᵃ15. bid sochaide atrefea indiut-su ⁊ bid fáilid nach oín ad-id-trefea.

     bid   3 sg. fut. cop.
     sochaide   f. 'multitude'
     atrefea   3 sg. fut. of *atreba* 'dwells, possesses'
     indiut-su   2 sg. of *i^n* 'in, into'
     fáilid   'joyous'
     nach   nom. m. 'any'
     ad·id·trefea   3 sg. fut. w. obj. infixed 'who shall dwell it' = 'who shall dwell such a dwelling' = 'who shall so dwell'
     'It will be a multitude that will dwell in you and anyone will be joyous who shall so dwell.'

17. Wb. 29ᵈ27. ní mebul lemm cia f-a-dam.

ní   neg. cop. pres.
mebul   f. 'shame'
fadam   1 sg. pres. subj. of *fo·daim* 'suffers'
'I do not consider it a shame although I may suffer it.'

18. Ml. 112ᵇ12. is toísigiu ad·ciam teilciud in bḗla, resíu ro·cloammar a gduth-sidi.

toísigiu   comp. of *toísech* 'first' = 'prior'
ad·ciam   1 pl. of *ad·cí* (probably nasalized, to be read [*ad·giam*])
teilciud   vn. of *do·léci* 'throws'
bḗla   gen. of *biáil* m. 'axe'
resíu   conj. 'before'
ro·cloammar   1 pl. pres. subj. of *ro·cluinethar* 'hears'
guth   m. 'voice, sound'
sidi   enclitic gen. of *suide* (emph.); here emphasizes *a*
'It is earlier that we see the throwing of the axe before we may hear the sound of it.'

GRAMMAR

51. Historical treatment of Old Irish: the Celtic branch of Proto-Indo-European

In the sections of the grammar included in Chapters XI to XX the point of view will be historical. Many of the topics discussed in the first fifty grammatical sections will be treated again from this point of view. The position of Old Irish as an Insular dialect of the Celtic branch of the Indo-European language family will also be noted.

Old Irish belongs to the Celtic branch of the Indo-European language family. Commonly held to be most closely related to the Italic branch, Celtic also exhibits similarities with Germanic. The characteristics Celtic shares with Italic have led some scholars to propose an Italo-Celtic branch; a notable similarity is the common change of $p \ldots k^w$ to $k^w \ldots k^w$, as in OIr. *cóic*, Lat. *quínque* 'five.' The two branches also share lexical characteristics, such as OIr. *tír*, Lat. *terra* 'earth,' and prepositions, such as OIr. *di-*, Lat. *dē* 'from.' For a thorough discussion of the problem, see "Italo-Celtic Revisited," by Calvert Watkins, in *Ancient Indo-European Dialects*, ed. Henrik Birnbaum and Jaan Puhvel (Berkeley: Univ. of California Press, 1966); Watkins considers the evidence inadequate for assuming an earlier "common" Italo-Celtic language, and accordingly he ascribes the shared features to mutual influences. Germanic has clearly borrowed from Celtic, as words like OE *ríce*, OHG *ríhhi* 'powerful' indicate; as Lat. *rēx*, *rēgis* 'king' illustrates, this must have had PIE *ē*, which became *i* in Celtic, as in Gaulish *-ríx*, OIr. *rí*, but *æ* in Germanic. The period between the initial expansion of the Indo-Europeans from the area north of the Black Sea around 3000 B.C. to our first recorded references to Celtic peoples around 400 B.C. is obscure. We may assume, however, that around the middle of this period the Celts were in contact with the Italic speakers, and that some time later, in the first millennium B.C., they were in contact with Germanic speakers. Subsequently, the Celts were overpowered by the Romans, as described by Caesar. A Celtic subgroup had invaded Britain around the middle of the first millennium. From this subgroup we have the only linguistic evidence of any extent. And the Celtic languages currently spoken have developed from Insular Celtic, as will be discussed in xii.G.56.

With Greek (or Hellenic), Celtic, Italic, and Germanic make up the Western group of the Indo-European language family. They are commonly designated as the centum group, because in them certain IE *k*-sounds were not modified, as in the word for 'one hundred': OIr. *cét*, Lat. *centum*, Gk. *hekatón*, Goth. *hunds.* The other branches of Indo-European known in the nineteenth century modified such *k*-sounds to sibilants: Baltic, Slavic, Albanian, Armenian, and Indo-Iranian; these are known as the satem group, after a modified form of the Avestan word for hundred: *satəm*. Some other branches of Indo-European are poorly attested, such as Thraco-Phrygian and Illyrian, which some scholars considered the dominant group in Central Europe before the Celts achieved such a position.

In addition to these branches, which had been extensively studied in the nineteenth century, two further language subgroups were discovered early in this century. Tocharian, with two dialects labeled A and B, was discovered in manuscripts from caves in Chinese Turkestan. Anatolian, with Hittite and Luwian as the two prominent dialects, was discovered in Asia Minor in 1906. Tocharian provided additional insights into the development of the Indo-European language family, in part because it maintained *k* in contrast with other Eastern languages. This characteristic led to downplaying of the centum-satem dichotomy. The Anatolian languages had an even more profound effect on Indo-European studies. The best-attested, Hittite, exhibited characteristics that had earlier only been hypothesized, notably a sound or sounds transcribed *ḫ*, *ḫḫ*, which correspond to previously proposed laryngeals. Knowledge of Hittite accordingly led to a revaluation of Indo-European phonology; our views of Indo-European syntax are also being revised, partly with the help of Hittite.

Hittite is consistently OV in structure, as illustrated by the following sentence:

> DUMU.É.GAL šūpi watar parā ēpzi
> nobleman pure water out he-holds
> 'The nobleman holds out pure water.'

Indo-European syntacticians, especially Delbrück, had pointed out OV characteristics in Vedic, such as the use of postpositions, preposed relative constructions, genitives, and adjectives—such as *šūpi* above. But until the syntax of Hittite was understood, little was made of these observations. On the basis of Hittite syntax, as well as that of Vedic Sanskrit, early Greek, and the other dialects, we must assume that Proto-Indo-European was OV in structure.

Since Old Irish is VSO, the Celtic languages underwent profound syntactic changes in the interval between 3000 B.C. and our first attested Old Irish materials of about 400 A.D. These will be discussed below.

52. Changes in inflection: *o*-stem nouns

Old Irish also differs considerably in its inflectional system from Proto-Indo-European, in large part because of losses of endings. Celtic introduced a strong initial stress accent, which replaced the pitch accent system of Proto-Indo-European. In the course of time this led to the weakening and loss of endings. But a characteristic feature of Old Irish is the residual effect of the old endings on the initials of following words. By noting the original endings, we can account for the phonological processes of lenition, nasalization, and palatalization, as well as the vocalism of the root.

The forms of the *o*-stem nouns *fer* 'man' and *scél* 'story' were given in I.G.3. Here they are listed with the old endings.

Sg.	N	fer	-os	scél^n	-om
	V	a fir	-e		
	A	fer^n	-om	scél^n	-om
	G	fir	-ī	scéuil	-ī
	D	fiur	-ōi	scéul	-ōi
Pl.	N	fir	-oi	scél	-ā
	V	firu	-ōs		
	A	firu	-ōns	scél	-ā
	G	fer^n	-ōm	scél^n	-ōm
	D	fer(a)ib	-obhis	scél(a)ib	-obhis
Du.	NA	fer	-ā	scél^n	-ā
	G	fer	-ou	scél	-ou
	D	fer(a)ib	-obhim	scél(a)ib	-obhim

Here only the source of nasalization in the indicated forms will be noted. Other such processes will be discussed later.

53. Verb inflection: the present indicative

The forms of the present, given in I.G.4, are listed here with their original endings. Details of their development will be noted later.

Sg.	1	biru	(-ō ?)	·biur	-ō
	2	biri	-esi	·bir	-ei
	3	berid, -ith	-eti	·beir	-et
	rel.	beres(s)			
Pl.	1	berm(a)i	-om . . .	·beram	-omos
	rel.	berm(a)e			
	2	beirthe	-te . . .	·berid, -ith	-ete
	3	ber(a)it	-onti	·berad	-ont
	rel.	berd(a)e bert(a)e			

As in many paradigms, the forms of the present cannot simply be accounted for as regular phonological developments of the Indo-European endings. The absolute endings have been differently interpreted by different scholars. For the time being, the endings supplied may assist in understanding the developments of the stem vowels.

54. The relation of the Old Irish phonological system to that of Proto-Indo-European

As noted in I.G.5, Old Irish had a phonological system consisting of six stops and six fricatives. In addition there were three nasals and the liquids r and l. The vowel system consisted of five short and long vowels and eight diphthongs. This system had changed considerably from that of Proto-Indo-European, which may be reconstructed as follows:

		Labials		Dentals		Velars		Labio-velars		Glottals	
Obstruents:	a.	p		t		k		k^w			
	b.	b	bh	d	dh	g	gh	g^w	g^wh		
	c.			s							
Laryngeals:								χ		ʔ	h
								γ			
Resonants:		m		n							
			w	r l		y					
Vowels:		e o									
		e									
		a									

There have been numerous points of dispute about this system, notably the analysis of the velars. Other problems have to do with the characteristic features of the phonemes symbolized d dh, etc. These were formerly assumed to be voiced and voiced aspirated stops in Proto-Indo-European, as in Sanskrit. But recent studies propose other pronunciations, partly on the ground that the Sanskrit voiced aspirates may have been remodeled on the basis of aspirated stops in the indigenous languages of India. The problem is of greater importance when dealing with the early dialects than with Old Irish; for in Old Irish /d dh/, etc. fell together.

Among other major differences is the loss of the laryngeals. In the subsequent restructuring long vowels resulted, which may already be posited for late Proto-Indo-European: $\bar{\imath}$ $\bar{e}$ $\bar{a}$ $\bar{o}$ $\bar{u}$. These vowels became phonemes in the early dialects, foreshadowing the five-vowel system of Old Irish. It must also be remembered that the resonants had vocalic as well as consonantal allophones. Proto-Indo-European, then, included the sounds [i u] as well as [y w].

In another major restructuring between Proto-Indo-European and Old Irish, the labio-velars were lost as separate entities; their reflexes fell together with those of the velars and labials.

Direct correspondences between the Proto-Indo-European system and that of Old Irish may be set up as follows:

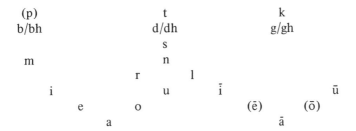

(p)		t		k
b/bh		d/dh		g/gh
		s		
m		n		
	r		l	
i		u	ī	ū
e	o		(ē)	(ō)
	a		ā	

Examples are given here to illustrate the major correspondences; combinatory changes will be dealt with later. Besides the reconstructed Proto-Indo-European form, an example from another dialect will be given, with preference for Italic and Gothic, in addition to an English cognate. When the English cognate varies in meaning from the Old Irish, it is put in parentheses.

Labials: PIE p > OIr.- The loss of *p* in Proto-Celtic is one of the notable developments of the Celtic branch.

	PIE patēr-	Lat. pater	Goth. fadar	OIr. athir	'father'
	PIE bher-	Lat. fert	Goth. bairip	OIr. berid	'carries, bears'

The /b/ often proposed may have been post-IE: cognates cannot be provided for many dialects, as may be clear from the lack of an example here.

Dentals:	PIE trey-	Lat. trēs	Goth. þreis	OIr. tri	'three'
	PIE dᵘō	Lat. duo	Goth. twa (nt.)	OIr. dá	'two'
	PIE dhur-	Lat. forēs	Goth. daur	OIr. dorus	'door'
Velars:	PIE kṃtom	Lat. centum	Goth. hunda	OIr. cét	'hundred'
	PIE gen-	Lat. genus	Goth. kuni	OIr. gein	'(kin), birth'
	PIE ghort-	Lat. hortus	Goth. gards	OIr. gort	'(garden), yard, enclosed field'
Labio-velars:	PIE kʷi-	Lat. quis	Goth. hʋas	OIr. cia	'who'
	PIE gʷen-	Gk. gunḗ	Goth. qino	OIr. ben	'(quean), woman'
	PIE gʷher-	Lat. formus	Goth. warms	OIr. gor	'warmth, heat'
Sibilant:	PIE septm	Lat. septem	Goth. sibun	OIr. sechtⁿ	'seven'
Nasals:	PIE mel-	Lat. molit	Goth. malip	OIr. melid	'(meal), grinds'
	PIE newm	Lat. novem	Goth. niun	OIr. nóiⁿ	'nine'
Resonants:	PIE rēg-	Lat. rēx	Goth. reiks (borrowed)	OIr. rí	'(rich), king'
	PIE plnos	Lat. plēnus	Goth. fulls	OIr. lán	'full'

(PIE y was lost; cf. Lat. iuvencus, Goth. juggs, OIr. oac 'young')
PIE w > OIr. f, as illustrated in the following example.

Vowels:	PIE wiros	Lat. vir	Goth. wair	OIr. fer	'were [wolf], man'
	PIE ekʷos	Lat. equus	Goth. aiƕa-, OE eoh	OIr. ech	'horse'
	PIE alyos	Lat. alius	Goth. aljis	OIr. aile	'(else), other'
	PIE oktō	Lat. octo	Goth. ahtau	OIr. ocht	'eight'
	PIE bhu-	Lat. fuisse	OE bēon	OIr. buith (dat. sg.)	'being'
ī	PIE rī-	Lat. ritus	OE rīm	OIr. rīm	'(rime), number'
ē > ī	PIE wēr-	Lat. vērus	OE wǣr	OIr. fír	'true'
ā	PIE bhrātēr	Lat. frāter	Goth. broþar	OIr. bráthir	'brother'
ō > á	PIE gnōto-	Gk. gnōtós	Lat. nōtus	OIr. gnáth	'known'
ū	PIE rū-	Lat. rūmor	Goth. rūna	OIr. rún	'(rune), secret'

The long vowel system was reduced by the mergers of $\bar{\imath}$ and $\bar{e}$, $\bar{a}$ and $\bar{o}$.

Since Proto-Indo-European had no diphthongs, the Old Irish diphthongs resulted from combinatory developments; these will be discussed later.

Reviewing the development of the Old Irish phonological system we observe that its system of simple short and long vowels is exactly like that of Latin. This parallelism may reflect the early contiguity of the Italic and Celtic peoples; approximately 1500 B.C. they are assumed to have been contiguous in Central Europe, as noted in XI.G.51.

On the other hand, the system of consonants more nearly resembles that of late Old English, with parallel series of voiceless and voiced stops and fricatives (though not in the sibilants) and a similar set of resonants with differences in the semivowels. Both Germanic and Celtic developed their consonant systems at a relatively late period, and as a comparison with the Proto-Indo-European consonants indicates the differences from Proto-Indo-European are great.

55. The home of the Indo-Europeans

Previous theories on the home of the Indo-Europeans around 3000 B.C. have now yielded to almost certain evidence that this was north of the Black Sea, in southern Russia. Archeological investigations have indicated a very good fit between the later locations of the various groups and this area, as well as with their early wanderings. Moreover, whatever inferences had been made concerning the culture of the Proto-Indo-European speakers are comparable to the findings of archeologists.

The culture identified as that of the Proto-Indo-Europeans has been given the label "Kurgan," a Russian word for burial mound. Marija Gimbutas has presented the findings in several excellent articles: "Proto-Indo-European Culture: The Kurgan Culture during the Fifth, Fourth, and Third Millennia B.C.," in *Indo-European and Indo-Europeans*, ed. George Cardona, Henry M. Hoenigswald, and Alfred Senn (Philadelphia: Univ. of Pennsylvania Press, 1970), pp. 155–97; "The Beginning of the Bronze Age in Europe and the Indo-Europeans: 3500–2500 B.C.," *The Journal of Indo-European Studies*, 1 (1973), 163–214. The Kurgan peoples had the horse, the wheel, and bronze weapons. With the aid of these they conquered various areas, including Europe to the northwest. One of the groups in this area was the forerunner of the Celts. We have little information about the possible ancestors of the Celts between 3000 and 1200 B.C. When we can identify with reasonable certainty Celtic groups at this second date, their culture had changed considerably from that of the Kurgan peoples of 3000 B.C. Presumably their language had too. But we can only speculate on these changes, and do little more than note differences between the poorly attested Gaulish of the beginning of our era and the Insular Celtic languages. This will be our aim in subsequent chapters.

chapter XII

READING AND TEXTUAL ANALYSIS, Section 12

The two further challengers, Munremor and Mend, are rapidly disposed of in this section.

1. 'Frithālid, a Ulto, in comram beus' ol Cet.
2. 'Nis·rainnfe indossa' ol Muinremor mac Gerginn.
3. 'Inn é so Muinremor?' ol Cet.
4. 'Is mé ro·ġlan mo ġoo fodéoid, a Muinremu⟨i⟩r,' ol Cet.
5. 'Ni·fuilet trí thráth and ō thucus-⟨s⟩a trī laíchcenn ūait im chenn do chétmeic ast ferunn.'
6. Dessid side dano.
7. 'In comram beus!' ol Cet.
8. 'Rot·bia són' ol Mend mac Sālchada.
9. 'Cīa so?' ol Cet.
10. 'Mend' ol cách.
11. 'Cid ane' ol Cet, 'meic na mbachlach cusna lesanmannaib do chomram cucum?
12. Ar ba mese ba sacart oc baistiud ind anma-sin fora athair, messe t⟨h⟩all a šáil de co claidiub conna·ruc acht oinchois ūaim.
13. Cid do·bérad mac ind oinchoisseda cucumsa?'
14. Dessid side dano.

---

1. frithālid   2 pl. impv. of *fris·áli* 'carries on; attends to, looks to'
2. nis·rainnfe   2 sg. fut. of *rannaid* 'divides,' following neg., w. 3 sg. f. pers. pron. referring to *mucc*
   indossa   'now'; stressed on *-o-*
3. inn   'is (it)?'

é 'he'

4. ro·glan   3 sg. *ro*-pret. of *glanaid* 'cleans,' used as rel. clause after *mé* 'I'

   goo   acc. pl. m. of *gaí* 'spear,' used w. *mo* 'my'

   fo·déoid   'at last'; this statement is taken as a martial saying, referring to "cleaning" spears on the bodies of enemies

5. ni·fuilet   3 pl. of *fil* = ·*tá* 'is,' after neg.; a late inflected form; for *fil* see VII.G.33.2

   trí thráth   see IV.3a.1

   ó   conjunction 'since, after'; lenites

   tucus   1 sg. *ro*-pret. of *do·beir* 'takes'

   laích-cenn   acc. pl. nt. 'warrior-head'

   úait   VIII.G.38.a

   im   prep. w. acc. 'about, round, including'

   ast   *a*^g prep. w. dat. 'out of, from' w. 2 sg. poss. pron.

   ferunn   dat. sg. nt. of *ferann* 'land'

8. són   nom. acc. nt. of *suide* (unstressed) 'that'

11. ane   'then, next'

    bachlach   gen. pl. m. 'herdsman, churl,' w. art.

    co n-   prep. w. dat. 'with,' w. pl. art. > *cusna*

    lesanmannaib   dat. pl. nt. of *les-ainm* 'nickname'; see IX.7.1

12. ar   conjunction 'for, because'; introduces principal causal clauses

    sacart   nom. sg. m. 'priest'

    baistiud   dat. sg. m. of *baisted* 'baptism' after *oc* 'at'

    messe t⟨hall⟩   see this expression in XI.11.13

    sáil   acc. sg. f. of *sál* 'heel'

    claidiub   dat. sg. m. of *claideb* 'sword'

    (conna)·ruc   3 sg. *ro*-pret. of *berid* 'bears'

    acht   'except'; after neg. *ní* and *conná*- 'only'

    oín-chois   acc. sg. f. of *cos* 'leg, foot,' w. prefixed 'one'

13. do·bérad   3 sg. condit. of *do·beir* 'bring'

    oínchoisseda   gen. sg. m. of *oínchoissiḍ* 'one-legged man'

    cucumsa   *co*^g prep. w. acc. 'to, up to,' w. 1 sg. pers. pron. affix

GLOSSES

19. Ml. 69ª21.   co n-epreḍ: 'du-gén a nnoíḃ sa ⁊ ní diḡén a n-ærgarthe se, ciḍ accubur lium'; ní eper in sin.

    co n-epred   *co* w. ind. in consecutive clause = 'so that'; used in an independent clause to support an inference rather than a consequence; frequent in glosses; *epred* 3 sg. impf. of *as·beir*

    du·gén   1 sg. fut. of *do·gní*

    noíḃ   'holy; a saint' here 'holy thing'

    diḡén   1 sg. fut. proto. (probably long *ē*) of *do·gní*

    ærgarthe   'forbidden' pass. pret. of *ar·gair*

    cid   'although it be'; *cia* + cop. pres. subj. 3 sg.

    accubur   nt. 'desire'; vn. of *ad·cobra*

    eper   1 sg. pres. subj. of *as·beir* or 3 sg. pres. ind. pass. (-*eperr*)

20. Wb. 29ª28.   biit al-aili and ro·finnatar a pecthe resíu do·coí grád
forru; al-aili is íaruṁ ro·finnatar: berir dano fri laa brātha.

biit   3 pl. consuetudinal pres. ind. of subst. vb.
al-aili   'other'; *al-aili . . . al-aili* 'some . . . others'
ro·finnatar   pass. pres. of *ro·finnadar* 'finds out'; special meaning fr. *ro
·fitir* 'knows/knew'
pecthe   nom. pl. of *pecad* 'sin'
resíu   conjunction 'before'
do·coí   3 sg. pres. perf. subj. of *téit*
grád   nt. 'grade, order' w. *téit* = 'be ordained'
berir fri   'is referred to'
brātha   gen. of *brāth* 'doom'

21. Ml. 67ᵈ14.   aṁal ru-n-d gab slīab Siōn andes ⁊ antūaiḋ dun chathraiġ
dia dītin, sic ru-n-d gaḃsat ar ṅdā thoīḃ du dītin ar n-inṁeḋōnach-ni.

ru-n-d gab   3 sg. perf. of *gaibid* w. nt. infix used in sense of 'to be' after
conjunction that takes a rel. and in indirect speech
andes   'from the south' (see IX.G.45; Thurneysen G.305)
antūaid   'from the north' (see IX.G.45; Thurneysen G.305)
dun   *do* + art.
chathraig   dat. of *cathir* f. 'city'
dia   *do* + 3 sg. f. poss. pron., referring to *cathir*
dītin   dat. of *ditiu* f. 'protection'
sic   Lat. = *is samlaid*
ru-n-d gabsat   3 pl. past, see above
thoīb   m. 'side'
in·medónach   'internal, inward,' pl. 'entrails'

GRAMMAR

56. The Celtic languages on the Continent

Julius Caesar (102?–44 B.C.) gives the first lengthy account of Celtic speakers
by a contemporary. In the celebrated passage of Book VI.11–20 of his *Gallic War*,
Caesar gives his views of the social system, the religion, and the economic and
political arrangements he found in Gaul. His description of this aristocratic society has been examined for its accuracy and compared with later accounts as
well as with archeological discoveries. For a recent survey, see Chapter i of *The
Celtic Realms*, by Myles Dillon and Nora K. Chadwick (London: Weidenfeld and
Nicolson, 1967; 2nd ed. 1972).

Among the reported customs was feasting, as in SMMD. Two passages are of
especial interest, recorded by Posidonius and quoted by Diodorus: "Brave warriors they honor with the finest portions of the meat." "In former times . . .

92

when the hindquarters were served, the bravest hero took the thigh-piece, and if another man claimed it, they stood up and fought in single combat to the death." Since such details concerning the practices of the mainland Celts agree with details in Old Irish story, it is reasonable to assume that the Celts who settled in Britain had earlier made up a group of the Continental Celts.

The date of the settlement in Britain is, however, uncertain. The Celts are associated with peoples who are especially distinguished, about the fourteenth century B.C., by a new burial practice in central Europe: cremation of the body and placing of the ashes in an urn, which was then deposited in an urnfield. The Urnfield culture developed the use of iron, especially near the Austrian city Hallstatt. With their technological advances they were the dominant people in Central Europe through the Hallstatt period (c. 800–450 B.C.) and the La Tène period (named from a site in Switzerland) (c. 450–50 B.C.). But whether the ancestors of the Old Irish first settled in Britain in the Hallstatt period, or as early as 1800 B.C. (*The Celtic Realms*, p. 214), is an open question. What is clear is that the Continental language, Gaulish, was SVO rather than VSO, and that it even preserved SOV features of Proto-Indo-European. Whatever the reason, Old Irish was strongly modified in structure.

The remains of Gaulish are unfortunately scanty. But names permit a contrast between the two subgroups. Thus, the Gaulish name *Dumnorix* attested by Caesar corresponds to Irish *rí an domhain* 'king of the world.' The preposed OV-type modifier of Gaulish is replaced by a postposed VO construction in Irish. Even verb-final sentences are found in some of the earliest Old Irish texts. The dominant VSO order of Old Irish then must be relatively recent. As noted above, this order has had a profound effect on the language.

57. The prepositional constructions of Old Irish

Along with the verb-initial constructions of VSO languages, the use of prepositions is highly characteristic. Old Irish has developed this characteristic in great degree, affixing to prepositions enclitic forms of pronouns. In such affixation, the prepositions are modified in various ways. The preposition *frith* 'against' may serve as example. It may appear in its full form in compounds, as in this lesson in the imperative form *frithálid*. It has this shape when stressed, or after the stress, in nominal and verbal compounds. When before the stress, as in the third singular present *fris·áli* 'carries on,' it has the final sibilant. Before nouns the final consonant is reflected in gemination of the following initial consonant, as in *fri-nnech* 'against someone,' or in -h, as in *fri h-ór* 'for gold.' The form *fri* spread from such forms to the compound forms with suffixed personal pronouns. The resultant forms were listed in II.G.7: first singular *frim, frium*; second singular *frit, friut*, third singular masculine *fris(s)*, and so on. In this way prepositions have developed into a variety of forms. The etymology of *frith* is assumed to be the PIE root *wert-* 'turn,' which is also reflected in Lat. *versus* 'toward' and NE -*ward*. Other such prepositional developments will be noted below.

58. Noun inflection: ā-stems

The forms of the ā-stems, as given in II.G.8, can be derived from earlier reconstructed forms, much like the o-stems. Those are instructive for understanding
the phonological developments in pre-Old Irish. The forms of *ben* 'woman,' for
example, are reconstructed as follows:

		OIr.	PIE
Sg.	N	ben	g^wén-ā
	V	ben	g^wén-ə
	A	mnaí	(g^wen-m̥, but modified by
		bein (archaic acc. is attested)	analogy w. dat.)
	G	mná	g^wn-(j)ās
	D	mnaí	g^wn-ái
Pl.	NV	mná	g^wn-ás
	A	mná	g^wn-áns
	G	ban	g^wn̥-ōm
	D	mnáib	g^wn-ábhis
Du.	NA	mnaí	g^wn-ái
	G	ban	g^wn̥-?
	D	mnáib	g^wn-ábhim

Among the readily recognizable changes are the reductions of the endings.
These are ascribed to the strong initial accent, which was introduced presumably in the millennium before our era. We must assume relatively late changes,
because the lost endings have left traces in the modifications of following words,
as noted in XII.G.60 and later.

Another notable effect of the strong stress accent is the reduction of the stem,
when the accent falls on the ending, as in the genitive and dative singular. After
the loss of the stem vowel *e*, the initial labial was assimilated to the following
nasal: *bn- > mn-*. In this way the inflected forms became relatively complex,
especially if the noun stem was monosyllabic, as for *g^wen-*.

59. Copula and substantive verb

As noted in II.G.9, forms of the copula are derived from a number of IE roots.
absolute forms, like the third singular *is* 'is,' are from the root *ʔes*, also found
in NE *be*; forms of the substantive verb like ·*tá* 'is' are from the root *(s)teh-*,
which is also found in NE *stand*. These roots have given rise to forms that are
complex in origin; some of them are as follows:

1 sg. *am*   PIE esmi, as in Skt. asmi, Gk. eimí
            (*a*- developed from *e*- in proclitic position)

2 sg. *at*   PIE esi, as in Skt. ási, Gk. eî
            (*-t*, the 2 sg. pron. was added to the regular development of this form)

3 sg. *is*   PIE esti, as in Skt. ásti, Gk. estí

94

The OIr. first plural *ammi* is derived from the assumed **es-mos*, modified in accordance with the first singular. The second plural and third plural, on the other hand, cannot be derived from the IE form reconstructed on the basis of reflexes in other dialects. Forms of the copula in this way have been greatly modified from the expected developments.

60. Historical background of lenition

As noted in II.G.10, lenition is a term used for relatively lax articulation of consonants. Like nasalization and gemination, it was caused by the final elements of preceding words. The processes may be related to the strong stress: phrasal groups were articulated as units, and the finals of some words then affected the initials of others.

Lenition was caused by final vowels. Examining the reconstructed forms of *o*-stems and *ā*-stems, we would then expect lenition after the nominative and vocative singular of *ā*-stems, the genitive singular of *o*-stems, as well as the dative singular of all genders, among other forms. See XI.G.52 and XII.G.58.

Lenition is particularly prominent after the article, and after pronominal and numeral forms that are in close relation to the following noun. It is also found when descriptive adjectives and genitives occur in phrases in which they are associated with nouns. The effect is clearest in *o*-stems and *ā*-stems, the forms which have been given in this and the previous grammar lessons.

Lenition occurs after verbal forms and after uninflected words such as prepositions, as noted above. The prepositions causing lenition are *amal, ar, cen, di, do, fo, im, ó úa, tre tri*. Conjunctions causing lenition are *ocus, no nu, ma, cía ce, co ó, ama(i)l*. It is also found after the vocative particle *a á*. In all of these forms the basic cause is the same: influence of a preceding vowel.

chapter XIII

READING AND TEXTUAL ANALYSIS, Section 13

In meeting the challenge of Celtchair, son of Uithechair (a hero who had made an appearance in ix.7.4), Cet shows increasing confidence, a situation that seems ominous for the ultimate success of Connaught, especially since Celtchair's retirement seems dishonorable. By this time the formulaic challenge and response are scarcely novel.

1. 'In comram beus!' ol Cet.
2. 'Rot·bia sōn' ol lāech líath mór forgránda di Ultaib.
3. 'Cïa so?' ol Cet.
4. 'Celtchair mac Uithechair sin' ol cách.
5. 'An bic, a Cheltchair,' ol Cet, 'manip dom thūarcain fo chētóir.
6. Rotānac-sa, a Cheltchair, co dorus do thiġe.
7. Ro·hēġed immum.
8. Tánic cách.
9. Tānacais-⟨s⟩iu dano.
10. Dot·luid i mbernai armo chenn-sa.
11. Do·reilgis gaï form-sa.
12. Ro·lēcus-⟨s⟩a gaï n-aill cucut-su co·ndechaid tret slīasait ocus tre hūachtar do macraille.
13. Ataí co ngalur fúail ōnd ūair-sin, nicon·rucad mac na inġen duit.
14. Cid dot·bérad cucum-sa?'
15. Dessid side dano.

---

2. líath 'gray-haired'
   forgránda 'very ugly, terrible'

5. bic   = *biuc*, as in X.9.5

thūarcain   dat. sg. f. of *túarcan* 'crush, battling'; vn. of *do·fuairc*

fo chét-óir   dat. sg. f. of *úar* 'time,' compounded w. *cét* 'first' = 'at once'

6. rotānac-sa   Thurneysen considers this an error for *ro·ánac-sa*, 1 sg. *ro*-pret. of *ro·ic* 'reaches, attains'

7. ro·héged   cf. the form in XI.11.8, from which you may assume the nonmandatory use of *-h-*

8. tánic   3 sg. pret. of *do·ic* 'comes'; the 2 sg. pret. of the next sentence has occurred previously in XI.11.9; the similarities between the contrasts in X.9 and XI.11 are worth comparing both for their dramatic effect and their reflection of storytelling techniques

10. dot·luid   3 sg. pret., w. infixed 2 sg. pron. of *do·tét* 'comes'; the impers. construction is found in other archaic texts = 'you came'

i m·bernai   dat. sg. f. of *berna* 'gap, breach' after i^n

armo chenn-sa   cf. *ar chenn*, as in VI.4.6

11. do·reilgis   2 sg. *ro*-pret. of *do·lé(i)ci*, as in XI.11.10

12. ro·lēcus-⟨s⟩a   1 sg. *ro*-pret. of *lé(i)cid*, *·lé(i)ci* 'throws'

co·ndechaid   3 sg. *ro*-pret. of *téit* 'hits, goes to' after *co n-*

slíasait   acc. sg. f. 'thigh'

hūachtar   acc. sg. m. 'upper part'

macraille   gen. sg. f. 'testicles'

13. ataí   2 sg. pres. of *·tá, atá* 'is'

galur   dat. sg. nt. of *galar* 'disease'

fúail   gen. sg. m. 'urine'; w. *galur* = 'urinary disease'

ōnd ūair-sin   prep. *ó* w. art. sg. 'from that hour, since then'

nicon·rucad   *·rucad* is pret. pass. of *berid* 'bears,' which here corresponds to Eng. 'begets'

ingen   nom. sg. f. 'daughter, girl'

14. dot·bérad   3 sg. condit., w. 2 sg. infixed pers. pron. of *do·beir* 'brings'; cf. the slightly varying sentence in XII.12.13

GLOSSES

22. Wb. 13^b12.   masu ġlé liḃ trā in precept ro·pridchus-sa .i. as-reracht Crīst hó marḃaiḃ, ciḋ dia léiciḋ cunduḃairt for drēcht ūaiḃ de resurrectione hominum?

masu   *ma* + 3 sg. pres. ind. 'if it is' (len.)

ġlé   'clear'

ro·pridchus-sa   1 sg. pres. *ro* perf. prefix w. pres. tense gives force of a perf.; *p* nasalized [b] in rel. clause

as·reracht   (< *ess-ro·ess·recht*) 3 sg. perf. of *as-érig* 'arises'

cid dia^n   'what [is it], from which, why?'

léicid   'leave, allow'

cundubairt   f. 'doubt'

drēcht   'portion'

ūaib   *ó* + 2 pl.

23. Ml. 32^{c}15.   amal as-robrad fri Dauíd do·rolgída a pecthi dō, ní eperr immurġu frin-ni, in tain du-luigter dūn ar pecthi.

   as·robrad   pass. perf. sg. of *as·beir* 'says'
   do·rolgida   pass. perf. pl. of *do·luigi* 'forgives'
   eperr   pass. pres. ind. of *as·beir*
   du·luigter   pres. pass. of *do·luigi*
   Phonetic /a fekθi/ . . . /ar bekθi/

24. Ml. 54^{d}7.   ro·lil dīm m'ernigde ⁊ nī dechuid hūaim.

   ro·lil   3 sg. perf. of *lenaid* 'follows, sticks to' (w. *di-*)
   ernigde   f. 'prayer'
   dechuid   3 sg. perf. proto. of *téit*

GRAMMAR

61. The Celtic languages in the British Isles

In the absence of early records the Celtic settlements in Britain can be dated only by evidence from archeology and the languages. Such evidence is inadequate for determining the earliest dates of the settlements in Britain, though much archeological work remains to be done.

Linguistic evidence permits the assumption of two waves of immigration, for the Celtic languages may be subdivided into two groups: Goidelic, or Q-Celtic, and Brythonic, or P-Celtic. (The earliest Roman historians referred to the P-Celts as Pritani, and the early Welsh texts to the main island as Prydain; the present spelling is in accordance with the name used by the inhabitants of the Roman province, Brittones.) Linguistic evidence for the subdivision of the Celtic languages is largely phonological, such as the contrasting words for 'five': OIr. *cóic* and Welsh *pump*. Gaulish shares the *p*, and accordingly is also P-Celtic. Another important phonological distinction is position of the accent: in contrast with the strong initial accent of Goidelic, Welsh has a stress accent on the penultimate. The location of the stress has had far-reaching consequences, both for losses of vowels in medial and final syllables, and for stylistic and poetic practices. Irish prose and poetry make great use of initial alliteration, a practice that can be ascribed to the strong stress on initial syllables. The effect of this stress on vowels has been illustrated in the paradigms of nouns and verbs given in the last two chapters; it will be discussed further in G.62.

The reasons for a strong initial stress accent instead of the free pitch accent of Proto-Indo-European can only be speculated on. In this accentual shift Celtic shows tantalizing similarities to Germanic, which also adopted a strong initial stress accent in the first millennium B.C. The date of the Germanic stress shift has been placed about 400 B.C., on the basis of internal linguistic evidence. Words in which the Proto-Indo-European accent followed *p t k k^w*, as illustrated by Sanskrit *pitár-* 'father,' show a voiced fricative in Germanic, as in Gothic

98

fadar; if the Proto-Indo-European accent preceded these stops or *s*, they remained unvoiced, as in Goth. *broþar* (cf. Skt. *bhrãta*). Subsequent modifications have introduced the same consonants in Eng. *father, brother*, and eliminated most of the variations within one set of words; but the consonant interchange in *was : were* is a result of the Proto-Germanic voicing. The phenomenon was definitively described by Carl Verner and is commonly referred to as Verner's law. If the stress shift in Celtic is ascribed to the same period as that of Germanic, and to the same cause, estimates concerning the invasion of Britain by Goidelic speakers would center around the middle of the first millennium B.C.

Whatever the date, Britain was already inhabited. Nothing is known of the language of the earlier inhabitants. Mythical accounts in Irish story ascribe strange features to them. One group, the Fomorians, were giants; another, the Firbolg, sometimes called the "bag people" because *bolg* means a bag, have been equated by T. F. O'Rahilly with the Belgae, one of the tribes of Continental Celts. O'Rahilly takes Belgae as the name of the people of the god Bolg, a sun god, and he equates Cuchulain's lethal *gai bolg* as the sun's rays or the thunderbolts— either is light from heaven. Some scholars have also proposed that the VSO structure of Irish is from earlier inhabitants. Such suggestions must be examined on the basis of general linguistic information regarding effects of one language on another. Little such information has been assembled. The reason for the VSO structure is accordingly difficult to propose. When scholars in addition suggested that the earlier inhabitants of Ireland were related to Hamito-Semitic speakers of North Africa, because their languages are also VSO, their assumptions were made on the basis of a series of speculations. Such far-ranging speculations have tended to discourage concern even with the establishable structural characteristics of Old Irish, especially its syntax. But these can be ascertained from the data, as in SMMD.

62. Effects of the initial stress accent on Old Irish

Examination of any of the paradigms in the two preceding chapters provides illustrations of the effects of the strong initial stress accent on final syllables. For example, the nominative singular ending *-os* has been lost by the time of Old Irish; on the other hand, Lithuanian with its pitch accent preserves to this day a bisyllabic form *výras* 'man.' Similarly, as noted in XII.G.58, OIr. *ben* has lost the final syllable; but this has been maintained in Gk. *gunḗ*, OCS *žena* 'woman,' and so on. In this way many forms of nouns have become monosyllabic in Old Irish.

In addition to the strong initial stress, weaker stresses fell on the third and subsequent alternate syllables. As a result, the vowels of these syllables were maintained in polysyllables, but the nonstressed vowels were lost. An example may be given by means of OIr. *apstal* 'apostle'; this was borrowed from Lat. *apostolus*. As in this example, the Old Irish rule of vowel loss requires that every other vowel be dropped. Moreover, as illustrated in the second syllable of *apstal*, the vowels in syllables not having the main stress accent were often modified to [ə], written *-a-*.

The Old Irish stress rule had a great effect on the forms of verbs. When finite verb forms were accompanied by preverbs, the accent fell on the first syllable of the second element. Thus the complex form made up of *ber-* 'bear, carry' and the preverb *ess-* from **eks-* is *as beir* 'he says' < **eks-béret*; as noted above, the unstressed **e* of the preverb became *a-*.

The interrogative particle *in*, negative particles, and particles with relative prepositions were also treated as preverbs, with regard to stress. Thus when **eks-beret* was preceded by one of these elements, the stress fell on the second preverb; this gave rise to the form *épur, épir*. Since the accented or tonic syllable in such forms is first, the resultant forms are called prototonic. Contrasts between selected prototonic and deuterotonic forms were given in x.G.49. For an account of the changes involved in such forms, such as the loss of *-ks-* in *épur*, Thurneysen's or Pedersen's grammars can be consulted. Compare also xiii.13.11 *do·reilgis* with xiii.13.12 *ro·lēcus-sa* and xi.11.10 *ro·lēcis*.

63. Noun inflection: *i-* and *u-*stems

The endings of these two inflections were parallel. They are similar to the endings of the *o*-stems, xi.G.52, though *i* or *u* rather than *o* preceded the termination. In Proto-Indo-European [i] varied with [y] and [u] with [w] in accordance with the Sievers-Edgerton law; basically, the vocalic [i u] stood between consonants and [y w] between vowels. Because of the parallelism in endings, these two inflections influenced each other in several of the Indo-European dialects. In Old Irish, the genitive singular of the *i*-stems was taken over from the *u*-stems; it was also used in the dual. To illustrate these parallelisms, the endings of *i*- and *u*-stems will be placed side by side here, after those of *o*-stems, and only the masculine *i*-stem *fáith* 'prophet' < **wātis* will be given here; other examples were given in iii.G.12.

		OIr.	*o*-stems	PIE *i*-stems	*u*-stems
Sg.	N	fáith	-os	-is	-us
	V	fáith	-e	-i	-u
	A	fáith n-	-om	-im	-um
	G	fátho	-ī	(-ous)	-ous
	D	fáith	-ōi	-ī	-ū
Pl.	NV	fáithi	-oi	-ejes	-ewes
	A	fáithi	-ōns	-ins	-ūns
	G	fáithe n-	-ōm	-ijōm	(-ijom)
	D	fáithib	-obhis	-ibhis	(-ubhis, modified)
Du.	NA	fáith	-ā	-ī	-ū
	G	fátho	-ou	(gen. sg.)	(gen. sg.)
	D	fáithib	-obhim	-ibhim	(-ubhim, modified)

The results of reductions of the endings may be determined from the attested forms, such as the nasalization caused by the accusative singular and genitive plural.

100

Chapter XIII

64. Imperfect and imperative forms

Examples of these forms were given in III.G.14. The earlier forms of the endings of the imperfect are obscure. If they had been based on the imperfect endings in Indo-European, they would have been similar to the present indicative conjunct endings. It is assumed that the imperfect endings, however, are based on Indo-European middle endings; thus the third singular ·*bered* would have developed from **bhere-to*. The other endings are too problematic for discussion here.

In the imperative, the second singular is based on the simple stem; *beir* is from **bhere*. In the third singular the middle ending **-to* was added. The plural forms are like those of the present indicative conjunct.

65. Historical background of nasalization

In its simplest form, nasalization adds an *n-* to a following word when this begins with a vowel, as in II.1b.8 *i nHērinn* 'in Erin,' *i n-īarthur* 'in the west.' The preposed *n* simply comes from the earlier form of the preposition *in*. Nasalization is accordingly caused by an earlier final *m* or *n*.

Before *b d g* nasalization is also written with *m* or *n*, as in II.1b.8 *i mBrēfni*; the nasal was also pronounced as the nasal corresponding to the stop. See III.G.15.

Before other consonants, the nasals had other effects. A following *p, t, c,* or *f* became voiced. Following *s, r, l, n, m* may have been unmodified, though double spellings suggest some modification. Because of the effects on *p, t, c, f* the term "nasalization" cannot apply in its literal sense; and accordingly the Irish term *eclipsis* has merit.

In a remarkable development the nasalization which was originally a matter of juncture, or sandhi, came to have a meaningful role as an indicator of relative constructions (Lewis and Pedersen, pp. 115–17). It may also be noted that gemination of a resonant has the same effect as nasalization and in the writing system is similarly indicated by doubling the resonant. Before vowels, of course, the two remain distinct, as: *a h-ingen* 'her daughter,' *a n-ingen* 'their daughter.'

chapter XIV

READING AND TEXTUAL ANALYSIS, Section 14

The last challenger, Cúscraid Mend Macha, is overcome with less humiliation but equal effectiveness. And as the last line of Section 14 indicates, Cet seems to have carried the day.

1. 'In comram beus!' ol Cet.
2. 'Rot·bia sōn' ol Cúscraid Mend Macha mac Conchobair.
3. 'Cuich so?' ol Cet.
4. 'Cūsc-raid' ol cách; 'is adbar ríg ar deilb.'
5. 'Ní buide frit' ol in gilla.
6. 'Maith' ol Cet.
7. 'Cucainni ceta·tudchad-so do chétgaisciud, a gillai.
8. Imma·tarraid dún issin chocrich.
9. Fo·rācbais trian do muintire, ocus is ⟨s⟩amlaid do·cūadaiss ocus gai trīat brāgit conna·ētai focul fort chenn i córai; ar ro·loitt in gai féthi do brāgat.
10. Conid Cúscraid Mend atot·chomnaic ōnd ūair-sin.'
11. Do·rat tár fon n-indas-sin forsin cóiced n-uile.

---

4. adbar   nom. sg. nt. 'material, suitable person,' followed by gen.
   deilb   dat. sg. f. of *delb* 'shape'
5. buide   nom. sg. f. 'good will, regard'; *Ní buide frit* = 'There is no thanks to you'
   frit   *fri* w. 2 sg. pers. pron. 'for you'
6. maith   'good'—used here as interjectional adj.
7. cucainni   *cu* w. 1 pl. pers. pron. 'to us'; note zero form of cop.: [It was] . . .
   ceta·tudchad-so   *ceta-* is adverbial form of *cét-* 'first' used before a vb.; 2 sg. *ro*-pret. of *do·tét* 'comes'
   -gaisciud   dat. sg. nt. of *gaisced* 'warlike deed'
8. imma·tarraid   3 sg. *ro*-pret. of *do·airret* 'meets,' used impersonally, w. *imma·* 'mutually'

issin   *i* 'in' w. dat. sg. art.; cf. *isin* I.1a.7

cocrích   see VIII.6.11

9. fo·rācbais   see v.3b.12 and, for form, x.9.9, IX.7.2

trian   acc. sg. nt. 'third part'

muintire   gen. sg. f. of *muinter* 'retinue'

samlaid   *amal* 'as' w. 3 sg. nt. pers. pron. 'like that, thus'

do·cúadaiss   cf. X.9.7

tríat   *tri* 'through' w. 2 sg. poss. pron.

brágit   acc. sg. m. of *brágae* 'neck, throat'; note gen. at end of sentence

conna·ētai   ·*étai* is 2 sg. pres. of *ad·cota* 'obtains,' after *co n-* and neg.

focul   acc. sg. nt. 'word, phrase'

fort   *for* 'upon, over' w. 2 sg. poss. pron.

córai   dat. sg. f. of *córa* 'fitness'; w. *i* = 'appropriately'

ro·loitt   3 sg. *ro*-pret. of *loittid* 'wounds, injures'

féthi   acc. pl. f. of *féith* 'sinew'

10. conid   *co n-* 'and, that' w. 3 sg. pres. of *is* 'is'

mend   'stammering'

atot·chomnaic   3 sg. pret. of *ad·cumaing* 'occurs' w. 2 sg. pers. pron. = 'which happened to you,' i.e., 'that you are [called]'

ōnd ūair-sin   see XIII.13.13 'from that hour, since'

11. do·rat   3 sg. *ro*-pret. of *do·beir* 'gives, puts, brings'

tár   acc. sg. nt. 'disgrace'

fon n-indas-sin   see X.9.10

forsin   *for* 'on' w. art. sg.; the acc. of *cóiced* is indicated by the following *n-*

GLOSSES

25. Wb. 18ᵈ3.   immu-n-cūalammar, nīmu-n-accamar.

immu-n-cūalammar   1 pl. perf. of *immu-s-cluinetar* 'we have heard one another'

nīmu-n-accamar   1 pl. perf. of *immu-sn-aiccet* 'we have seen one another'; neg.

26. SG. 31ᵃ6.   di airisin do·rataḋ foir a n-ainm sin, ar iss eḋ laithe in sin ro ngénair-soṁ, ni airindī ro·ngenaḋ-soṁ isind luc sin.

airisin   dat. sg. f. of *airisiu* 'story, history'

do·ratad   perf. pass. sg. of *do·beir*

laithe   'day'

ro·ngénair-som   3 sg. perf. of *gainithir* 'is born'

airindī   'because'

ro ngenad-som   3 sg. past subj.

luc   'place'

27. Ml. 82ᵃ7.   ní dēnti dūiḃ-si anīsin, air atá nech duḃar ṅdeicsin .i. Dīa.

dēnti   verbal of necessity of *do·gní*

ndeicsin   f. 'beholding'

28. Ml. 120^{d}2. amal du-n-eclannar étach ṅderscaigthe hi tiġ cennaiġi do
buith immin ríġ, is samlaiḋ du-érglas ind soilse sainriuḋ asnaiḃ dūliḃ do
imthimchuil in choimded.

du-n-eclannar   pres. pass. sg. of *do·eclainn* 'searches out'
ētach 'garment'
ṅderscaigthe pass. pret. part. of *do-róscai* 'distinguished, of surpassing excel-
    lence'
cennaigi gen. sg. 'merchant'
buith f. 'being' vn. of subst. vb.
du-érglas pass. perf. of *do·eclainn*
soilse 'light'
sainriud 'in particular' (*sainred* 'specialty')
asnaib dūlib   prep. *a(s)* 'out of, from' + dat. pl. art. + dat. pl. of *dúil* f.
    'element'
imthimchuil 'surrounding'
coimded gen. sg. of *coimdiu* 'Lord'

GRAMMAR

66. The five provinces of Ireland

In the prose saga, the *Táin Bó Cúailgne* 'The Cattle-Raid of Cooley,' Ireland is
divided into *cóiceda* 'fifths.' These were: Ulaid 'Ulster,' Connachta 'Connaught,'
Laigin 'Leinster,' Mumu 'Munster,' and a further province which is not men-
tioned. Later, this fifth province is referred to as Mide 'Meath.' The first three
of these provinces feature prominently in SMMD.

Although present-day dialects are associated with some of these divisions, notably Ulster and Munster, we cannot associate differences in the languages of
the early texts with geographically distinct dialects. Our inability to make such
distinctions may be a result of the literary tradition, by which all the ancient
stories are transmitted in a general language, something like the generalized epic
language of Homer. It may also be a result of inadequate study. The five provinces are clearly delineated in story, and might well be expected to exhibit distinct dialect characteristics, yet communication may have been adequate to elim-
inate these.

67. Exceptions to the VSO structure

In some of the earliest texts, patterns are found in which verbs are final. These
were identified by Bergin, and the phenomenon is referred to as Bergin's law.
(See Osborn Bergin, "On the Syntax of the Verb in Old Irish," *Ēriu*, 12, 1938,
197–214 and Thurneysen G.327–28.) When simple verbs stand at the ends of
clauses, they have conjunct forms; when compound verbs occupy this position,
they have prototonic forms.

Examples are:

brechtaib ban mberar 'by the spells of women he is taken' (conjunct)
mor mairg mor deilm diulaing 'great woe, great wailing it causes' (prototonic)

These archaic patterns indicate that Irish was OV at an earlier time. As indicated earlier, a VSO pattern was adopted at some stage and became predominant in the Insular languages. (Calvert Watkins, "Syntax of the Old Irish Verb," *Celtica*, 6, 1963, 32–37.)

68. Inflections of consonantal stems (dentals and velars)

In Proto-Indo-European, consonant stems add case endings directly to the base of the noun. When final consonants and vowels were lost in Old Irish, the case endings disappeared almost entirely, as illustrated here. The final losses will be summed up in xv.G.74 and 75. It can be observed from the nominative singular forms of both *rí* and *car(a)e* that two final consonants were lost, as were syllables consisting of a short vowel or a vowel followed by a single consonant.

		Final endings		
Sg.	N	-s	rí < -gs	carae < -ants
	V	--	rí	carae
	A	-m	ríg	carait
	G	-os	ríg	carat
	D	-(a)i	ríg	carait
Pl.	NV	-es	ríg	carait
	A	-ns	ríga	cairtea
	G	-ōm	ríg	carat
	D	-obhis	rígaib	cairtib
Du.	NVA	-e	ríg	carait
	G	-ou	ríg	carat
	D	-obhim	rígaib	cairtib

In the accusative plural of *carae*, the ending *-ant + ns* had become *-edd-(+ās)*; this then developed as in *cairtea*. The datives plural and dual underwent the same modification of ending as did *rí*. These examples of consonant stem inflections illustrate modifications and losses which Old Irish underwent because of the adoption of a strong initial stress accent.

69. The development of the copula and the substantive verb

As noted in II.G.9, Old Irish developed a distinction between the copula and the substantive verb. The distinction is not found in Germanic nor in other ancient Indo-European dialects. It is comparable, however, to the contrast between the absence of *be*, that is, ø, versus *be* in Black English; Black English *he sick* simply states a fact, while *he be sick* indicates a continuing state, or in the customary grammatical terminology, a consuetudinal present, for which the substantive verb but not the copula has a special form in Old Irish. The source of the Celtic distinction between copula and substantive verb is unknown. The similar distinction between Sp. *ser* and *estar* may or may not be useful to investigators seeking to account for its origin; for the Spanish contrast may be based on Celtic rather than on a pattern of an earlier indigenous language which may also have been found in Britain and thus have influenced Celtic as well as Spanish.

Whatever the source of the distinction, the paradigm of the verb and the particles that mean 'be' is based on several Indo-European roots, as it is in English. Proto-Indo-European apparently had no copula initially, but before the time of the dialects the root **ɔes-*, **es-* was used in this sense. In some dialects the root **bhew-* 'become' came to be used in this way as well. In addition, the root **steh-*, **stā-* 'stand' came to be used in Celtic for the substantive verb; forms of this root were also used in Spanish, possibly providing an indication that Celtic was the source of the Spanish distinction. The Old Irish forms of 'be' illustrate the effects of modifications which probably were introduced from one or more non-Indo-European languages, presumably the speech of the earlier inhabitants of Britain.

The details of the history of each Old Irish form based on these roots are complicated, as noted in XII.G.59. The complexities are of more interest to specialists concerned with historical linguistics than to students wishing to understand Old Irish. The comprehensive grammars may be consulted for the standard views on the assumed history of the individual forms. For other verbs, see the form of *gaibid* in XII.Gl.21; see also Thurneysen G.480.

70. Historical background of palatalization

The losses of final vowels were late enough to leave effects on elements preceding them. When final high front vowels were lost, that is, *i ī, e ē,* or *j* + vowel, they left the effect on preceding elements known as palatalization. Examination of the paradigms given in this lesson and preceding lessons indicates the forms that may have been expected to produce palatalization, such as the genitive singular ending of *o*-stems: *-ī*. The genitive singular form of *mac: mic* or *meic* and *scél: scéuil* provide illustrations of palatalization through *i ī*. The third singular present *do·beir* < *-*bheret* provides illustrations of palatalization through *e ē*. Palatalization is regular in the *i*-stems, e.g., *súil, fáith*, as well as the *io-* and *iā*-stems. The regular developments have been modified by systematic modifications in paradigms, that is, by analogy. Details can be found in the comprehensive grammars, as in Thurneysen G.55–57, 99–102.

chapter XV

READING AND TEXTUAL ANALYSIS, Section 15

When Cet is about to enjoy his apparent success, Conall Cernach enters. His challenge is quite different from those of his predecessors. The exchange between him and Cet is made in an alliterative speech with statements of generally four syllables, apparently an archaic literary text incorporated by the author. In the Book of Leinster an "R" is placed in the margin beside each 'Fochen.' These passages (9 and 11) are good examples of the Old Irish *retoiric*, now usually called *rosc* or *roscad*. These passages are early forms of alliterative verse; neither of them is completely regular in syllable count or alliterative pattern. In general the alliteration binds lines together as well as being internal in the line.

1. In tan diḋiu ro⟨n⟩d·mbertaiġestar ocon ṁuicc ocus scían inna láiṁ co·n-accatar Conall Cernach is·tech.
2. Is and tarḃlaing for lár in tiġe.
3. Ferait Ulaiḋ fāilti móir fri Conall.
4. Is and ro·lá Conchobar in cenniḋi dia chinn ocus nos·mbertaiġeḋar.
5. 'Is maith lenn ar cuit do thairiuc' ol Conall.
6. 'Cia rannas dúiḃ?'
7. 'Ro·ddét dond ḟiur nod·ranna' ol Conchobar '.i. Cet mac Māġach.'
8. 'In ḟīr, a Cheit,' ol Conall, 'tusso do rainn na-mmuicce?'
9. Is and as·bert Cet:
     'Fochen Conall,   criḋe licce,   londbruth loġa,   luchair eġa,
   guss flann ferge   fo chích ċuraḋ   crēchtaiġ cathbūaḋaiġ.
10. At comsa mac Findchoiṁe frim.'
11. Et dixit Conall:
     'Fochen Cet,   Cet mac Māġach,   maġen curaḋ,   criḋe n-eġa,
   ethre n-ela,   err trén tressa,   trethan áġach,   caín tarḃ tnúthach,
   Cet mac Māġach.
12. Biḋ menn innar n-imchoṁruc-ni ón' ol Conall, 'ocus biḋ menn inar

107

n-imscaraḋ; biḋ airscēla la fer mbrot, biḋ fīaḋnaise la fer manath; ar ar·cichset airg loman londgliaiḋ na da err eḃlait ēcht ar ēcht, reġaiḋ fer dar fer is·taiġ-seo innocht.'

---

1. tan   f. 'time' *In tan* = 'when'
   rond·mbertaigestar   *ro*-pret. of *bertaigidir* shakes, brandishes'; w. rel. -*n*- and infixed pers. pron. 3 m. used reflexively
   co·n-accatar   3 pl. pret. of *ad·ci* 'sees'
   is·tech   *i n*-'(come) into' and *tech* acc.
2. tarblaing   3 sg. *ro*-pret. of *do·air-ling* 'leaps down'
   lár   acc. sg. nt. 'floor, middle (of a hall)'
3. ferait   3 pl. pres. of *feraid* + *fáilti* = 'welcomes'
4. ro·lá   3 sg. *ro*-pret. used w. *fo·ceird* 'puts, throws'
   cennidi   acc. sg. f. 'headgear'
   nos·mbertaigedar   3 sg. pres., w. 3 sg. f. infixed pers. pron.; cf. VI.4.1
5. lenn   *la*ᵍ 'with, by' w. 1 pl. pers. pron.
   cuit   nom. sg. f. 'portion'
   tairiuc   dat. sg. nt. of *tairec* 'obtaining'; the cognate vb. *do·airec* 'comes to an end' is used in XVI.17.5
6. rannas   3 sg. pres. rel. of *rannaid* 'divides, carves'
7. ro·ddét   *ro*-pret. pass. of *daimid* 'concedes, suffers'
   nod·ranna   3 sg. pres. rel., w. nt. pers. pron. affixed to *no*·, a ptc. used without meaning to support pron.; the nt. pron. refers to the act of dividing
8. tusso   'thou'
9. cride   nom. sg. nt. 'heart'; also in sent. 11
   licce   gen. sg. f. of *lecc* '(flag)stone'
   londbruth   nom. sg. m. *bruth* 'heat' w. adj. *lond*- 'angry, harsh,' used also in Conall's remarks, sent. 12
   loga   gen. sg. m. of *lug* 'lynx' usually in transferred sense 'hero'
   luchair   nom. sg. f. 'glitter, brightness'
   ega   gen. sg. f. of *aig* 'ice'; also in sent. 11
   guss   nom. sg. m. 'vigor, strength'
   flann   'red'; note that postposed adj. position requires association w. *guss*
   ferge   gen. sg. f. of *ferg* 'anger'
   cích   dat. sg. f. 'breast'
   curad   gen. sg. m. of *cur* 'hero, champion'; also in sent. 11
   créchtaig   gen. sg. of *créchtach* 'full of scars/wounds'
   cathbúadaig   gen. sg. m. of *cath-búadach* 'victorious in battle'
10. at   2 sg. pres. of *is* 'is'
    comsa   possibly the gen. sg. m. of *commus* 'comparison' = 'thou are comparable to me'
    mac   the nom., rather than the voc., makes this a strange construction, an appositive to the sub. in the vb.
11. magen   nom. sg. f. '(dwelling)place'
    ethre   nom. sg. nt. 'end, tail'—possibly 'plumage'
    ela   gen. sg. f. 'swan'
    err   nom. sg. m. 'nobleman fighting in a chariot'; note du. in sent. 12

trén 'strong'

tressa   gen. sg. m. of *tress* 'combat'

trethan   nom. sg. m. '(stormy) sea'

ágach   'warlike, with many battles'

caín   'good, beautiful'; preposed possibly in marked order

tarb   nom. sg. m. 'bull'

tnúthach   'jealous, angry, fierce'

12. menn   'clear, distinct'

imchomruc   dat. sg. nt. of *imchomrac* 'meeting'

ón   like *són*, nt. form of *side*, unstressed form of *suide*, nt. *sodain* 'that, this'

imscarad   nom. sg. m. 'separation'

airscéla   nom. sg. nt. 'famous tale'

brot   gen. pl. m. 'goad' after acc. sg. of *fer* 'man'

fiadnaise   nom. sg. nt. 'testimony'

manath   an obscure word; Thurneysen hesitantly cites Pokorny's emendation to *menath* 'awl,' proposing that 'even the lower people will remember the fight' or *monach* 'dexterous, skilled' (reading of one MS)

ar·cichset   3 pl. fut. of *ar·cing* 'marches forward (to the encounter)'

airg   nom. pl. m. of *arg* 'prominent warrior'; or acc. sg. of *airg* 'trouble, difficulty'; by this second interpretation *na da err* would be the sub. of *ar·cichset*; further, *loman*, which is quite obscure, could be taken as gen. pl. of *lom(m)án* 'branch or trunk stripped of its bark' = 'spear-staff'

-gliaid   possibly acc. sg. nt. (?) of *gléo* 'fight'

eblait   3 pl. fut. of *agid* 'drives, performs'

écht   acc. sg. m. 'violent deed, exploit'

regaid   3 sg. fut. of *téit* 'goes'

is·taig   note form in acc. in sent. 1; here place rather than change of place is indicated since the dat. is used

GLOSSES

29. Wb. 10ᵈ5.   cani epir? náte! at·beir.

cani   interrog. expecting affirm. answer

epir   3 sg. pres. ind. proto.

náte   'no'

at·beir   3 sg. pres. w. infixed obj. pron. 3 sg. nt. leniting

30. Wb. 20ᵃ10.   ní nach aile ass-id-beir.

ass-id-beir   3 sg. pres. w. infixed obj. 3 sg. nt.

31. Ml. 93ᵈ14.   is ed as-berat-som, is gau dún-ni innahí ad-fiadam di Chrisst, hūare nād n-acat hi frecndairc gnimu cosmaili du dēnum du Christ indas as-n-da-fiadam-ni du-n-da-rigni.

as·berat-som   3 pl. pres. of *as·beir*

gau   f. 'falsehood' *is gau dún-ni* 'it is a lie for us' = 'we lie'

ad-fíadam   1 pl. pres. of *ad·fét* 'tells'
n-acat   3 pl. pres. of *ad·cí*
frecndairc   'present'; f. 'at present'
cosmail(i)   'like'
indas   nt. 'state'; nasalizing 'how, as'
as-n-da-fíadam-ni   1 pl. pres. w. infix anticipating obj. of dependent clause
du-nda-rigni   3 sg. perf. of *do·gní*

32. Ml. 17^c7.   is ed as-berat ind heretic as laigiu deacht Maicc in-daas deacht Athar, air is hō Athir ar-roét Macc cumachtae. is laigiu didiu intí ara-foim indaas intí hō n-eroimer.

as-berat   3 pl. pres. of *as·beir*
laigiu   'less'
deacht   f. 'divinity'
ar-roét   3 sg. perf. of *ar·foím* 'receives, assumes'
cumachtae   nt. 'power'
hō n-   prep. *ó* 'from' w. rel.
eroimer   3 sg. pres. pass. of *ar·foím*

GRAMMAR

71. The Book of Leinster (LL): manuscript abbreviations

The manuscript here is from the facsimile of the Book of Leinster published by the Royal Irish Academy (pp. 111–14). This portion begins in your text at sentence 4.

Note the abbreviation of *Conchobar* at the end of the first line. At the beginning of the next line *ī* with superscript stroke is *in*; this is a very common abbreviation for *n*. See also lines 3 and 4, etc. In the same line *-bert-* has a similar abbreviation for *-er-* as does line 6, but one that occurs less commonly. It is used in *Conchobar*, already referred to, for *ar*. The abbreviation of *-ar* in *nos·mber-taigedar* is very common—an *a* with lengthened final stroke with cross-stroke (see also l. 3 of MS). More difficult is the raised *i* in *cride* for *ri*; also *frim* at the end of line 8. Other letters with *r* can be similarly raised. In *cride* the *de* has been made into a digraph. In MS line 7 note the way of writing *air* in the first word. In *gus* the scribe uses a sort of cursive *z* for *us*. This is fairly common. The abbreviation *m̄c* is usual for any case of *mac*. (The vocative would be preceded by leniting *a*.)

In line 9 note that your text reads *Magach* for MS *matach*. Only in LL and only in this place does this form appear. If you compare the manuscript form of *t* with the top of *g* in the next word, you can see the likelihood that a damaged manuscript might at some time have given rise to the form the scribe wrote. See also line 11. At the end of this line *m̄d* for *mend* gives an alternative spelling for text *menn*. In line 12, notice the form of the superscript for *m*. The insular hand regularly contrasts the abbreviations of *m* and *n*.

Facsimile of a portion of page 113^b of the Book of Leinster, published by Royal Irish Academy House, 1880 (Dublin).

72. The development of the pronominal forms

The personal pronouns were generally unaccented, placed either after accented forms as enclitics, or before accented forms as proclitics. As a result they have been greatly modified; the modified forms have also influenced one another, leading to further departures from the expected forms. Through such changes there is no longer a variation between the forms of the nominative and the oblique forms, as in *I: me*, Lat. *ego: mē*. The forms that are found can only be tentatively reconstructed to compare with those in the other dialects.

The first singular personal pronoun *mé* is related to the oblique forms; on the other hand, the second singular *tú* is related to the Indo-European nominative, as in Lat. *tū*. The first plural *sní* and the second plural *sí* are related to the forms found also in Lat. *nos, vos*; but the Old Irish forms are derived from forms with an initial *s-*, the source of which is unclear, possibly IE movable *s* as in xv.15.1 *is·tech*. These few forms alone illustrate that the history of the pronouns presents a great number of problems, and contributes little to an understanding of the forms found in the Old Irish texts. Moreover, the origin of the second syllables in the emphatic forms *messe* and *tussu* is unknown; *-se* and *-su* have been related to the demonstrative particles, and the two forms interpreted: 'I here,' 'thou there.' The third person forms are also difficult to explain; the singular forms *(h)é, sí, (h)ed* correspond to Gothic *is, si, ita*, with modifications in vocalism; the plural *(h)é* is obscure in origin.

The oblique forms of the personal pronouns are also difficult to account for. As with many weakly stressed forms, they underwent various modifications and cannot be directly equated with the forms reconstructed from the evidence in other dialects. Explanations of the various pronominal forms are suggested in the comprehensive grammars, and remain a topic of concern to specialists.

73. Inflection of the *r*-stems

The kinship terms in *-r-* may serve to illustrate how a relatively simple inflection was modified by sound changes, and also by analogical changes. The initial consonant of the word for 'father' was lost like all initial *p-*. The medial *-t-* was lenited between vowels. The endings were lost because of the strong initial stress accent but left modifications on preceding elements in accordance with statements made above, as in xiv.G.70. In the singular forms the *th* is nonpalatal in the nominative, accusative, and dative by analogy with the genitive; because of the following *-e-* vowels, *th* should have been palatal. Similarly, in the plural, *th* is palatal in the genitive and dative by analogy with the nominative and accusative.

	Sg.		Pl.		Du.	
	OIr.	PIE	OIr.	PIE	OIr.	PIE
N	ath(a)ir	pətḗr	a(i)thir	pəteres	*athir	pəter-e
A	ath(a)ir	paterm̥	aithr(e)a	paterns		
G	athar	patros	aithre	pətrijõm	athar	pətrou
D	ath(a)ir	pateri	aithrib	pətr̥bhis	athr(a)ib	pətrobhim

111

Like other paradigms, the declension of *r*-stems illustrates the results of sound changes and analogical modifications.

74. Forms made from preterite stems

As noted in III.G.13, the preterite indicates simple past, or punctual action. Thus the form *tarblaing* XV.15.2 means 'he leapt down' in contrast with 'he used to leap,' a meaning expressed by the imperfect. In this way the Old Irish preterite corresponds to the aorist of Greek, and the perfect of Greek and Latin, in contrast with their imperfect; the *ro*-forms correspond closely in meaning to the perfect.

Although the meaning of the forms is clear, the forms themselves are very problematic in origin. Thurneysen G.415–40 lists the various forms according to three methods of formation: *s*-preterites, *t*-preterites, and suffixless preterites, which may be reduplicated or unreduplicated. The weak verbs take the *t*-preterite. Strong verbs with some final resonants and final *-g* in the root take the *t*-preterite; other strong verbs take the suffixless preterite. The origins of these forms have been indicated by Calvert Watkins in his book, *Indo-European Origins of the Celtic Verb* (Dublin: Institute for Advanced Studies, 1962). The *s*- and *t*-preterites, as well as *s*-subjunctives, are historically *s*-aorists. The reduplicated preterites are historically perfects. Some forms derive from root and thematic aorists. In this way the preterite formation incorporates forms of various origins, as does the Latin perfect: *scrībō, scrīpsī* 'write' has an *s*-aorist form; *videō, vīdī* 'see' has a perfect form.

The details of development of the various subclasses are highly complex, and must be left for individual study or specialized courses in Irish historical linguistics. It is important to observe that Old Irish has maintained earlier grammatical categories, such as preterites. To express such categories, however, it has made use of various formal possibilities, creating highly irregular methods of formation for relatively precise categories of meaning.

75. Historical background of gemination

The process known as gemination resulted initially from the lengthening of an initial consonant after some final elements, often *-s*; if such elements were found before initial stressed vowels, these were preceded by *h*-. Thus, after the genitive singular feminine, the nominative plural feminine and neuter, and the accusative plural of the article *inna, na* gemination occurred, as in XV.15.8 *na-mmuicce* 'of the pig.' Other contexts for gemination were given in V.G.25. Gemination also resulted when identical consonants were contiguous, as in *cummasc* < **commisc* 'mixing.'

In late Old Irish geminates were being eliminated; they are often written with a single symbol. Moreover, the geminated and nasalized forms of *s*-, *r*-, *l*-, *m*-, *n*- are identical, that is, both are unlenited. As a result, gemination is no longer an independent phonological process. Traces of it remain, however, even in New Irish.

chapter xvi

READING AND TEXTUAL ANALYSIS, Sections 16 and 17

In Sections 16 and 17 Conall, the champion of Ulster, accepts the challenge of Cet, but quickly overwhelms him. No other warrior of Connaught proceeds to challenge Conall. Accordingly, he gains the champion's portion.

Section 16

1. 'Eirg ón ṁuicc diḋiu!' ol Conall.
2. 'Ciḋ dano dot·ḃéraḋ-su cucce?' ol Cet.
3. 'Is fír' ol Conall '⟨Cet⟩ do chunġiḋ choṁraṁe cuccum-sa.
4. Do·bér oı̄nchoṁraṁ duit, a Cheit,' ol Conall.
5. 'Tongu na·tongat mo thuath, ō ro·ġaḃus gaı̄ im láiṁ nad·raḃa cen ġuin duini do C⟨h⟩onnachtaiḃ cach ōenlaithi ocus orcain fri daiġiḋ cech n-ōenaiḋchi, ocus niro·c⟨h⟩otlus riaṁ cen c⟨h⟩enn Connachtaiġ fom ġlūin.'
6. 'Is fír' ol Cet, 'at ferr do lāech indó-sa.
7. Maḋ Ānlūan no·beth is·taiġ, do·bēraḋ coṁram ar araile duit.
8. Is aniṁ dún naḋ·fil is·taiġ.'
9. 'Atá immurġu' ol Conall, oc taḃairt chinn Ánlúain assa chriss; ocus do·lēici do Chet dara ḃruinni co·rrōeṁiḋ a loim fola fora ḃēolu.
10. Ro·gaḃ siḋe immurġu ón ṁuic, ocus dessiḋ Conall acci.

---

1. eirg 2 sg. impv. of *téit* 'goes'
   ón prep. *ó* + art. = 'Get away from the pig!'
2. dot·bérad-su see XIII.13.14
   cucce *co* 'to, up to' w. 3 f. pers. pron.
3. Cet supplied by Thurneysen, to complete the meaning
   chomrame gen. pl. m. of *comram* 'contest'
4. do·bér 1 sg. fut. of *do·beir* 'takes, accepts'

113

5. tongu   1 sg. pres. of *tongid* 'swears,' of which *·tongat* is 3 pl.
    na   MIr. based on OIr. *a n-* 'that which' and *nī* 'that which'
    ro·gabus   1 sg. *ro*-pret. of *gaibid* 'takes'
    nad·raba   1 sg. *ro*-pret. of *·tá* 'is,' after *nad·* 'that not'
    guin   vn. acc. sg. of *gonaid* 'kills, wounds'
    duini   gen. sg. m. of *duine* 'man'
    cach óen-laithi   gen. sg. nt. of *lathe* = 'every single day'
    orcain   vn. acc. sg. of *orgid* 'slays, destroys'
    daigid   acc. sg. f. of *daig* 'flame, fire'
    ni-ro·chotlus   1 sg. *ro*-pret. of *con·tuili* 'sleeps'
    riam   *ría* 'before' w. nt. pers. pron. = 'never' after *ni*
    glūin   dat. sg. nt. of *glún* 'knee'
6. ferr   see the similar comp. construction in X.10.3
7. no·beth   3 sg. past subj. of *tá* 'is'
    ar   prep. confused w. prep. *for* 'on, over'
    araile   acc. sg. m. 'other'
8. anim   nom. sg. f. 'blemish; pity'
    nad·fil   conj. form of *·tá* 'is' after neg.; w. 3 sg. infixed pron. (*nad* is the form of the
        neg. used in rel. clauses)
9. oc   'at'; often used w. vn., as here w. the vn. of *do·beir* 'takes' w. force of participle
    chriss   dat. sg. m. of *cris(s)* 'belt, girdle'
    dara   prep. *tar* 'over, across' w. 3 sg. poss. pron.
    bruinni   acc. sg. f. of *bruinne* 'breast, chest'
    co·rrōemid   3 sg. *ro*-pret. of *maidid* 'breaks (out),' after *co n-* 'so that'
    a   nom. sg. nt. of art. *in* 'the' (or perhaps 3 sg. nt. poss. pron.)
    loim   nom. sg. nt. 'draught, gush'
    fola   gen. sg. f. of *fuil* 'blood'
    béolu   acc. pl. m. of *bél* 'lip'; pl. 'mouth'
10. ro·gab   3 sg. *ro*-pret. of *gaibid* 'takes'; used here w. *ón muic* in the meaning 'left'
    dessid   3 sg. *ro*-pret. of *saidid* 'sits down'

Section 17

1. 'Tecat don chomram a fecht-sa!' ol Conall.
2. Ni·frīth ón la Connachta lāech a thairisme.
3. Do·ratad immurgu damdabach dona boccótib immi im⟨m⟩a c⟨h⟩ūairt, ar
    ro·boí drochcostud is·taig do chloindībircthib la drochdaīni.
4. Luid īarum Conall do rainn na-mmucce.
5. Ocus gebid dano cenn in tarra ina bēolo, co·tairnic do rann na-mmucce.
6. Ro·sūig in tairr .i. ere ind nónbair cona·farcaib bannai de.

---

1. tecat   3 pl. impv. of *do·ic* 'comes'
    a fecht-sa   'this time, now'
2. ni·frīth   3 sg. pret. pass. of *fo·gaib* 'finds, gets'; cf. X.9.1

3. do·ratad   pass. *ro*-pret. of *do·beir* 'puts'
   damdabach   nom. sg. f. 'large vat, enclosing shelter' (made here with shields)
   boccótib   dat. pl. f. of *boccóit* 'shield, buckler'
   imma   prep. *im* 'around' w. 3 sg. poss. pron.
   cúairt   f. 'circuit'; here amplifies *imma* = 'all (around) him'
   drochcostud   compd. consisting of *droch-* 'bad' and *costud* nom. sg. m. 'usage, custom'
   chloindibircthib   compd. of *cloin-* 'slanting, iniquitous' and *diburcud* dat. pl. m. 'shoot-
       ing of darts'
   la   indicates agent
   drochdaini   acc. pl. m. of *droch-* and *duine* 'man'
4. luid   3 sg. pret. of *téit* 'goes'
   do rainn na-mmucce   contrast XI.11.1 *in mucc do rainn*
5. gebid   3 sg. pres. of *gaibid* 'takes, seizes'
   tarra   gen. sg. of *tairr* 'belly,' w. preceding art. after *cenn* 'end'
   co·tairnic   3 sg. pret. of *do·air-ic* 'comes to an end'; after *co·* 'so that'
6. ro·súig   3 sg. *ro*-pret. of *súgid* 'sucks'
   ere   acc. sg. nt. 'load'
   nónbair   gen. sg. m. of *nónbar* 'nine men'
   cona·farcaib   3 sg. *ro*-pret. of *fo·ácaib* 'leaves (behind)'
   bannai   acc. sg. f. of *bannae* 'drop, bit'

GRAMMAR

76. The Book of Leinster (LL): problems of spelling

The reading passage is included on the portion of the Book of Leinster given in Chapter XV. You will notice, however, differences of spelling and sometimes of expression between the LL version and the text. For example, in the first sentence (ll. 15 and 16 of the fascimile) *ol* is written *or* (Thurneysen normalized all variants to *ol* in his text) with an *r*. The *r* here is like the Arabic numeral 2. This form is frequently used after *o* and occasionally after the similarly shaped letter *b*.

The abbreviation *dā* is regularly expanded *dano* as it has been in your text. This word is rarely written out. In line 16 the initial of *cucci* is lenited and this time the manuscript reads *ar Cett* for *ol Cet*. None of the manuscripts have the form ⟨Cet⟩ that Thurneysen supplies. In the next line *chucumsa* uses the superscript for *m* to represent the syllable *um*. This abbreviation is fairly common, especially for unstressed syllables. In line 17 *oen* with tall *e* replaces *oin-* of the text.

Line 19 departs from the text: *nach menic robá cen chend Connachtaig fóm chind oc cotlud.* ⁊. *cen guin duine cechoen lá* ⁊ *cech oen aidchi.*

The abbreviation *nā* for *nach* parallels the abbreviation of *Conchobar* in line 4 of the facsimile and for *cech* below. *Nach* = 'why not, that not.' For *menic* see IX.7.1. The abbreviation *im̄* in line 22 for *immurgu* is very common, as is *f* with superscript for *for* in line 25. The letters following *muic* in this line are the usual ampersand when ⁊ is not used; it corresponds to tall *e* + *t*. Notice also the two forms of *s* in *dessid*, with *de* written as a digraph.

77. The ogam writing system

The peculiarly Irish or Celtic writing system was ogam, named from the deity Ogma who especially represented learning and culture. Ogam inscriptions were chiseled on the edges of standing stones and because of weathering they are often difficult to read. In the *Auraicept na n-Éces* 'The Scholars' Primer,' ed. George Calder (Edinburgh: John Grants, 1917), a discussion of the ogam signs is added to a grammar at least partly from Isidore of Seville and Virgilius Maro. Traditionally the grammar is ascribed to Cenn Faelad who is recognized as an Irish scholar who died in 679, forty-three years after the death of Isidore.

The account of ogam is fanciful, but we learn the order of the letters and their names. They were classified according to shape and named for trees. From the stories we know that they were carved on sticks for magic purposes and in this respect are related to the runic *futhark*. The ogam symbols are based on Latin with a few added because they seemed necessary for indicating distinctions. Palatal and velar consonants, for example, were not distinguished in the original alphabet (the Irish call it the Beithe-Luis-Nin), but special vowel symbols were added later. Furthermore, though a symbol for *h* was at the head of one group, it is not used in transcriptions. When ogam is inscribed on a vertical stone, the characters are read from the bottom up. See chart opposite.

78. Inflection of *io-* and *iā*-stems

These stems inflect like the *o-* and *ā*-stems but have reflexes of *-i-*. These reflexes are clearly observable when the Old Irish endings of both types of inflection are compared, as in the nominative singular: *fer* 'man': *céle* 'companion,' *scél* 'story,' *cride* 'heart,' *túath* 'people,' *soilse* 'light.' The *io-* and *iā*-stems accordingly provide insights into the losses of final elements. The original nominative singular ending *-os* was lost in both **wiros* and **keilios*, but the *-i-* was maintained, though with modification to *-e*. The contrasts between the neuter and feminine nouns above have a similar basis. Comparison of such forms then helps to illuminate the earlier history of Old Irish and the Celtic languages.

This history is also determined from the early inscriptions, such as those in ogam. In the inscription cited opposite the genitive singular of *macc* still has final *-i*. This vowel must accordingly have been lost in late Old Irish. Other evidence of the earlier forms is provided by the Gaulish inscriptions, and by the Gaulish names cited by Classical authors. Even the nominative singular ending is maintained in the Gaulish names *Segomarus, Cernunnos*, and in the ordinal *decametos* 'tenth.' The losses of endings must accordingly be dated since the beginning of our era. Such a date also permits the further assumption that the stress accent causing these losses was introduced relatively late. The pitch accent of Proto-Indo-European must have been maintained in Celtic as late as the first millennium before our era. These assumptions have important implications for the history of Old Irish verse; alliterative verse is likely only when a language has a strong initial stress accent. The implications have not yet been worked out adequately; they promise fascinating topics of investigation once we master the difficult early poetic and prose texts.

116

OGAM CHARACTERS

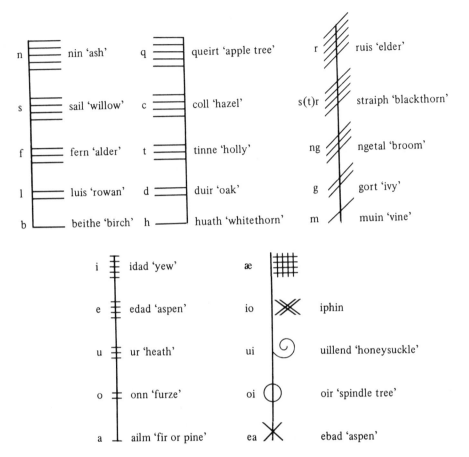

Names on ogam stones are in the genitive, signifying 'the stone of x' as in this inscription from Cornwall:

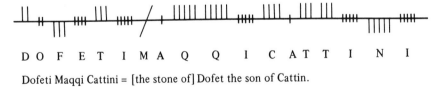

D O F E T I M A Q   Q I C A T T I N I

Dofeti Maqqi Cattini = [the stone of] Dofet the son of Cattin.

117

Equally intriguing problems are provided by the changing linguistic forms. The ogam form *maqqi* or *maqi* 'of the son' has no indication of the palatalization of the medial consonant. Such indication is found after loss of the final *i*, as in *maicc*. An explanation may be indicated by observing the changes in spelling during the Germanic umlaut change. In Old High German the word for 'door' was spelled *turi*; in Middle High German it is spelled *tür*. Indication of the change is necessary only when the conditioning element is lost. The medial consonant of *maqi* was probably palatalized at the time of the ogam inscriptions, much as -*u*- was probably fronted in Old High German times. But as long as the conditioning element remained, the modified sound was simply considered a variant, not a separate phoneme. Determining the changing structure of the language presents problems of great linguistic interest.

79. Forms made from the future stem

Investigation of the history of Old Irish future forms provides topics of further interest. The *f*-future of weak verbs cannot be related to any formation in other Indo-European dialects, or even to a formation in the Britannic branch of Celtic. It must therefore have been developed in the Goidelic branch of Celtic, that is, relatively recently. It is accordingly similar in origin to the "weak" formations of other Indo-European dialects: the Germanic dental preterite, the Lat. -*b*- imperfect and future, the Gk. *k*-perfect, and others. In each of these formations a suffixal element was developed as a tense marker, but its origin is unclear. Many theories of origin have been proposed; for those of the origin of the *f*-future, see Thurneysen G.398. Watkins, "Origin of the *f*-Future," *Ériu*, 20 (1966), 67–81, gives a good survey of previous explanations and his own (not widely accepted) solution. Without further materials from the preliterate periods of these dialects, none of the theories can be established to the exclusion of others. It is important to observe that in each of the dialects a suffixal marker was selected to indicate a grammatical category; this device is in accordance with the grammatical structure of languages shifting from an OV to a VO order.

The future forms of strong verbs can be related to Indo-European formations. Both the *ē*-future and the *s*-future are related to a desiderative formation found in Indo-Iranian. When the -*s*- followed a vowel, it was lost, giving rise to the *ē*-future. The Old Irish future of strong verbs accordingly is based on forms that underwent a shift in meaning from 'I want' to 'I will.' For further details, see Thurneysen G.414–15. The future tense then is a development after the period of Proto-Indo-European, and is based on inflectional markers which earlier had a different force.

80. Verbal nouns

The verbal nouns of Old Irish can best be understood as a distinctive formation made with forms that can be related to those of other Indo-European dialects. As a formation the verbal noun is characteristic of VSO languages; syntactically a noun somewhat like an infinitive, it differs from infinitives in having subjects or objects expressed in the genitive, as in *guin duini* XVI.16.5. Like *guin*, the verbal noun of *gonaid* 'kills,' verbal nouns may be made in one of the noun classes. The form *guin* is a neuter *i*-stem. The verbal noun *suide* 'sitting' of *saidid* 'sits' is a *io*-stem. Like many other verbal nouns, these have no consonantal affix. Others have a final dental, e.g., *brith* of *berid* 'bears.' Others end in a nasal, e.g., *orcun*, accusative *orgain* of *orgid* 'slays.' A few are unrelated in form to their root, e.g., *gal* of *fichid* 'fights.' For more details, see Thurneysen G.444–55. All the Indo-European dialects developed nominal forms of verbs, though from different formations. The Germanic infinitive ending *-an* < *-onom* is an accusative; the Gk. *-ein* is a locative; the Lat. *-se/-re* is also a locative in origin. These came to be incorporated in the structure of their languages, as the varying uses of the English infinitive may indicate. Their specific origin is accordingly less important for their understanding than is the framework of the language in which they were developed.

chapter XVII

READING AND TEXTUAL ANALYSIS, Sections 18 and 19

In Sections 18 and 19 the inevitable battle occurs between the men of Connaught and the men of Ulster. The men of Ulster win out in accordance with the pre-eminence of their champion. Unfortunately, Ailbe, the cause of the strife, does not do so well; the outcome of the battle may seem unusual when compared with stories in the European tradition.

Section 18

1. Ni·tarat immurġu do Chonnachtaiḃ acht dā c⟨h⟩ois na-mmucce foa bráġit.
2. Ba becc dano la Connachta a cuit.
3. At·raġat siḋi, at·raġat dano Ulaiḋ, co·rroacht cách araile.
4. Ro·boí trā buille dar áo i suiḋiu, combo coṁard ra sliss in tiġe in ċarnāil ro·boí for a lár, co·mbātar na srotha din chrú forna doirsiu.
5. Maiḋith dano in slúaġ forna doirsi⟨u⟩ co·rralsat soïmōl for lár ind liss .i. cāch oc trūastaḋ a chēli.
6. Is and gaḃais Fergus dōiḃ daur mór ro·boí for lár ind liss assa ḟrēnaiḃ.
7. Maiḋit immach dano assind liss.
8. Do·berar in cath i ndorus ind liss.

---

1. ni-tarat   3 sg. *ro*-pret. of *do·beir* 'gives,' after neg.
   chois   acc. du. f. of *cos* 'leg, foot'
   foa   prep. *fo* 'under' w. 3 sg. poss. pron.
   bráġit   acc. sg. m. of *bráġae* 'neck, throat'
2. ba   3 sg. pret. of *is* 'is'; followed by the prep. *la* 'in the opinion of'; *ba* may be trans-lated 'it seemed'
   cuit   nom. sg. f. 'portion,' after a^n 'their'
3. at·ragat   3 pl. pres. (historical) of *at·raig* 'rises, jumps up'

120

co·rroacht 3 sg. pret. of *ro·saig* 'attains, comes to,' after *co n-* 'until; so that'

araile acc. sg. m. 'the other [of two]'

4. buille nom. sg. f. 'blow, stroke'

áo acc. sg. nt. 'ear' after *tar, dar* 'across'

i suidiu dat. sg. nt. of anaphoric pron. *suide* = 'that' after prep. *i^n* 'thereby, then'

combo 3 sg. pret. of *is*, w. *co n-*

comard ra (*ra = fri-a*) 'as high as'

sliss acc. sg. m. 'side, sidewall'

carnáil nom. sg. f. 'heap [of corpses]'

lár dat. sg. nt. 'floor' after *for*; see sent. 5; note the rel. use of *ro·boí* 3 sg. *ro*-pret. of *·tá*

srotha nom. pl. nt. of *sruth* 'river, stream'

chrú dat. sg. nt. of *crú* 'blood'; note lenited initial after prep. *di* w. art. 'of, in consequence of'

doirsiu acc. pl. nt. of *dorus* 'door,' after prep. *for* w. art. 'on, over'

5. maidith 3 sg. pres. 'breaks out'

slúag nom. sg. m. 'host'

co·rralsat 3 pl. *ro*-pret. of *fo·ceird* 'performs'

soïmól acc. sg. nt. 'a good drinking round'—an example of a gruesome sense of humor

liss gen. sg. m. of *les* 'the enclosed space around a dwelling'

trúastad dat. sg. m. 'striking'

6. gabais 3 sg. pret. of *gaibid* 'takes, seizes'

dōib prep. *do* 'against' w. 3 pl. pers. pron.

daur acc. sg. nt. 'oak'

lár dat. sg. nt. 'middle'

frénaib dat. pl. f. of *frén* 'root,' after prep. *a^g* w. 3 sg. poss. pron. 'from'

7. im·mach 'out' (implies motion); *i^n* + *mag* 'field, place'; see *is·tech* and *is·tig*; and *im·maig* 'outside' completes the pattern

8. do·berar pass. of *do·beir* 'gives' = 'takes place'

Section 19

1. Is and luid Mac Dathó immach ocus in cú inna láim, co·rrailced etorro dús cia díb do·ngegad .i. rús con.
2. Do·rraíga in cú Ulto ocus ro·lēci for ár Connacht, ar ro·mebaid for Connachta.
3. As·berat-som is i m-Maigib Ailbi ro·gab in cú fertais in charpait fo Ailill ocus Meidb.
4. Is and do·n-áraill Fer Loga .i. ara Ailella ocus Medba co·rrala a cholainn for leth ocus corro·an a chenn i fertais in charpait.
5. As·berat dano is de atá Mag n-Ailbi .i. Ailbe ainm in chon.

---

1. luid 3 sg. pret. of *téit* 'goes'

láim dat. sg. f. of *lám* 'hand'

co·rrailced 3 sg. past *ro*-subj. of *léicid* 'lets loose'

etorro   prep. *itir* w. 3 pl. pers. pron. 'among them'

dús   (*do fius*), dat. sg. of *fess* vn. of *ro·fitir* 'in order to know'; cf. *·fitir* 'knows'

do·ngegad   3 sg. condit. rel. of *do·goa* 'chooses'

rús   nom. sg. m. 'instinct'

2. do·rraíga   3 sg. *ro*-pret. of *do·goa* 'chooses'

ro·léci   3 sg. *ro*-pret. of *léicid* 'lets loose' = 'he let himself loose, rushed (against)'

ár   acc. sg. nt. 'slaughter'

ar   conj. 'for, because'

ro·mebaid   3 sg. *ro*-pret. of *maidid* 'breaks' = 'Connaught men were routed'

3. as·berat   3 pl. pres. of *as·beir* 'says'

Maigib   dat. pl. of *mag* 'plain'; here a place-name *Mag n-Ailbi*, a plain 'of the fair woman'
        extending from County Leix to County Kildare

fertais   acc. sg. f. 'chariot-shaft' (two shafts extended from the *carpat*)

4. do·n-áraill   3 sg. *ro*-pret. of *do·aidlea* w. infixed 3 sg. pers. pron. 'hits, runs over'

ara   nom. sg. m. 'charioteer'

co·rrala   3 sg. *ro*-pret. of *fo·ceird*; here intrans. 'it fell'

colainn   nom. sg. f. 'body'

leth   acc. sg. nt. = 'to the side, aside'

corro·an   3 sg. *ro*-pret. of *anaid* 'stays'

5. de   prep. *di* w. 3 sg. pers. pron. = 'as a result of that'; a typical explanation of a name in
        heroic story

GRAMMAR

81. Old Irish in monasteries of Europe

After the ogam inscriptions the oldest Irish written materials are found in monasteries in South Germany, Switzerland, and Italy. Among these materials are the glosses included in Chapters VI through XV; they are particularly important for our knowledge of Old Irish because they provide evidence of the language at the time they were written down. Texts transmitted orally, and written in manuscripts of the eleventh century and later, have been modified, and actually represent Middle Irish in great part.

The wanderings of ancient Irish monks are among the fascinating events of the early Middle Ages. Christianity was introduced into Ireland as early as the fifth century. In the sixth century pilgrims, or *peregrini*, set out to establish religious communities in other areas, including the Continent. The most notable was St. Columbanus, who set out for the Continent about 590 A.D. with twelve disciples. After traveling through France and Switzerland, where one of his disciples, St. Gall, founded the monastery named after him, Columbanus himself founded the monastery of Bobbio in northern Italy. In the course of their teaching these early monks wrote glosses in Latin texts, and in this way left behind valuable evidence on the language. The practice of glossing texts is also of great importance for our earliest information on Old English and Old High German. Besides the interlinear notations, which can be readily interpreted, the writers included other material, such as poems. Of the surviving glosses the earliest were written at Würzburg around the middle of the eighth century. Those from Milan,

St. Gall, and other monasteries are not much later. These earliest texts have been compiled by Whitley Stokes and John Strachan in the *Thesaurus Palaeohibernicus*, 2 vols. (Cambridge, Eng.: Univ. Press, 1901–03). It may seem strange that similar texts were not found in Ireland; scholars assume that any manuscripts with Irish glosses were worn out by use in Ireland, but not in the monasteries of Europe, where they would have had no readers after the practice of wandering to the Continent ceased.

82. Compound sentences

With the initial verb in the principal clause, subordinate clauses commonly follow the main clause in complex sentences. Exceptions are conditional clauses introduced by *ma* 'if' and temporal clauses, such as those introduced by *in tan* 'at the time, when.' But subordinate clauses introduced by *co n-* follow, as illustrated by the numerous *co* clauses in this lesson and earlier. Subordination of various meanings is introduced by *co-* 'until, so that,' or simply a connective; it, and other conjunctions, may also be accompanied by the negative: *cona*. It may be noted that *co* corresponds to a preposition (*co* 'to') as do other conjunctions. Another group of conjunctions correspond to nouns, such as *tan* 'time.' Such conjunctions are then followed by a nasalizing relative clause. In this way, many subordinate clauses are comparable to nominal constructions, whether introduced by prepositions that have come to be conjunctions or by nominal phrases.

Accordingly, the relationship of subordinate to principal clauses is comparable to that of verbal nouns, which are often related to the principal clause by means of the preposition *do* 'to' as in XI.11.1 *do rainn*. Complementation, like subordinate clauses, then occupies a nominal relationship to principal clauses.

Coordinate conjunctions, notably *ocus* 'and' and *no, nu* 'or,' and in its most frequent use co^n 'and so,' may also relate clauses. Like the subordinating constructions, these contribute to a relatively simple syntactic structure, with the force of each sentence carried by the principal verb.

83. Prepositions

The close interrelationship of syntactic elements in a sentence and their dependence on the initial verb are also brought about by heavy reliance on prepositional constructions. Examples may be readily found, as in XVII.18.1, where the verb js followed by two nominal phrases introduced by the prepositions *do* and *fo*, in addition to the object. These phrases illustrate that the prepositions are closely related to the elements they govern, as the lenition after *do* and compound forms like *foa* indicate. The VSO structure of Old Irish then led to heavy reliance on prepositional constructions, and these in time to the compound forms made up of prepositions and pronominal elements.

The widespread use of preverbs with verbs is in accordance with this structure. Virtually all of the prepositions are also used as verbal prefixes. When prototonic, they merge with the following verb, giving rise to forms differing considerably from the deuterotonic equivalent, e.g., *tarat* of XVII.18.1 as compared with the deuterotonic *do·rat*. In this way the grammatical structure of Old Irish led to morphological patterns differing considerably from those of earlier forms of the language and those of related languages like Latin.

84. The passive

One of the characteristic features of Old Irish is the development of a new passive inflection. This is based on *r*-endings found also in other Indo-European dialects, notably Italic, Tocharian, and Hittite. In Old Irish this is found in third singular and plural forms, as in the conjunct third singular *·berar* and third plural *bertar* 'is, are carried.' These forms are supplemented with forms for the other persons, which are made by infixing pronouns, e.g., *no-m-berar* 'I am carried.' In this way inflections were developed throughout the various tenses and moods.

As in XVI.17.3 *do·ratad* 'was made,' the passive was often used in an impersonal sense, but with the subject clear. In the course of its development Irish used the passive more and more widely, often accompanied by an accusative which indicated the object of the action. The so-called passive may then be viewed as an impersonal construction, though the agent may be indicated by means of a prepositional phrase. The characteristic Irish use of the passive is found in the last sentence of this story; the form *ro·lēced* indicates an action with no specific agent, but comparable in meaning to 'they let him go.'

85. The deponent

The term "deponent" is taken over from Latin grammar, where it refers to a verb form with passive endings but an active meaning, such as *loquor* 'I speak.' Irish deponents, in contrast with Latin deponents, may make passive forms. The most common type of deponents in Irish are made from adjectives, and have causative or factitive meaning, such as 'make tall' and 'cause to seat' = 'place.' Already in early Old Irish the deponent inflection was defective. During the course of Old Irish it gradually dies out, and is replaced by active inflections.

chapter xviii

READING AND TEXTUAL ANALYSIS, Section 20

Section 20 concludes the story anticlimactically, at least for some modern readers. Though Conchobar and the men of Ulster had won the contest, Fer Loga, the charioteer of Ailill, seems to come off best.

1. Do·lluid a-mmaiḋm andess for Beluch Sen-Roírenn, for Áth Miḋbine i m-Maistin, sech Cill nDara, sech Rāith Imġain, hi Fiḋ nGaible do Áth Mac Luġnai, sech Druim-Dá-Maiġe, for Drochet Coirpri.
2. Oc Áth Chinn Chon i mBiliu, is and ro·lá cenn in chon asin charput.
3. Oc techt īar fraíchruḋ Miḋi síar, is and do·n-ārlaic Fer Loġa isin fraích .i. ara Ailella, ocus ro·ling isin carpat īar cúl Conchobair co·rraġaḃ a chenn dara aiss.
4. 'Emḋe, a Chonchoḃair!' olse.
5. 'T'ōġrĩar!' ol Conchoḃar.
6. 'Niba mór,' ol Fer Loġa '.i. mo ḃrith latt co Emain Macha ocus ṁná ōentaṁa Ulaḋ ocus a n-ingena macdacht do ġaḃāil chepóce cecha nóna immum co·n-ērḃrat: Fer Loġa mo lennān-sa.'
7. Ba écen ón, ar ní·laiṁtis cena la Conchoḃar.
8. Ocus ro·lēceḋ Fer Loġa dar Āth Lūain síar dia ḃliaḋna ocus dī gaḃair Conchobair leis co n-allaiḃ óir friu.
9. Scēla muice Meic Ḋathó in sin.

---

1. do·lluid   3 sg. pret. of *do·tét* 'goes to'
   maidm   nom. sg. nt. of vn. of *maidid* = 'flight'; note the initial nasalization indicating the 3 pl. pron. 'their'
   andess   'from the south, northward'
   for . . . sech   'over . . . past'; the place names have been identified with places in County Kildare
   Áth   'ford'

Druim-Dá-Maige   Drumomuy = 'hill of two plains'
Drochet Coirpri   Drehid = 'bridge of Coirbre'
3. techt   dat. sg. f. of vn. of *téit* 'goes'
   fraichrud   dat. sg. m. 'heath' after *íar n-* 'along'
   síar   'westward'
   do·n-árlaic   3 sg. *ro*-pret. of *do·léici* 'throws' w. 3 sg. infixed pers. pron. = 'he jumped down'
   fraích   acc. sg. m. 'heath'; nasalized by acc. sg. art.
   ro·ling   3 sg. *ro*-pret. of *lingid* 'leaps'
   cúl   dat. sg. m. 'back'
   co·rragab   3 sg. *ro*-pret. of *gaibid* 'seizes' after *co n-* 'and'
   aiss   acc. sg. f. 'back'; *dar-a* = 'over his back, from behind'
4. emde   interj., from impv. 'beware'
5. t'ógriar   nom. sg. f. 'full wish,' after *t'* < *do* 'thy'
6. brith   nom. sg. f. of vn. of *berid* 'takes'—after *mo* 'my,' objective gen. w. *brith*
   latt   prep. *la* 'with' + 2 sg. pers. pron.
   óentama   nom. pl. f. 'single'
   ingena   nom. pl. f. 'daughter'
   macdacht   indecl. adj. 'marriageable'
   gabáil   dat. sg. f. of vn. of *gaibid* 'sings; obtains'
   cepóce   gen. sg. f. of *cepóc* 'choral-song,' probably erotic
   nōna   gen. sg. f. of *nóin* 'ninth canonical hour' here 'evening'
   co·n-érbrat   3 pl. *ro*-pres. subj. of *as·beir* 'says'; the function of *ro-* may be modal here
   lennān   nom. sg. m. 'darling'
7. écen   nom. sg. f. 'necessity'
   ón   nom. sg. nt. of *suide* 'that' (unstressed)
   ni·laimtis   3 pl. impf. of *ro·laimethar* 'dares,' w. loss of *ro·* after prefixed *ni·*
   cena   prep. *cen* 'without' w. 3 sg. nt. pers. pron. = 'otherwise'
8. ro·lēced   3 sg. pass. of *léicid* 'lets loose, sends'
   blíadna   gen. sg. f. of *blíadain* 'year'; + *dia* an old word for 'day' = 'a year from that day'
   dí gabair   nom. du. f. of *dá* 'two' and *gabar* 'horse [with white spot (?)]'
   allaib   dat. pl. nt. of *all* 'bridle'
   óir   gen. sg. nt. of *ór* 'gold'
9. scéla   nom. pl. nt. of *scél* 'tale, story'

GRAMMAR

86. The transmission of the ancient literature

In the earliest period of Insular Celtic, literature was transmitted orally. Preservation of literature, traditions, laws, and so on was one of the functions of the filid. Like the men of law, the leeches, and craftsmen, the filid belonged to the class named *oes dána* 'men of art.' In Irish society this class was lower than the *flaithi* 'nobles' and higher than the *grád féne* 'order of farmers,' the independent freemen. These three classes have been compared by Dumezil in his imaginative studies with the three higher castes of Ancient Indian society: *brahmans*, *kshatriyas* 'warriors,' and *vaiśyas* 'townsmen.' In Ireland, however, the warriors represented the highest class in a *tuath* 'people, state.' The fili is also often compared to the *druid* of Continental Celtic society, described by Caesar. Unlike the *brahman* and the *druid*, the fili had no priestly functions. He was, however, required to complete a rigorous course of training, in which he came to learn the literary and other monuments which were to be transmitted.

When ogam was introduced, it was not aimed for the transmission of longer texts; it is comparable in this way to the Germanic runes and to the early Greek script known as Linear B. The writing of extended documents was first applied to Christian texts. The earliest Irish manuscripts are copies of the Gospels and the Psalms in Latin; St. Columba's *Cathach*, written near the end of the sixth century, is the earliest which has survived. As noted above, Irish copyists began to include secular materials, such as nature poems, in the manuscripts. Apparently they also produced manuscripts of the ancient literature, as early as the ninth century. This inference is based on the form of the language, for unfortunately none of the old manuscripts devoted to native secular literature have survived.

The manuscripts that have preserved for us the oldest forms of Old Irish texts were written in the twelfth century. The two most important are the Book of Leinster (LL), also called the Book of Noughaval, in which the text of the SMMD is found, and the Book of the Dun Cow (LU). Folio manuscripts on vellum, they both contain an enormous amount of material, written in compact form, as the facsimile given above illustrates. Later centuries produced other important manuscripts, such as the Yellow Book of Lecan of the end of the fourteenth century, which also includes SMMD. Many stories, as well as much of the early literature, have been lost. The literature that has survived we owe to the patient work of monks, and to the peaceful transition between the pagan filid and the Christian men of the church.

87. Sketch of the characteristics of Old Irish, and some of the changes it has undergone

The grammatical discussions presented above have discussed individual characteristics of Old Irish grammar. Some of them will be summarized here, in a brief sketch of the Old Irish language.

Old Irish, except for its Insular Celtic neighbors, is the only Indo-European language that has the structure VSO. Through recent linguistic study we know that various other characteristics are to be expected in such languages. Notable among these is the position of nominal modifiers; these follow nouns, whether expressed in relative clauses, adjectival constructions, or genitives. Further, constructions involving government of syntactic entities, such as prepositions and comparatives, observe the same order as do verbs with regard to their objects. Since these characteristics are in accordance with universals of language, they have nothing to do with genealogical relationship. Moreover, there is as yet no secure means of accounting for syntactic changes, like that which Insular Celtic underwent when verbs came to stand initially in clauses. It may be attractive to try to account for them, as did Pokorny, by proposing that the invading Celts re-patterned their language after the language of the earlier inhabitants of Britain.

127

Since we are uninformed about the language of those inhabitants, we cannot substantiate such a hypothesis. For the time being linguists might do best by trying to determine the characteristics of Old Irish, and of other VSO languages, in their aim to understand them more fully.

Besides the characteristic position of nominal modifiers after nouns, VSO languages also tend to have subordinate clauses follow principal clauses. Moreover, nonfinite constructions, such as infinitives and verbal nouns, are prominent in VSO languages. It has been proposed that the use of the English gerund as a verbal noun is the result of Celtic influence, e.g., "His imitating amused the audience." In the other Germanic languages, e.g., German, the present participle is not used in this way. Speakers of English are accordingly prepared for the use of the Old Irish verbal noun with an objective genitive, as in "His dismissal was accepted." The use of verbal nouns as complements comparable to subordinate clauses is far more developed in Irish, however, and is one of the constructions that needs further study, both for its origins and for its role in the language.

88. Morphological characteristics of Old Irish

VSO languages are strongly prefixing. This morphological characteristic has had an important effect on the Old Irish verbal system, although it has become substantially weaker in the modern language.

The forms that are found must be explained on the basis of two other features of the language. One is the strong initial stress accent which was introduced into Celtic, and Germanic, during the first millennium B.C. As a result of this accent, many medial and final syllables were lost. One rule of loss that may be observed is that "every final syllable went out." If a prefix was placed on a verb, and if it was accented, the prefixed form would then come to differ considerably from its erstwhile nonprefixed form. This is the basis for the differences between prototonic and deuterotonic forms, as well as for other changes in verb forms.

The second feature of verbal systems that assists in understanding the Old Irish verb is the inherited structure of the Indo-European verb. In Proto-Indo-European a verbal root could be inflected for various meanings; Vedic Sanskrit maintains this situation, inflected verbal roots in a present system, a perfect system, an aorist system, and a future system. The particular form of any verb in one system had little to do with that in another. There were ten classes in the Sanskrit present system. A root might be inflected in one or more of these; it might also be inflected in the aorist, but the particular one of seven aorist classes selected had no reference to the present class. This verbal structure gave rise to suppletion, that is, the use of forms from two or more roots in one paradigm. Suppletion is evidenced still by English verbs like *go, went,* or by Latin verbs, such as *ferō, tulī, lātum* 'bear.'

These three features led to the highly complex verb forms found in Old Irish. An explanation of their origin may assist in understanding them; for mastery of the forms, however, there is little help but memorization.

Fortunately, the nominal forms are far less complex. The loss of inflectional endings, however, has resulted in distinctions between forms solely on the basis of palatal or nonpalatal quality of final consonants.

Because of the loss of inflectional endings the relationships expressed by case forms in earlier stages of the language are expressed largely by prepositions. The prominent role of prepositions in VSO languages may also be the basis for one of the notable features of Irish: suffixing prepositions, which have also been called conjugated prepositions. Enclitic forms of pronouns are frequently found in VO languages, as in French. These came to be closely associated with the strongly accented prepositions and led to the paradigms presented above. Mastery of the inflected prepositions is second only to mastery of the verbal inflection for facility in reading Old Irish.

89. Phonological characteristics of Old Irish

A strong initial stress leads to weakening of elements in subsequent syllables of words. Apart from the weakening and loss of final elements, this weakening also affected the other sounds of words and word groups. These were pronounced as units. With major energy expended on the stressed vowel, subsequent consonants between vowels were weakened so that intervocalic stops came to be fricatives, in the process known as lenition; other consonants also came to be produced with more lenis articulation.

Moreover, when the second element of a "word unit" followed nasals, it was modified, in the process known as nasalization. The occurrence of nasalization in turn permits us to determine the combinations that were articulated as units. It is interesting, for example, that nasalization is found consistently after prepositions like *i*, cf. Lat. *in*, NE *in*, but not after prepositions with suffixed pronouns; these were apparently articulated as independent units, and accordingly were not necessarily subject to nasalization by a preceding nasal.

The fourth of the phonological processes at work in Old Irish can also be ascribed to the unitary articulation of word groups: gemination. When appropriate final consonants came to stand before certain initial consonants, assimilation brought about gemination, in a process like that at work in *un-/in-* + *licit* = *illicit*. For the understanding of the Old Irish phonological modifications then, it is important to note the introduction of a strong initial stress accent and the articulation together of word groups.

The elements of the system are symmetrical, with three voiceless and voiced stops and fricatives, and five short and long vowels, in addition to the resonants. By observing the positional variation of these, due to the phonological processes described here, the phonological system can be readily understood.

90. Some notes on the Old Irish lexicon

The bases of the Old Irish lexicon are Indo-European. Although lexical items may have undergone characteristic phonological change, such as OIr. *athir* in contrast with Lat. *pater*, Gk. *patēr*, and so on, a large part of the vocabulary can be related directly to Proto-Indo-European. Whitley Stokes has compiled the most extensive listing of the Celtic words in the Indo-European tradition in *Urkeltischer-Sprachschatz*, Vol. II of *Vergleichendes Wörterbuch der indogermanischen Sprachen*, ed. August Fick (Göttingen: Vandenhoeck & Ruprecht, 1894). These include most of the words for common elements of society and culture.

Many Celtic innovations in vocabulary are shared with Italic. The innovations show no characteristic cultural patterns; both Celtic and Italic have introduced new words for 'son' and 'daughter,' though the words are not related: Lat. *filius*, OIr. *mac*; Lat. *filia*, OIr. *ingen*. It may be however that a supposed cultural group consisting of Celtic and Italic speakers introduced the kinship system of a different culture, changing the terms in the process.

The innovations common to the two subbranches of Indo-European, such as the prepositions OIr. *con-*, Lat. *cum* 'with,' and OIr. *di*, Lat. *de* 'from,' give little evidence for assuming new vocabulary in accordance with specific cultural changes. Instead, the Old Irish vocabulary provides evidence for conservatism in vocabulary. The word for 'king,' OIr. *rí* corresponds to Skt. *rāj-* as well as to Lat. *rēx*. The word for 'horse,' OIr. *ech* corresponds to the widely attested word found in Skt. *aśva-*, Gk. *híppos*, Lat. *equus*, OE *eoh*, and so on. Moreover, one of the Celtic goddesses is named *Epona*, a goddess of horses for wagons or chariots. Verbs like *berid* 'bears' also correspond to the normally expected roots, as in Skt. *bharati*, Gk. *phérō*, Lat. *fero*, and so on. In short, the Old Irish vocabulary is fully as conservative as that of any other Indo-European language of its time.

LYRIC POEMS

chapter XIX

The following are examples of the Old Irish lyrics that have been preserved, many on the margins of manuscripts. End-rhyme and syllable-counting are the structural principles of their form. (Observe the elision in the last line of the first lyric.) The translations are free, keeping something of the metrical restrictions of the original. Prepare your own literal versions.

POEM 1

> Ní fetar
> cía lassa fífea Etan
>   acht ro-fetar Etan Bán
>   nícon fhífea a hoenurán.
>
> Blush redden?
> Who knows who sleeps with Edan?
> But I know that Edan's bed
> is not for one intended.

---

1. fetar   1 sg. pres. *ro·fitir* 'knows'
2. cía lassa   w. following prep. as antecedent of a nasalizing rel. clause 'with whom'
     fífea   3 sg. fut. of *foaid* 'spend the night'
3. Bán   adj. 'white, fair-haired'
4. a hoenurán   (also *oenarán* dim. of *oenar*) 'alone' w. f. poss.

POEM 2

> A Rí rinn,
> cid dub mo thech nó cid finn
> nícon íadfaider fri nech
> nár íada Críst a thech frimm.

133

Starry King,
black or white my house within,
none shall find that closed it be
lest Christ close to me His inn.

---

1. rinn   also *rind* nt. and m. gen. pl. 'constellation, star'
2. cid   conj. 'though'; *cia* + 3 sg. pres. subj. of cop.
      dub   adj. 'black'
      thech   nt. 'house'
      finn   adj. 'white'
3. íadfaider   fut. pass. of *íadaid* 'close, shut'
4. nár   *ná* + *ro* neg.
      íada   3 sg. pres. subj.

Four poems on the seasons are included in a story from the eleventh century. They have been assumed to be illustrations of archaic verse for students. Unrhymed, they alliterate and are fixed in their number of syllables per line—seven and five. They are fine examples of early nature poetry. The poems on autumn and winter are given in this chapter; the two remaining, in Chapter xx.

The framework in which we find these poems is a tale called "The Guesting of Athirne," ed. Kuno Meyer, *Ériu*, 7 (1914), 2–5, from the Book of Leinster (L), p. 118a, and Harleian 5280 (H) fol. 77a. A third copy from RIA 23 N 10, pp. 15–16, is edited by Rudolf Thurneysen, pp. 197–98 of the same volume of *Ériu* (R); the abbreviations are used below to refer to variants. Kenneth Jackson, in *Studies in Early Celtic Nature Poetry* (London: Cambridge Univ. Press, 1935), gives his own translation of the four poems, pp. 128–30, with notes on problems, pp. 45–46. David Greene has emended and translated the poems, in David Greene and Frank O'Connor, *A Golden Treasury of Irish Poetry* (London: Macmillan, 1967), pp. 140–43 (Greene's version in brackets).

The setting for the poems is a visit by Athirne to his foster son who detains him by reciting one of these songs against traveling in any season.

POEM 3: AUTUMN

1. Raithe fó foiss fogamar
2. feidm and for cech [ech] oenduine
3. fri tóeb [oíb] na llá lángairit
4. Loíg brecca a broind oisseillti [i ndiaid deisseilte,]
5. dítnit^L (dianit^H/diánad^R) [dínit] rúadgaiss raithnigi.
6. Reithit daim a dumachaib
7. fri dordán na damgaire.
8. Dercain subai i síthchailltib

134

9. slatta etha imm ithġurtu
10.   ós íath domuin duinn.
11. Draiġin, drissi delgnacha
12. fri tóeb [duai] in láir leithlissi,
13. lán do mess tromm teinnithir (tairnith^L)
14. [do-] tuittit cnoí cuill . . . caínmessa
15.   do [cuill], robilib [robili] ráth (rathi ^R)

Time of harvest, homesteading;
holdings here for everyone;
ever the days dwindling;
deer, flecked fawns from holtwood-hinds
5 hide on plains of purple-heath;
proud stags, from hills hurrying,
hearing bold herds bellowing.
Berries, fruit from forestlands,
fields of clustered cornstubble
10   cover the broad bounds.
Blackthorn, brambles—bristling;
broken half a hermitage;
heavy, crop-filled countryside;
cast by hazels, handsome-nuts,
15   high trees of old time.

In the last two lines Greene has moved *do* up a line and *cuill* down a line to preserve the alliterative pattern of the first stress of each line alliterating with the last two stressed syllables of the preceding line. There are seven syllables in each line and a trisyllabic ending except lines 10 and 15 which are five syllables long with monosyllabic endings.

---

1. raithe   f. 'a period of three months, a season'
   fó 'good'
   foiss   gen. sg. of *foss* m. 'rest, remaining in a place' (gen. sg. used as attrib. adj.)
   fogamar   m. 'autumn'
2. feidm   nt. later m. 'load, stress; effort; burden, service; work, duty'; Meyer translates
      'work,' Jackson 'occupation,' and Greene (who substitutes *ech* for *cech*) 'load'
   ech   m. 'horse'
3. fri tóeb   m. *taeb* 'side,' but after *fri* or *la* 'beside, near; along; in comparison with; in
      respect to'; this passage is cited w. Meyer's translation 'throughout'
   oíb   Greene has *oíb* f. and m. 'appearance; beauty; vigor; prosperity' and translates it
      'harvest'
   lángairit   *lán* 'full, completely' (here prefixed for alliteration) + *gairit* 'short'
4. loíg   pl. of *lóeg* m. 'a calf, a fawn'

brecca   pl. adj. 'speckled, freckled, dappled'

broind   dat. of *bru* f. 'belly'; Meyer 'from the midst,' Jackson 'from the side'; Greene has *i ndiaid* fr. *dead* f. 'end'; *i ndiaid* 'behind; following, looking for'; Greene translates 'drop in the wake'

oisseillti   *os(s)*: m. 'a deer' + *elit* f. 'a doe, a hind'; gen. pl. *ellti*; Meyer 'deer-herd,' Jackson 'hinds'; Greene's *deisseilte* alliterates on *d-*; he apparently assumes that *broind* was written for *diaid* because of the alliteration w. *brecca*; he does not explain the form *deisseilte*, but translates the line 'Dappled fawns drop in the wake of hinds'; perhaps he takes the last word as past adj. of a compd. of *silid* 'drops, drips'—w. palat. *l*—or of *silaid* 'sows, breeds, springs'; another possible compd. that preserves alliteration and is closer to the vocalism of the MSS would be *doss* 'bush, thicket' w. *elit* 'the does of the thicket'

 5. dítnit   3 pl. pres. of *dítnid* 'shelters, protects'; Meyer and Jackson accept this reading: 'affords a shelter, shelters them'

dianit/diánad   cop. in rel. clause 'to which they are/it is'; it is doubtful this would be stressed adequately for alliteration; Greene *dínit* or *dínu* nt., or m. pl. 'lamb, suckling'

rúadgaiss   'red' + *gas* orig. nt., later m. 'spring, shoot, twig'

raithnigi   gen. sg. of *raithnech* 'heather'

 6. reithit   3 pl. pres. *reithid* 'runs'

daim   m. pl. of *dam* 'stag'

dumachaib   f. pl. dat. of *dumach* 'bank, mound'; Meyer 'mound,' Jackson 'knolls,' Greene 'dunes'

 7. dordán   m. as vn. of *dordaid* 'makes a *dord*' = 'buzzing, humming, droning, intoning' (of stags, mermaids, birds, bulls, human beings, etc.); Meyer 'chorus,' Jackson 'belling,' Greene 'clamor'

damgaire   f. 'a herd of stags or deer, the bellowing or roaring of a stag'; Meyer 'bellowing of the hinds,' Jackson 'of the deer-herd,' Greene 'of the herd'

 8. dercain   nt. and f. pl. of *dercu* 'acorn'

subai   f. pl. of *sub* 'berry, strawberry'; Meyer and Jackson treat it as an adj. 'sweet,' Greene translates 'acorns and berries'

sithchailltib   *sith-* 'long' + f. dat. pl. of *caill* 'wood, forest'; Meyer 'long-leaved woods,' Jackson 'high woods,' Greene 'peaceful woodlands' from *síd/síth* 'peace'

 9. slatta   f. pl. of *slat* 'rod, lath, twig; branch'; Meyer 'blades,' Jackson and Greene 'cornstalks'

etha   gen. sg. nt. of *ith* 'corn, grain'

ithgurtu   *ith-* + *gort* m. 'field, land; corn crop'

10. ós   prep. w. dat. 'over, above'

íath   nt. 'land, country'

domuin   gen. sg. m. 'world, earth; country'

duinn   gen. sg. m. adj. *donn* 'brown'

11. draigin   m. 'blackthorn, sloe'

drissi   gen. pl. f. of *dris* 'bramble, briar, thornbush'

delgnacha   gen. pl. of *delgnach* adj. 'thorny, prickly, bristly'

12. duai   gen. sg. m. of *doé* 'rampart' (supplies alliteration)

láir   'surface, ground, floor, middle, interior'; Meyer 'by the site,' Jackson 'by the midst,' 'of the house site'

leithlissi   'half' + *les* 'enclosed space around a house, courtyard'; Greene *shlissi* fr. *slis*

136

'sidewall, edge,' Meyer 'half-ruined fort,' Jackson 'ruined court,' Greene 'with the broken wall'

13. mess   m. 'tree fruit, mast, acorns'

tromm   adj. 'heavy'

tairnith   Meyer takes this as part of *do-airndim* 'I let down,' but it leaves the line a syllable short; H reads *tindithir*, R *teinnithir*; Jackson and Greene take *lán* as an adj. and the last word as a compd.: *tend* + *ithir* 'firm, hard' + 'arable land, pasture land; earth, ground'

14. tuittit (Greene *do-tuittet*)   3 pl. pres. *do-tuit* 'falls'

cnoí   pl. *cnó* 'nut'

cuill   gen. sg. of *coll* 'hazel'

caínmessa   'fine, good, beautiful' + Meyer and Jackson 'crop,' Greene 'fruit'

15. robilib   *ro-* intensifier, w. concrete noun 'large; venerable'; *bile* nt. 'a large or old tree' used of what are thought to have been sacred trees of pagan Ireland; Greene has dat. sg.

ráth   m. and f. 'rampart, fort'; alternate form of gen. sg. *ra(i)thi*

POEM 4: WINTER

1. Dubaib raithib rogeimred
2. robarta tonn túargabar
3.   iar toíb betha blaí.
4. Brónaig eóin gach [Brónach cach én] íathmaige
5. acht fíach fola fordeirge
6.   fri fúaim geimrid gairg.
7. Garb [Gaim] dub dorcha dethaite.
8. díumassaig coin chnámchomaig
9. cuirthir ar aed íarnlestar
10.   íar ló dorcha dub.

Darkest of times: truewinter.
Tides of ocean energy
  on edge of world's wastes.
Woe to larks of levelland;
5 look—ravens, red, ravaging,
  as rough winter wails,
weary, dreary, darkening;
dogs are bold at bone-crushing.
Bear to the fire food-kettles,
10   for cold, dusky days.

---

1. dubaib   adj. 'black, dark'; Greene *dubu* nom.

raithib   dat. pl. of *raithe*, see XIX.P.3.1 (Ch. XIX, Poem 3, l. 1; references to poems will follow this form) 'in the darkest seasons'

gemred/gaimred   nt. 'winter' (w. *ro-* intensive prefix 'deep')

2. robarta   m. 'full tide, flood tide; impetuous course'

   tonn   f. 'wave'; Meyer 'heavy seas,' Jackson and Greene 'storm of waves'

   túargabar   perf. proto. stem of *do-fócaib* (later forms pres.) here pres. pass. pl. 'are lifted up, raised'

3. iar toíb   Meyer 'along the side,' Jackson 'along the expanse,' Greene 'against the border'

   betha   gen. sg. m. of *bith* 'world'

   blaí   f. 'field, plain'; Meyer 'of the world's region,' Jackson 'of the world,' Greene 'of the earth's lands'

4. brōnaig   pl. 'sad, sorrowful'

   eóin   nom. pl. m. of *én* 'a bird'

   íathmaige   *íath* nt. 'land, country; territory' + *maige* gen. sg. of *mag* 'field, plain'; this compd. 'meadow-field,' Jackson 'meadow-plain'; Greene has *brónach cach én*, probably so as not to interrupt the alliterating sequence and he translates 'plain'

5. acht   'but, except'

   fíach   'a raven'

   fola   gen. sg. f. of *fuil* 'blood'

   fordeirge   adj. gen. sg.; Meyer 'dark red,' Jackson 'crimson,' Greene 'red and bloody raven'

6. fúaim   nt. later m. 'sound, noise'; Meyer 'uproar,' Jackson 'clamor'

   geimrid   see l. 1

   gairg   'rough, blunt, fierce'

7. garb   'rough, rugged, coarse; rude, harsh'; Greene *gaim* 'winter storm, winter'

   dorcha   adj. *dorchae* 'dark, gloomy'

   dethaite   'smoky, sooty, dusky'

8. díumassaig   fr. *díummsach* 'proud, haughty, arrogant'; Jackson 'vicious,' Meyer 'insolent'

   chnámchomaig   *cnám* m. 'bone' + *comach* vn. 'breaking, pounding'

9. cuirthir   pres. pass. of *cuirid* 'put'

   aed   nt.? 'fire'

   íarnlestar   *íarn* 'iron' + *lestar* nt. later m. 'a vessel'

   íar   Meyer 'throughout,' Jackson 'after,' Greene 'at the end of'

POEM 5: THE OCEAN

1. Féġaiḋ úaiḃ
2.   sair fo thúaiḋ
3.   in muir múaiḋ
4.   mílach;
5.   aḋḃa rón
6.   reḃach, rán,
7.   ro-gaḃ lán
8.   línaḋ.

Look, there rides—
   northeast glides
   torrent tides
      teaming;

138

home of seals,
wanton whales
flood-tide gales,
gleaning.

---

1. fégaid (also féc(h)aid)   2 pl. impv. 'look, keep a lookout'
   úaib   ó prep. leniting w. dat. 'from, away from' + pl. pron.
2. sair   'eastward'
   túaid   'north, in the north' w. *fo/fa* 'northward' (here 'to the northeast'; not to be confused w. prep. *fo* 'under')
3. muir   nt. and m. 'sea'
   múaid   adj. (meaning uncertain, occurs in poetic style) usually translated 'noble, proud'
4. mílach   (*míl* 'animal') 'abounding in animals'
5. adba   f. vn. of *ad-fen* 'dwelling place, home'
   rón   m. (cf. OE *hran/hron* 'smaller kind of whale') 'seal'
6. rebach   adj. 'skilled in feats of strength, etc.; nimble; playful'
   rán   'very noble, glorious' (chiefly in poetry)
7. lán   adj. 'full,' as noun 'tide'
8. línad   vn. of *línaid* 'fills,' of tide 'flowing, flood'

GRAMMAR

91. The early background of Old Irish literature

Inadequately known, Old Irish literature is the most important of the literatures of the early Middle Ages. In addition to a distinct imagination, Old Irish literature maintained its traditional matter and form, with little modification from Greco-Roman tradition imported with Christianity; by contrast, this influence brought about the loss of virtually all native Germanic literature on the Continent, and it strongly modified the literatures of England and the North Germanic areas. Moreover, apart from its own achievement, the literature of Celtic Britain is important for its influence on European literature of the Middle Ages and later. The subject matter of the Arthurian tales, those of Tristan and Isolde, of Percival, and many others are taken from British story. Besides the content, many of the forms of medieval literature may also have been based on those of the Celts.

The early Irish literature reflects the culture of the Gauls and Britons as described by Caesar, *Gallic War*, Book VI.13–20 and Book V.2. According to Book VI.14 the Gauls did not transmit their literature in writing; students learned by heart a great number of verses (*magnum numerum versuum*) during a period of training which may have extended as long as twenty years. Presumably such a situation was maintained also in Britain; the ancient Celtic literature was maintained without disruption by such schools of poets until it was eventually written down. Preservation of the form and content of verse, tales, and laws is more accurate when oral, in that errors are not recorded. Though Irish is not written until quite late, it is more ancient in the world it depicts than are Old English and the other Germanic dialects.

Yet internal evidence also provides insights into changes, especially of the poetry. This brief sketch will survey some of the principal forms.

92. The archaic verse; cadenced verse

Songs of praise represent the oldest literary tradition. The fili had as one of his duties the obligation of praising great men, and memorializing them after their death. The earliest Old Irish verse provides examples of this custom. Much of this verse is composed in a meter with a fixed number of syllables, often seven, with a word boundary after the fourth syllable of seven; the fifth syllable then must be stressed and the sixth unstressed; the seventh, though it is usually unstressed, is unregulated with regard to stress, as is the first part of the line. For an example see the first line below (*Māl . . .*).

This meter has been related to forms of Sanskrit and Greek, and used as evidence for assuming an Indo-European metric pattern. It also included a shorter line of five syllables, as in the second half-line below (*macc . . .*). Like the seven-syllable line, this could be modified further. For a full discussion, see Calvert Watkins, "Indo-European Metrics and Archaic Irish Verse," *Celtica*, 6 (1963), 194–249. See also Charles W. Dunn, who has contributed the essay on Celtic in *Versification: Major Language Types*, ed. W. K. Wimsatt (New York: New York Univ. Press for the MLA, 1972), pp. 136–47. Most of the surviving poems are bound by alliteration, as in the following poem taken from Kuno Meyer, *Über die älteste irische Dichtung* (Berlin: George Reimer, 1914), p. 6.

Māl adrūalaid īathatmarb, macc sōer Sētni,
selaig srathu Fomoire   for dōine domnaib.

Di ōchtur Alinne   oirt trīunu talman,
trebunn trēn tūathmar   Mess-Delmann Domnan.

A prince has passed to the fields of the dead, the noble son of Setna;
he ravaged the valleys of the Fomorians   over worlds of men.

From the height of Alenn   he slew the strong of the earth,
a tribune strong, great in people Mess-Delman, the Dumnonian.

The archaic characteristics of the poem are reflected in its syntax; the verb follows the noun in the first line, and the expression *dōine domnaib* has the genitive preceding its noun. Moreover, besides archaic vocabulary, it contains the compound *tūathmar*; later verse, like the later language, includes few such compounds.

The poem may have been longer than these two stanzas, as Meyer suggests. Yet it illustrates the song of praise, which has been asserted to be the primary type of poem in the early Indo-European tradition. See Rüdiger Schmitt, *Dichtung und Dichtersprache in indogermanischer Zeit* (Wiesbaden: Harrassowitz, 1967), especially Chapter ii, pp. 61–102.

Examples of the shorter line are available in the rhetorics of SMMD 15: *Fochen Conall, cride licce, londruth loga*. These rhetorics exemplify another type of ancient poem, the challenge. Still others, such as charms, prayers, incantations, curses, are poorly documented. Legal lore, however, was handed down in verse, as noted in Watkins' "Indo-European Metrics." Moreover, in contrast with Old English we have treatises on Irish versification. These permit a deeper understanding of Old Irish verse than is possible for early Germanic verse, as is evident in treatises like Gerard Murphy's *Early Irish Metrics* (Dublin: Royal Irish Academy, 1968).

93. Úaim; alliteration

Both the rhetorics in SMMD and the poem cited above illustrate the Old Irish form of alliteration. After a nonalliterating first word, successive sequences are connected by continuing consonant or vowel alliteration. The principles of Irish alliteration are thus different from those of Germanic verse, which require one or two alliterations in the first half-line, one in the second half-line of a long line (with possible crossed alliteration), as in the well-known lines from the Old Norse "Hávamál":

> deyr fé   deyia frændr,
> deyr siálfr it sama

> Cattle die,   kin die,
> dies the soul itself

The differing Celtic use may be indicated by the Irish word *úaim*, literally 'stitching.' By contrast the Icelandic poet and metrist, Snorri, called the alliterating element in the second half-line the *hǫfuðstafr* 'head-stave' and those in the first half-line *stuðlar* 'supports.' Alliteration is thus distributed by lines in Germanic; in Irish, on the other hand, it often continues through a second line, which is determined by syllable counting rather than initial elements of words.

The elements of alliteration were, however, comparable in the two linguistic areas, at least in the earliest periods. Vowels alliterated with other vowels; consonants only with each other, including the special clusters *sp, st, sk*. In Old Irish, eclipsis did not prevent alliteration, as of *b* and *mb*; nor did lenition, except for *f* (the lenited form of which is zero), *p* (the lenited form of which is *f*), *s* (the lenited form of which alliterates only with lenited *s*). These principles indicate that the poetic conventions for alliteration were determined before eclipsis and lenition took place, and were subsequently maintained by tradition. Alliteration can only have been effective after a strong initial stress accent was introduced; it must then be ascribed to the first millennium B.C., and the nonalliterating verse which has survived is in accordance with poetic techniques in force before this time. The similarities, as well as the differences, between Celtic and Germanic verse, can thus be explained on the basis of their earlier contiguity and subsequent separation, or because similar linguistic structures led to similar metrical developments.

94. The later lyric; rhyming syllabic verse

Latin verse introduced into Ireland with Christianity also contained end rhyme. This was adopted by Irish poets, but, as in alliteration, with distinct conventions.

Each vowel after the stressed vowel must rhyme; the consonants, however, are classed by sets determined for quality and phonetic classes. The phonetic classes are:

voiced stops [b d g]
voiceless stops [p t k]
voiceless fricatives [f θ χ]
voiced fricatives and lenis liquids [v v̄ ð γ l n r]
emphatic, fortis liquids [m L N R]
[s]
any final vowel

Examples of these sets are found in the poem of SMMD 3, e.g., *airi* : *aili*, *gním* : *thír*, *cutal* : *tucad*, and so on. Besides end rhyme, Irish syllabic verse uses internal rhyme, consonance, and other forms of phonetic agreement.

The later lyric is notable for its love of nature, of solitude, and of God. The first of these themes is treated in the celebrated set of poems on the seasons included in Chapters XIX and XX. The other themes are readily found in Irish verse from the early period to the present, as in the following initial stanza of a longer poem:

Dúthracar, a Maic Dé bí,
a Rí suthain sen,
bothnat deirrit díthraba
commad sí mo threb.

I would like, O Son of God the living,
O king eternal, ancient,
a hut, secret, in the wilds,
so that for me it would be my house.

This verse is fixed in the number of syllables, and the first part of the line is relatively free. The last syllable is stressed, occurring often after a break, as in the lines cited here.

The widely used *deibide*, or cut stanza, follows this pattern, as in the poetry of SMMD 3. In *deibide* the first line rhymes with the second, the third with the fourth, and each line normally consists of seven syllables. As an example the following self-descriptive quatrain is often cited (Gerard Murphy, *Early Irish Metrics*, p. 65; Dunn, in *Versification*, p. 140); the *scailte* 'scattered' variant suggests the absence of connection between couplets, or the lack of consonants to bind lines together.

Deibide scaílte na scél
ní híside nád aithgén;
is í seo ind aiste bláith bras
i ngnathaigther in senchas.

The deibide scailte of story
is not one I do not recognize.
It is the meter smooth, swift
in which are presented the traditions.

142

As this quatrain suggests, *deibide* served as a poetic form for fixing traditional and historical events. Many examples are found in the stories of the past.

95. Heroic tales and cycles

The song of praise is a simple poem commemorating heroes and events. Traditions were also preserved in prose, as in SMMD. These prose stories reflect the heroic activities: warfare, banqueting, raids, voyages, courtships, and love accounts. The later stories are brought together in large cycles: the Ulster Cycle, the Cycle of the Kings, the Fenian Cycle, and stories of mythology and the other world (see Dillon and Chadwick, pp. 239–69). Our story stands outside these cycles, representing an even earlier age. Ulster and its prime rival, Connaught, are indeed represented in SMMD. But the supreme hero of Irish story, Cú Chulainn, is not yet included among the warriors of Ulster.

In form, the heroic tales are comparable to SMMD; the main story is narrated in prose, with poetry included often at high points. The Icelandic sagas also have this form, probably by imitation of the Old Irish tales. Some scholars have proposed that some of the stories were originally transmitted from one generation to another by means of the verse, and that the prose was added by later, literate generations.

Summaries with commentary of notable heroic tales can be found in Dillon and Chadwick and other publications, such as the collection of essays *Irish Sagas,* ed. Myles Dillon (Cork: Mercier, 1968). Probably the best known is the *Táin Bó Cúailgne* 'The Cattle-Raid of Cooley.' Depicting conflict between Ulster and Connaught over cattle, the story deals primarily with the hero of Ulster, Cú Chulainn, and his battles. Various tales have been incorporated in the stories relating to him, including that of a father killing his son, as Cú Chulainn does Conla, a story maintained also in the Old High German *Hildebrandslied* and in Slavic and Persian tradition. Another story, the challenge of a giant to let Cú Chulainn cut off his head if he in turn may cut off the head of Cú Chulainn, is found in the Middle English poem, *Sir Gawain and the Green Knight*, and also in Old French.

The Cycle of the Kings recounts the traditions of the origins of the Irish rulers and the later kings. The Fenian Cycle is the latest. Many of its ballads are dialogues between Oisín (Ossian), the son of Finn, and St. Patrick. The mythological and voyage tales include imaginative accounts much more fanciful than those in other European story. In the *Voyage of Mael Dúin* the travelers find an island with a remarkable beast on it who could turn its flesh and bones in its skin without moving it; they pass under a stream of water and are able to spear salmon above themselves, and so on. Among these stories is also a parody, *The Vision of Mac Con Glinne*, a highly amusing satire on contemporary monastery life.

Old Irish literature is still too poorly known. Besides its importance for the understanding of the subsequent literature of Western Europe it is of great interest in its own right.

Chapter XX

Chapter XIX gave two songs of the seasons from "The Guesting of Athirne," those on autumn and winter. The first two poems here complete that series. As before, Greene's readings are given in brackets, other texts in parentheses with superscript initial ("J" for Jackson's suggestions).

POEM 6: SPRING

1. Glass úar errach aiġiḋe,
2. úacht ina ġaíth giġnither,
3. glaiḋsit [glaedait] lachain linnuisci,
4. luind cenḋach[R] [luinnécnach] (luinnéach[J]) corr crúaḋéigme
5. Cluinit cúana [daiṁ] a ndíthreḃaiḃ
6. fri h·éirġe [dúsacht] moch matanraiḋ
7. dúscit [meḋraiḋ] eónu a hinnsénaiḃ (indḟeraid[L])
8. mór bfiaḋ riasu bfirteititt [imḋa fíaḋ ré fírtheiċit]
9.   a fiḋ, a féor ġlass.

   Green, cool, quiet, quivering—
   cold in the wind wakening;
   wailing ducks on distant-ponds,
   doleful cranes are chorusing.
   Calls are heard on highlandmoors.
   Hurry, daybreak, dawninghour
   darting fowl from far-off isles
   fleeing wildbeasts, wanderers
      from wood, waste, and green.

---

1. glass   of weather 'fresh, raw, sharp' orig. 'gray'?
   úar   'cold'

errach   m. 'springtime'
aigide   'icy'
2. úacht   m. 'coldness'
gaíth   dat. of *gaeth* f. 'wind'
gignither   3 sg. fut. of *gainithir* 'is born; is produced, arises, originates'
3. glaidsit   3 pl. pret. 'have cried out'; *glaedait* 3 pl. pres. 'stick fast, adhere to'
lachain   nom. pl. f. of *lachu* 'duck, female duck'
linnuisci   f. *linn* 'pool, pond' + *uisce* m. 'water'
4. luind cendach   Greene 'wild and mournful' *lonn-* 'fierce, vehement' + *écn(d)ach* nt. vn. 'reviling; complaining of; grieving over'; R *luind cendach* is obviously corrupt; Jackson would read *luinnéach* 'song, chorus'
corr   f. 'crane, heron'
crúadéigme   'hard, harsh' + f. 'a cry, scream'; Meyer 'harsh-shrieking cranes set up their blasphemous chorus'; Jackson 'eager and . . . is the harsh-shrieking crane'; Greene 'wild and mournful is the crane of the harsh cry'
5. cluinit   3 pl. act. form of earlier deponent *ro-cluinethar* 'I hear'
cúana   f. 'wolf pack, hound pack'; Greene substitutes *daim* pl. m. 'oxen, stags,' which preserves the alliterative pattern
díthrebaib   dat. pl. f. 'desert, wilderness'
6. éirge   m. 'rising, arising'; Greene substitutes m. *dúsacht* 'awaking, arousing'
moch   'early'
matanraid   m. 'morning time'
7. dúscit   3 pl. pres. of *dúscid* fr. earlier *do-fíuschi* 'wakes'
medraid   'is exhilarated; excites'; Greene 'wakes'
innsénaib   Jackson suggests from Bergin that this is a collective fr. *inis* f. 'an island'
8. mór   m. 'many'; Greene *imda*: as indef. pron. 'many a'
fíad   m. 'wild animal,' later 'deer, stag'
riasu (Greene *re*)   'before which'
firteititt   *fír* 'true, truly' + 3 pl. pres. *teichet* or *teithet* 'flees, runs away'
9. a   prep. geminates 'out of'
fid   m. 'a tree, a wood'
féor   nt. 'grass'
glass   adj. (see l. 1 of this poem); also 'gray; green; blue'

POEM 7: SUMMER

1. Fó sín samrad sithaister,
2. samdal [sám] fid forard forglide
3. nach fet gaíthe glúaiseba [glúaiss];
4. Glass clúm caille clithaige,
5. soaid [cerba] srotha saebuisci,
6. tes [sén] i fótán fó.

Good, soft season—summertime:
silent wood, wild, wonderful;
no wind breathes or blows.

145

Bright, fine, feath'ry foliage,
freshwell waters, wandering,
warm on ground so good.

---

1. fó   see XIX. P.3.1
   sín   f. 'storm; season, weather'
   samrad   m. 'summer'
   sithaister   Meyer does not translate this word; Jackson derives it fr. *sith-* 'peace' and
   translates 'peaceful'; Greene derives it fr. *sith-* 'long' and translates 'for long journeys'
2. samdal or sám   'peaceful, calm'
   fid   see XX.P.6.9
   forard   *for-* intensive + *ard* 'high, tall'
   forglide   participle of *for-gella* 'attested, proven, true; chosen, choice'
3. fet   f. 'whistle'; Greene 'breath'
   glūaiseba   3 sg. fut. (Royal Irish Academy Dict. *glúasid* col. 113 l. 50) 'which not a puff
   of the wind will set in motion,' Greene *glúaiss* 'stirs'
4. glass   see XX.P.6.1, 9
   clúm   f. 'feathers, down; hair'
   caille   see XIX.P.3.8 *caill* f. 'wood, forest'
   clithaige   adj. *clithach* 'sheltering, protective'
5. soaid   fr. *do·soí* 'turns'
   srotha   m. pl. of *sruth* 'stream, river, current'; *cerba* fr. *cerbaid* 'cut off, cut short'
   saeb   'crooked, askew'; Greene 'wandering' + *uisce* 'water'
6. tes(s)   m. 'heat, warmth'
   sén   'sign, omen; good sign, blessing'
   fótán   m. (dim. of *fót*) 'a small sod or clod of earth'; Greene 'fine turf'

The following poem was edited in *Eigse* I, p. 248, and by James Carney,
Medieval Irish Lyrics (Dublin: Dolmen, 1967), pp. 78–79. Notice that the first
line rhymes with lines 2 and 4, and that the third line has extensive internal
rhyme *(aicill)* with line 4: *talam/anam*; *bráen/náem*, and in the last line also *cén/
dér*. Note alliteration also.

POEM 8: PRAYER FOR REPENTANCE

1. A Dhé, tuc dam topur ndér
2.   do díl mo chinad, ní chél;
3. ní toirthech talam cen bráen,
4.   ním náem cén anam cen dér.

Wells of tears may God me yield,
   pay for guilt of mine revealed;
without a tear, my own soul
   unwhole—a sear, unsown field.

146

1. A Dhé   voc. of *Día* 'God'
   tuc   2 sg. impv. of *do·beir*
   dam   1 pers. pron. w. *do*
   topur   m. 'well, spring'
   dér   nt. 'a tear' gen. pl. nasalized by preceding acc. sg.
2. díl   m. 'legally taking the place of, requital, recompense, payment'
   cinad   m. pl. of *cin* 'fault, guilt, crime'
   chél   1 sg. fut. conj. of *ceilid* 'hides, conceals'
3. toirtech   'fruitful, fertile'
   talam   m. 'the earth, ground'
   bráen   m. (also *bróen*) 'drop, rain, shower'
4. ním   'I am not'; see Thurneysen G.485
   náem   earlier *noíb* adj. 'holy'
   cén   (for *céin = fadéin*) 'myself'
   anam   f. 'soul,' usually *ainim(m)* or *anaim(m)*
   dér   see 1. 1 above

POEM 9: THE BLACKBIRD SONG [text from Carney, *Medieval Irish Lyrics,* p. 82]

1. Ach, a luin, is buide duit
2.   cáit 'sa muine i fuil do net,
3. a díthrebaig nád clinn cloc,
4.   is binn boc síthamail t'fet.

Ah, blackbird, great thanks to you!
In what brake does your nest lie?
Hermit bird, let ring no bell,
you sing well your soft, sweet sigh.

1. luin   voc. of *lon* 'blackbird, ousel'
   buide   f. 'thanks; pleasure, satisfaction'
2. cáit   (esp. w. *i* and subst. vb.) 'where is'
   'sa   *i* + art.
   muine   m. 'brake, thicket; bush'
   i fuil   *i* 'in which' + rel. form of the subst. vb.
   net   m. 'nest'
3. díthrebaig   voc. of *díthrebach* 'hermit, recluse'
   clinn   3 sg. pres. conj. of *clinnid* 'rings, sounds'
   cloc   m. 'bell'
4. binn   'melodious, tuneful, sweet-sounding'
   boc   'soft, tender, mild'
   síthamail (also *sídamail*) 'peaceful, tranquil'
   fet   see XX.P.7.3 here 'whistle'

147

POEM 10: STORM ON THE GREAT MOOR

1. Úar ind aḋaiġ i Móin Móir
2. feraiḋ dertan ní deróil;
3. dordán fris tiḃ in ġaeth ġlan
4. geissiḋ ós caille clithar.

Cold the night on the Great Moor,
not small the stormy downpour.
The wind laughs, shrieks without rest
above the shelt'ring forest.

---

1. úar   see XX.P.6.1
   adaig   f. 'night'
   móin   f. 'bog, peat-moss; turf, peat'
2. feraid   3 sg. pres. 'pours, showers, sheds'
   dertan   also *derdán* m. and f. 'storm, bad weather'
   deróil   adj. 'mean, insignificant, small'
3. dordán   see XIX.P.3.7
   fris   'at which'
   tib   w. *fri* 'touches; laughs, smiles at'
4. geissid   'cries out, roars, shrieks'
   ós   *úas* 'above, over'
   caille   dat. sg. of *caill*; see XX.P.7.4
   clithar   'sheltering, protective'

GRAMMAR: Bibliographical Notes

96. Bibliographical tools

Students of Irish are fortunate in having available two excellent compilations produced by an outstanding bibliographer, R. I. Best:

> *Bibliography of Irish Philology and of Printed Irish Literature.* 1913; rpt. New York: Johnson Reprints, 1970.

> *Bibliography of Irish Philology and Manuscript Literature.* 1942; rpt. Dublin: Institute for Advanced Studies, 1969. Publications 1913–41, by R. I. Best.

Any work published before 1941 can readily be located by means of these handbooks. They list the journals, work in Irish philology (lexicography; grammar; metrics; inscriptions; glosses and manuscripts) and on the literature (tales, sagas; poetry; religion, ecclesiastical; historical; legal; miscellaneous) and include indices. They are supplemented by a "report" produced in 1953 by Julius Pokorny:

> *Keltologie,* in Vittore Pisani, *Allgemeine und vergleichende Sprachwissenschaft—Indogermanistik.* Vol. 2 of Wissenschaftliche Forschungsberichte. Bern: Francke, 1953. Pp. 95–184.

This work is in the form of a lengthy review. It covers roughly the same areas as do the works of Best, but as the title suggests it deals with Celtic studies in general, not merely Irish.

Subsequent work can be found listed in the *MLA International Bibliography*, and in specialized works, such as the *Linguistic Bibliography*. With these bibliographical aids, virtually any desired publication can be readily located. Furthermore, the Dublin Institute is currently at work trying to bring the bibliography up to date.

97. Grammatical works

Besides numerous specialized studies there are two copious grammars devoted to Old Irish:

Pedersen, Holger. *Vergleichende Grammatik der keltischen Sprachen*. 2 vols. Göttingen: Vandenhoeck & Ruprecht, 1908–13. I, Einleitung und Lautlehre, 1908–09. II, Bedeutungslehre (Wortlehre), 1911, 1913.

Thurneysen, Rudolf. *Handbuch des Alt-Irischen*. Heidelberg: Winter, 1909. I, *Grammatik*. II, *Texte mit Wörterbuch*.

Thurneysen's grammar was translated, revised, and enlarged by D. A. Binchy and Osborn Bergin, and published as:

A Grammar of Old Irish. Dublin: Institute for Advanced Studies, 1946.

The translation has been reprinted numerous times subsequently. Every student of Old Irish should own this grammar.

Pedersen's grammar was abridged, revised, and published in English, under the title:

Lewis, Henry and Holger Pedersen. *A Concise Comparative Celtic Grammar*. Göttingen: Vandenhoeck & Ruprecht, 1937. (The unabridged grammar is essential especially for the verbal system.)

These grammars are in the tradition established by the neogrammarians around 1875. They are historical in format, though Thurneysen's is less so than Pedersen's. The phonology is treated at length, as is the morphology. Any material on syntax is included in the morphology. A comprehensive syntax of Old Irish is among the greatest requirements in Celtic studies.

98. Lexicography, glosses, and manuscripts

The standard Modern Irish-to-English desk dictionary is:

Dinneen, Patrick S. *An Irish-English Dictionary*. Dublin: Irish Texts Society, 1927 (and subsequently reprinted). Unfortunately, it is not always available and is currently out of print.

The Royal Irish Academy has long been at work on a comprehensive dictionary. This has been produced under various editors, and, accordingly, coverage is uneven. Not yet complete, the dictionary is already being revised. Details on the early fascicles may be found in Best, as can additional data on lexicographical work.

Information on the glosses and on the manuscripts and their publication can also be found in Best. The fundamental collection of glosses was published in 1901 to 1903 (Vol. I in 1901, Vol. II in 1903):

Stokes, Whitley and John Strachan. *Thesaurus Palaeohibernicus*. 2 vols. Cambridge, Eng.: Cambridge Univ. Press.

99. Works on Old Irish literature and culture

For an excellent introductory text on Irish literature and culture, see:

Dillon, Myles and Nora Chadwick. *The Celtic Realms.* London: Weidenfeld and Nicolson, 1967. 2nd ed., 1972.

It deals with the history of the Celts "from its remote beginning through the formation of the separate Celtic kingdoms in the British Isles, and down to the end of their independence." Like any such capable work it includes useful bibliographical references. These supplement the lists in Best and Pokorny.

For access to the literary monuments two excellent collections of individual texts are available:

Mediaeval and Modern Irish Series, published by The Dublin Institute for Advanced Studies.

Publications of the Irish Texts Society, London.

The Mediaeval and Modern Irish Series include brief introductions on texts and story, glossaries of varying completeness, with some notes. The Irish Texts Society publications include parallel translations and notes. Unfortunately, not all volumes in either series are kept in print.

100. Current works and means of access to them

Thanks to the interest and subsidies of the Irish government, a continuing set of publications may be found to deal with various questions in Irish civilization and history. Many of these are paperbacks, such as:

Irish Sagas. Ed. Myles Dillon. Cork: Mercier, 1968.

Early Irish Poetry. Ed. James Carney. Cork: Mercier, 1965.

Both of these volumes are collections of essays prepared for radio broadcasts. The authors are among the most distinguished Irish scholars.

It would be difficult to list the most useful works dealing with literature in translation. A good collection of the tales is:

Ancient Irish Tales. Ed. Tom Peete Cross and Clark H. Slover. Chicago: Univ. of Chicago Press, 1937. (Now taken over by Barnes and Noble, New York, and Harper; rev. 1969 by Charles W. Dunn with improved bibliography.)

For verse the following collections may be noted:

Murphy, Gerard. *Early Irish Lyrics.* Oxford: Oxford Univ. Press, 1956.

A Golden Treasury of Irish Poetry, A.D. 600–1200. Ed. and Trans. David Greene and Frank O'Connor. London: Macmillan, 1967.

Medieval Irish Lyrics. Trans. James Carney. Dublin: Dolmen, 1967.

Copies of these, when available, may be secured most readily from the bookstore that is an Irish institution: Hodges Figgis & Co., Stephen Court, Stephen's Green, Dublin, Ireland. Because of subsidies provided by the Government, Irish books are published in relatively inexpensive form. Any student of Irish can readily acquire an extensive library of original materials and secondary materials at little expense, particularly of those books published by the Irish Academy, the Dublin Institute for Advanced Studies, and the Irish Texts Society.

GLOSSARY

The glossary includes all words of the texts, including proper nouns. References are made to the chapter in which each text occurs, and then to the specific text; for example:

    References to SMMD: VII.5.1   = Chapter VII, Section 5, sentence 1
    References to glosses: XIV.Gl.28   = Chapter XIV, Gloss 28
    References to individual poems: XIX.P.3.4 = Chapter XIX, Poem 3, line 4

References to the grammar sections are given as follows:

    II.G.10.1 = Chapter II, Grammar 10, part 1

References to Thurneysen's *Grammar of Old Irish* are given as follows:

    Thurneysen G.561

The numeral refers to the page in the 1946 grammar and subsequent reprintings.

The words are listed alphabetically; yet derived forms are defined only under the main entries. For example, the various forms of *a·tá* are defined under this heading; a cross-reference is given, however, for each form in its alphabetical listing, such as *táthut*, pres. ind. 3 sg., which follows *tarsnu* in the glossary. Variant forms in the poems may be explained only in the notes to the texts, especially if they are problematic. Moreover, prenasalized and aspirated forms, especially those in the late chapters, may simply be listed under their unmodified forms.

The abbreviations are those listed before Chapter I.

A

a (1) leniting ptc. prefixed to vocatives; VII.5.5; VIII.6.7; IX.7.1; X.9.5; XII.12.1; XII.12.4; XIII.13.5; XIII.13.6; XIV.14.7; XV.15.8; XVI.16.4; XVIII.20.4; XIX.P.2.1; XX.P.8.1; see II.G.10.1

a (as) (ass) (2) prep. + dat.; out of, from; gem. IX.7.1; XIX.P.3.4; XIX.P.3.6; XX.P.6.7; XX.P.6.9

  asin XVIII.20.2 + art. dat. sg.
  asind VIII.6.8 + art. dat. sg.
  assind X.10.1; XVII.18.7 + art. dat. sg.
  asnaib XIV.Gl.28 + art. dat. pl.
  asmo VI.4.9; XI.11.10 + poss. pron. 1 sg.
  asdo XI.11.11; XI.11.13 + poss. pron. 2 sg.
  ast XII.12.5 + poss. pron. 2 sg.
  assa XVI.16.9; XVII.18.6; + poss. pron.
  3 sg.; see Thurneysen G.507-10

a (3) poss. pron. 3 sg. m. and nt. leniting; I.1a.1; III.2.3; III.2.4; IV.3.2; IV.3.7; IV.3.8; V.3.11; V.3.12; VIII.6.9; IX.7.4; IX.8.2; X.9.1; X.9.6; X.10.12; X.10.13; XI.Gl.18; XII.12.12; XIII.Gl.23; XVI.16.9; XVI.17.2; XVII.18.4; XVII.18.5; XVII.19.4; XVIII.20.3; XIX.P.2.4

For forms when suffixed to prepositions, see individual prepositions. See III.G.11.1.

a (4) poss. pron. 3 sg. f.; her, its; gem.; VIII.6.8; XI.11.2; XIX.P.1.4

For forms when suffixed to prepositions, see

individual prepositions. See III.G.11.1.

a^n (5) poss. pron. 3 pl. all genders, nasalizing; their; III.2.1; III.2.2; VI.Gl.2; VIII.6.1; VIII.Gl.8; IX.7.1; X.Gl.15; XII.Gl.20; XVII.18.2; XVIII.20.6

For forms when suffixed to prepositions, see individual prepositions. See III.G.11.1.

a^n (6) rel. ptc. used as antecedent for a rel. clause; see Thurneysen G.298; nasalizes a following segment but takes a leniting rel. clause (see X.G.46.1) = all that . . . , that which . . . ; II.1b.11; VIII.6.4; IX.Gl.11

  an IX.Gl.11
  na XVI.16.5

a^n (7) II.1b.12; IX.7.2; IX.Gl.10; XII.Gl.19; XIV.Gl.26; XVI.17.1; XVIII.20.1; see *in*

acaib X.9.6; see *oc*

·acat XV.Gl.31; see *ad·cí*

acci XVI.16.10; see *oc*

ach XX.P.9.1; exclamation

accubur XII.Gl.19; desire; vn. of *ad·cobra*

acht but, except; IV.3.1; VIII.6.8; VIII.Gl.7; XII.12.12; XVII.18.1; XIX.P.1.3; XIX.P.4.5

acum-sa IX.7.1; see *oc*

adaig XX.P.10.1; f.; night

  aidchi VI.4.3; acc. pl.
  n-oénaidchi XVI.16.5; acc. sg. of *oénadaig*, a compd. of *oén* one (see *oín*) and

adaig; cech n-oénaidchi every single night; see *cech*

ad·aig drives to, changes, reduces to;
atan·ebla v.3.13; fut. 3 sg.; deut. w. infixed pron. 1 pl.

adba xix.P.5.5; dwelling place; vn. of *ad·fen* requites

adbar nt.; material, makings; xiv.14.4

ad·chiam ix.Gl.11; see *ad·cí*

ad·cí (·aicci) sees;
at·chi x.9.3; pres. ind. 3 sg. w. meaningless infixed pron. 3 sg. nt.
n-ad-chiam ix.Gl.11; pres. ind. 1 pl. deut. nasalized by *a ⁿ* (6)
ad·ciam xi.Gl.18; pres. ind. 1 pl. deut.
atot·chiat xi.11.12; pres. ind. 3 pl. w. infixed pron. 2 sg.
n-acat xv.Gl.31; pres. ind. 3 pl. proto. nasalized by *húare ⁿ*
nimu-n-accamar xiv.Gl.25; perf. 1 pl. proto. preceded by *imma ⁿ* to indicate 'mutually' + infixed pron. 1 pl. = we have seen one another, w. neg.
in-dom-acca xi.11.6; pret. 2 sg. preceded by prep. *i ⁿ* w. rel. force and w. infixed pron. 1 sg.; see *cairm*
co·n-accatar xv.15.1; pret. 3 pl.
at·chondarc-sa xi.11.5; perf. 1 sg. w. meaningless infixed pron. and emph. suffix; see iv.G.18.1

ad·ciam xi.Gl.18; see *ad·cí*

ad·cota (·éta) vb.; obtains, gets;
·étai xiv.14.9; pres. ind. 2 sg. proto.

ad·cumaing vb.; occurs, befalls;
atot·chomnaic xiv.14.10; pret. 3 sg. w. infixed pron. 2 sg.; lit. = that befell you, that you are called

ad·fen (·aithfen) vb.; repays, gives in recompense;
·aithenar iv.3.9; pres. ind. pass. sg.

ad·fet vb.; tells, relates;
ad·fiadam xv.Gl.31; pres. ind. 1 pl. deut.
as·nda·fiadam-ni xv.Gl.31; pres. ind. 1 pl. deut. w. infixed pron. 3 pl. and infixed nasalization caused by conj. *indas ⁿ* + emph. suffix 1 pl.; see iv.G.18.1

ad·fiadam xv.Gl.31; see *ad·fet*

ad·gládathar (·aiccildethar) speaks to, ad-

dresses;
nícos-n-árlastar iv.3.5; ro-pret. 3 sg. preceded by neg. marker *nícon* w. infixed pron. 3 sg. f. *-s* nasalizing
corot·aicciller x.9.5; subj. 1 sg. preceded by conj. *co ⁿ* (4) + perf. *ro* + infixed pron. 2 sg.

ad-id-trefea xi.Gl.16; see *ad·treba*

ad·treba dwells, inhabits, possesses;
atrefea xi.Gl.16; fut. 3 sg.
ad-id-trefea xi.Gl.16; fut. 3 sg. w. infixed pron. 3 sg. nt.

aed nt.; fire; xix.P.4.9

aél m.; flesh-fork;
n-aél ii.1b.11; acc. sg. nasalized by preceding art. acc. sg.

aergarthe xii.Gl.19; see *ar·gair*

ag nt.; calf, cow, ox, beast, stag;
ag ix.7.1; nom. sg.
n-ag ix.7.2; nom. sg. nasalized by preceding nt. art.
aige viii.6.4; nom. pl.

ágach adj.; warlike, with many battles; xv.15.11

agaid f.; face;
aigthi vii.5.9; nom. pl.

agid drives;
eblait xv.15.12; fut. 3 pl.

aí x.Gl.15; partitive gen.; see *indala*

·aicciller x.9.5; see *ad·gládathar*

aidchi vi.4.3; see *adaig*

aig f.; ice;
ega xv.15.9; xv.15.11; gen. sg.

aige viii.6.4; see *ag*

aigide xx.P.6.1; icy

aigthi vii.5.9; see *agaid*

Ailbe i.1a.4; v.3.15; xvii.19.5; name of a legendary hound belonging to Mac Dathó, a legendary king of Leinster;
Ailbi xvii.19.3; xvii.19.5; gen. sg.
Thurneysen suggests that the name derives from the place-name Mag n-Ailbi *'Plain of Ailbe' 1951:64; but it has also been suggested that it represents an old god-name.*

Ailbi xvii.19.3; xvii.19.5; see *Ailbe*

aile other; declined like *io-iā* stem except that the nt. nom. acc. sg. is *aill;*

154

aile VII.5.7; X.Gl.15; XV.Gl.30

aili v.3.10; m. gen. sg.

a n-aill II.1b.12; nt. acc. sg.

n-aili XI.11.13; f. acc. sg.

n-aill XIII.13.12; m. acc. sg. (irregular)

Ailella XVII.19.4; XVIII.20.3; see *Ailill*

aili v.3.10; see *aile*

ailid (·ail) nourishes, feeds, supports;
no-d n-ail VIII.Gl.7; pres. ind. 3 sg. conj.
w. infixed pron. 3 sg. m. (nasalizing)
supported by *no*
no-t ail VIII.Gl.7; pres. ind. 3 sg. conj. w.
infixed pron. 2 sg. supported by *no*

Ailill I.1a.5; III.2.3; v.3.13; VI.4.5; VIII.6.6;
VIII.6.7; VIII.6.10; XVII.19.3; a legendary
king of Connaught; husband of Queen
Medb;
Ailella XVII.19.4; XVIII.20.3; gen. sg.

aill II.1b.12; XIII.13.12; see *aile*

aimser f.; time, period;
aimsir II.1b.8; dat. sg.

aimsir II.1b.8; see *aimser*

ainm nt.; name; I.1a.1; I.1a.4; XIV.Gl.26;
XVII.19.5;
anma XII.12.12; gen. sg.
anman VI.Gl.2; acc. pl.

air XIV.Gl.27; XV.Gl.32; see *ar* (2) conjunction

airdircus m.; fame, renown; I.1a.4; dat. sg.

airec nt.; finding, obtaining; vn. of *ar·ic*;
airiuc III.2.1; dat. sg.

airg XV.15.12;
(a) nom. pl. of *arg* = famous champion?
(b) acc. sg. of *airg* = trouble, difficulty?

airi v.3.10; VII.Gl.5; see *ar* (1)

airindí XIV.Gl.26; conjunction; 'because'
followed by leniting rel. clause; made up of
ar (prep.) + art. dat. sg. + stressed deictic
ptc. *í*

airisin XIV.Gl.26; see *airisiu*

airisiu f.; story, history;
airisin XIV.Gl.26; dat. sg.

airiuc III.2.1; see *airec*

airle f.; advice; v.3.14

airscéla XV.15.12; great tidings, great stories;
see *scél*

aiss f.; back;
dara aiss XVIII.20.3 = from behind (him),

lit. over his back

·aithenar IV.3.9; see *ad·fen*

al-aili XII.Gl.20; see *araile*

all nt.; bridle;
n-allaib XVIII.20.8; dat. pl. nasalized by
preceding prep. *co^n* (3)

allaib XVIII.20.8; see *all*

am VII.Gl.5; see *is*

ám X.10.5; indeed

amal conjunction nasalizing
(a) + ind. = as; XII.Gl.21; XIV.Gl.28
(b) + past subj. = as if; XIII.Gl.23

amrae adj.; wonderful, famous; I.1a.1

an IX.Gl.11; see *a^n* (6)

an X.9.5; XIII.13.5; XVII.19.4; see *anaid*

anaid (·ana) waits, remains, stays;
anait VI.4.3; pres. ind. 3 pl.
an X.9.5; XIII.13.5; impv. 2 sg.
corro·an XVII.19.4; pret. 3 sg. preceded
by *co^n* (4) and perf. *ro*

a n-aill II.1b.12; see *aile*

anair VII.5.1; from the east; in origin a prefix *an* + *air* 'east'; see IX.G.45; Thurneysen
G.305

anait VI.4.3; see *anaid*

anam XX.P.8.4; f.; soul

and IV.3.2; IV.3.6; X.10.7; X.Gl.15; XII.12.5;
XII.Gl.20; XV.15.2; XV.15.4; XV.15.9;
XVII.18.6; XVII.19.1; XVII.19.4; XVIII.20.2;
XVIII.20.3; XIX.P.3.2; see *i^n*

andes XII.Gl.21; see *andess*

andess XVIII.20.1; adv.; from the south,
northward;
andes XII.Gl.21;
In origin prefix *an* + *dess* 'south'; see
IX.G.45; Thurneysen G.305

and-so X.10.2; XI.11.3; see *i^n*

ane VIII.6.8; ptc. used after adverbs of place,
apparently meaningless

ane XII.12.11; then, next

aníar VII.5.1; IX.7.1; adv.; from the west,
eastward; in origin prefix *an* + *iar* 'west';
see *íarthar*; see IX.G.45; Thurneysen G.305

anim f.; blemish, defect; XVI.16.8;
is anim dún . . . = it is a pity for us . . . ;
see *do* (2); VIII.G.37.a

ani-sin XIV.Gl.27; see *intí*

Anlúain XVI.16.9; see *Anlúan*

155

Anlúan XVI.16.7; a hero of Connaught, by some versions the brother of Cet mac Mágach;
   Anlúain XVI.16.9; gen. sg.
anma XII.12.12; see *ainm*
anman VI.Gl.2; see *ainm*
a nnoíb-sa XII.Gl.19; see *noíb*
antuaid XII.Gl.21; adv.; from the north, southward; see *tuaid*; see IX.G.45; see Thurneysen G.305
anuas VIII.6.8; adv.; from above, downward; in origin prefix *an* + *uas*; see IX.G.45; see Thurneysen G.305
áo XVII.18.4; nt.; ear
apaide occurs only w. prep. *ar*;
   ar apaide VII.5.5; nevertheless
ar (1) prep. w. acc. and dat. leniting; before, in front of, for, in return for, on; often confused with *for*; IV.3.9; VI.4.6; VI.Gl.1; VIII.6.8; IX.Gl.10; X.Gl.14; XIV.14.4; XV.15.12; XVI.16.7; XIX.P.4.9;
   ara VI.4.10 + poss. pron. 3 sg. m.
   ara VII.5.4 + poss. pron. 3 pl.
   arar X.9.4; X.10.1 + poss. pron. 1 pl.
   armo XIII.13.10 + poss. pron. 1 sg.
   airi VII.Gl.5; V.3.10 + pron. 3 sg. nt.
   See VIII.G.38.c; Thurneysen G.497-99
ar (2) conjunction; for, because; VII.5.5; XII.12.12; XIV.14.9; XIV.Gl.26; XV.15.12; XVI.17.3; XVII.19.2; XVIII.20.7;
   air XIV.Gl.27; XV.Gl.32
   See IX.G.41.5; Thurneysen G.559-60
ar^n (3) poss. pron. 1 pl.; our; XII.Gl.21; XIII.Gl.23; XV.15.5
ár nt.; slaughter, destruction; VII.5.14; XVII.19.2
ara VI.4.10; VII.5.4; see *ar* (1)
ara m.; charioteer; XVII.19.4; XVIII.20.3
Arad IX.7.1; see *Araid*
ara·foím XV.Gl.32; see *ar·foím*
Araid a tribe of West Munster;
   Arad IX.7.1; gen. pl. in *Senláech Arad* 'Senláech of the Araid'
araile noun; substantival form of adj. *aile* 'other, the other'; IV.3.1; XVI.16.7; XVII.18.3;
   arailiu VII.5.10; acc. pl.
   al-aili XII.Gl.20; nom. pl.
arailiu VII.5.10; see *araile*

arar X.9.4; X.10.1; see *ar* (1)
archenae VIII.6.1; adv.; besides
ar·cichset XV.15.12; see *ar·cing*
ar·cing marches forward (to an encounter);
   ar·cichset XV.15.12; fut. 3 pl.
ar·foím receives, assumes;
   ar·roét XV.Gl.32; perf. 3 sg.
   ara·foím XV.Gl.32; pres. ind. 3 sg. deut. w. infixed pron. 3 sg.
   n·eroímer XV.Gl.32; pres. ind. pass. sg. nasalized because clause dependent on prep. + rel. ptc. (*hō*)
ar·gair forbids, prevents;
   aergarthe XII.Gl.19; past participle pass. used as a noun = what is forbidden
·árlastar IV.3.5; see *ad·gládathar*
armo XIII.13.10; see *ar* (1)
a-rrann VIII.6.8; XI.11.2; see *rannaid*
ar·róet XV.Gl.32; see *ar·foím*
as XV.Gl.32; see *is*
as·beir (-eper) says, speaks;
   as·biur-sa VI.Gl.1; pres. ind. 1 sg. deut. w. emph. suffix
   ·epur VI.Gl.2; pres. ind. 1 sg. proto.
   at·biri-siu V.3.15; pres. ind. 2 sg. deut. w. infixed pron. 3 sg. nt. (leniting) and emph. suffix
   at·beir XV.Gl.29; pres. ind. 3 sg. deut. w. infixed pron. 3 sg. nt.
   assid·beir XV.Gl.30; pres. ind. 3 sg. deut. w. infixed pron. 3 sg. nt.
   as·beir VIII.Gl.9; pres. ind. 3 sg. deut. rel.
   ·epir XV.Gl.29; pres. ind. 3 sg. proto.
   ·eperr XIII.Gl.23; pres. ind. pass. sg. proto.
   as·berat XV.Gl.32; XVII.19.5; pres. ind. 3 pl.
   as·berat-som XV.Gl.31; XVII.19.3; pres. ind. 3 pl. deut. + emph. suffix
   n-epred XII.Gl.19; impf. 3 sg. proto. nasalized by *co^n* (4)
   as·bert IV.3.9; XV.15.9; pret. 3 sg. deut.
   as·robrad XIII.Gl.23; ro-pret. pass. sg.
   ·eper XII.Gl.19; pres. subj. 1 sg. proto.
   n·érbrat XVIII.20.6; pres. subj. 3 pl. w. infixed *ro* nasalized by *co^n* (4)
   at·bertha V.3.10; past subj. 2 sg. w. infixed pron. 3 sg. nt.
as·berat XV.Gl.32; XVII.19.5; see *as·beir*

as·berat-som xv.Gl.31; xvii.19.3; see as·beir
as·bert iv.3.9; xv.15.9; see as·beir
as·biur-sa vi.Gl.1; see as·beir
ascada vi.4.6; vi.4.11; see ascaid
ascaid f.; gift, present;
  ascada vi.4.6; nom. pl.
  ascada vi.4.11; acc. pl.
asdo xi.11.11; xi.11.13; see a (2)
as·érig arises;
  as·reracht xiii.Gl.22; ro-pret. 3 sg.
asin xviii.20.2; see a (2)
asind viii.6.8; see a (2)
as·luí (·élai) escapes;
  at·rulais x.9.9; ro-pret. 2 sg. w. meaning
  less infixed pron. 3 sg. nt.
asmo vi.4.9; xi.11.10; see a (2)
asnaib xiv.Gl.28; see a (2)
as·n·da·fíadam-ni xv.Gl.31; see ad·fet
as·reracht xiii.Gl.22; see as·érig
as·robrad xiii.Gl.23; see as·beir
assa xvi.16.9; xvii.18.6; see a (2)
ass-id·beir xv.Gl.30; see as-beir
assind x.10.1; xvii.18.7; see a (2)
as·soí turns away; iv.3.8
ast xii.12.5; see a (2)
at vii.Gl.6; xv.15.10; xvi.16.6; see is
a·tá subst. vb.; is, exists; the preverb a(d) is
deleted when another prefix is added or
when pronouns are affixed;
  attó vii.Gl.4; pres. ind. 1 sg.
  atai xiii.13.13; pres. ind. 2 sg.
  i-tai iv.3.2; pres. ind. 2 sg. prefixed by
  prep. i^n in rel. construction = in which
  you are
  cid-no-tai iv.3.4; pres. ind. 2 sg. prefixed
  by no followed by nasalization (not
  shown) to indicate rel. force; idiomatic
  usage = what is the matter with you?
  a-tá iv.3.3; xiv.Gl.27; xvi.16.9; xvii.19.5;
  pres. ind. 3 sg.
  cid diatá x.10.4; pres. ind. 3 sg. cid +
  prep. de + rel. ptc. + pres. ind. 3 sg.; lit. as
  a consequence of what is...? why is...?
  táthut v.3.14; pres. ind. 3 sg. w. suffixed
  pron. 2 sg. = there is to you, you (sg.)
  have; note absence of preverb a
  ataat viii.6.4; pres. ind. 3 pl.; atát
  viii.6.11
  i-taat viii.6.8; pres. ind. 3 pl. prefixed by

prep. i^n w. rel. force = in which they are
biit xii.Gl.20; 3 pl. consuetudinal pres.
fil form used after neg. and in rel. constructions; used impersonally w. acc. to
indicate its sub.
  nad·fil xvi.16.8; preceded by form of
  neg. participle used in rel. clauses
  fuil xx.P.9.2; rel.
  ni-fuilet xii.12.5; later form—in classical
  OIr. fil had a 3 sg. form only; here a 3 pl.
  ending added = these are not
biaid iii.2.4; fut. 3 sg. (abs.?)
  ros-bía vi.4.6; vi.4.11; 3 sg. fut. (bia) w.
  infixed pron. 3 pl. (-s-) in dat. relation;
  ptc. ro used to support infixed pron. (always in 2nd position in verbal complex) =
  there will be to them = they will have
  ni-m-bia x.Gl.14; 3 sg. fut. w. infixed
  pron. 1 sg. in dat. relation = there will not
  be to me = I shall not have
  rot-bia xii.12.8; xiii.13.2; xiv.14.2; fut.
  3 sg. w. infixed pron. 2 sg. (-t-) in dat. relation; ptc. ro used to support infixed
  pron. = there will be to you = you will
  have
boí i.1a.1; i.1a.2; pret. 3 sg.
  co·mboí x.10.12; pret. 3 sg. nasalized by
  conjunction co^n (4)
  boithi iv.3.7; pret. 3 sg. w. suffixed pron.
  3 sg. dat. = there was to him = he had;
  perhaps the pret. should be interpreted as
  a modal pret. = he would have
  bátar vii.5.9; pret. 3 pl.
  co·mbátar vii.5.3; xvii.18.4; pret. 3 pl.
  preceded by conjunction co^n (4)
  ro-bá-sa vi.4.5; perf. pret. 1 sg. deut.
  (+ emph. suffix)
  nad-raba xvi.16.5; perf. pret. 1 sg. proto.
  prefixed by neg. participle used in rel.
  clauses
  ro-boí ii.1b.8; vii.5.11; xvi.17.3;
  xvii.18.4; xvii.18.6; perf. pret. 3 sg. deut.
  co·rrabae xi.11.10; co·rrabe iv.3.1; perf.
  pret. 3 sg. proto. preceded by and nasalized by conjunction co^n (4)
beith v.3.13; pres. subj. 3 sg.
  no-beth xvi.16.7; past subj. 3 sg.
bith iv.3.8; vn. (f.)
  buith xiv.Gl.28; vn.

cáit XX.P.9.2; where is
See *II.G.9; VII.G.33; Thurneysen G.475–83*
ataat VIII.6.4; see *a·tá*
ataí XIII.13.13; see *a·tá*
a·taibred II.1b.11; see *a^n* (6); see *do·beir*
atan·ebla V.3.13; see *ad·aig*
atát VIII.6.11; see *a·tá*
at·bail dies; (*as·bail* w. a petrified infixed
pron. 3 sg. nt.);
   ·epled V.3.10; past subj. 3 sg. proto.
at·beir XV.Gl.29; see *as·beir*
at·bertha V.3.10; see *as·beir*
at·biri-siu V.3.15; see *as·beir*
at·chí X.9.3; see *ad·cí*
at·chondarc-sa XI.11.5; see *ad·cí*
áth m.; ford; frequent in place-names;
XVIII.20.1; XVIII.20.2; XVIII.20.8
athair m.; father;
   athair-sium X.10.4; dat. sg. + emph. suffix, dat. sg.
   ath(a)ir XII.12.12; XV.Gl.32; dat. sg.
   athar XV.Gl.32; gen. sg.
Athar XV.Gl.32; see *athair*
Áth Chinn Chon XVIII.20.2; see *Áth Cinn Chon*
Áth Cinn Chon a ford in Co. West Meath,
lit. ford of the dog's head;
   Áth Chinn Chon XVIII.20.2; dat.sg. after
prep. *oc*; hence lenition of *Cinn* (after
dat. sg. *Áth*)
athesc nt.; account, report;
   n-athesca III.2.2; acc. pl. nasalized by preceding poss. pron. 3 pl.
athesca III.2.2; see *athesc*
athir XV.Gl.32; see *athair*
Áth Lúain XVIII.20.8; a ford on the Shannon
near the modern town of Athlone
Áth Mac Lugnai XVIII.20.1; a ford in Co. Of-
faly
Áth Midbine XVIII.20.1; a ford on the river
Liffey
atot·chiat XI.11.12; see *ad·cí*
atot·chomnaic XIV.14.10; see *ad·cumaing*
at·racht VI.4.1; see *at·raig*
at·ragat XVII.18.3; see *at·raig*
at·raig rises; (*as·raig* w. infixed pron. that
originally agreed in person and num. w. the

sub.; in texts as late as SMMD, this pron. has
been petrified as 3 sg. nt.);
   at·ragat XVII.18.3; pres. ind. 3 pl. deut.
   at·racht VI.4.1; pret. 3 sg. deut.
atrefea XI.Gl.16; see *ad·treba*
at·rulais X.9.9; see *as·luí*
attó VII.Gl.4; see *a·tá*

B

ba I.1a.4; V.3.11; IX.7.1; IX.7.2; X.Gl.15;
XII.12.12; XVII.18.2; XVIII.20.7; see *is*
bachlach m.; herdsman, churl, wretch;
   mbachlach XII.12.11; gen. pl. nasalized
by preceding art. gen. pl.
bad VI.4.2; VI.4.10; see *is*
báire gen. sg. in phrase: *cenn a báiri* X.9.6;
= his destination, his goal, lit. end of the
hunting match
baisted m.; baptism, baptizing;
   baistiud XII.12.12; dat. sg.
baistiud XII.12.12; see *baisted*
bale m.; place;
   bale i^n VIII.6.8 = there where . . .
bannae f.; drop, small particle;
   bannai XVI.17.6
bárach VIII.6.4; tomorrow; see *i mbárach*
bas III.2.3; V.3.12; see *is*
bás nt. *o*-stem; death;
   mbás IX.Gl.10; nasalized by preceding nt.
art. nom. sg.
   bás IX.Gl.10; acc. sg.
bátar VII.5.9; XVII.18.4; see *a·tá*
bec(c) adj.; little, small; VII.5.8; XVII.18.2;
   biuc X.9.5; dat. sg. used adverbially = a
little, a little while
   bic XIII.13.5 = *biuc*
   laigiu XV.Gl.32; comp.; less
béim IX.7.4; see *benaid*
beith V.3.13; see *a·tá*
bél m.; 'lip,' in pl. 'mouth';
   béolu XVI.16.9; acc. pl.
   béolo XVI.17.5; acc. pl.
   bélaib X.9.4; X.10.1; dat. pl.; w. prep. *ar*:
ar bélaib + gen. = in the presence of; *arár*
mbélaib-ni X.9.4, X.10.1 = in our presence; *ar* + poss. pron. 1 pl. + *bélaib* +
emph. suffix 1 pl.
béla XI.Gl.18; see *biáil*

bélaib x.9.4; x.10.1; see *bél*

Beluch Sen-Roírenn XVIII.20.1; a pass in Co. Kildare (*belach* = path, road, pass)

ben f.; woman, wife;
ben IV.3.2; IV.3.6; IV.3.8; v.3.10; v.3.14; nom. sg.
mnaí v.3.10; acc. sg.
mná IV.3.9; gen. sg.
mná XVIII.20.6; nom. pl.
mnáib IV.3.9; dat. pl.

benaid strikes, slays, cuts (off);
béim IX.7.4; vn. dat. sg.

béolo XVI.17.5; see *bél*

béolu XVI.16.9; see *bél*

·bered II.1b.12; see *berid*

berid (·**beir**) bears, carries off, takes away, obtains;
·berir XII.Gl.20; pres. ind. pass. sg.;
berir . . . fri = reference is made to . . .
·bered II.1b.12; impf. 3 sg. conj.
bértait VI.4.6; VI.4.11; fut. 3 pl. abs. w. meaningless suffixed pron. 3 sg. nt.
·mbert x.10.12; XI.11.11; pret. 3 sg. conj. nasalized by *con* (4)
Perf. forms supplied by ro·ucc (·rucc)
·ruc XII.12.12; *ro*-pret. 3 sg. proto.
·rucad XIII.13.13; *ro*-pret. pass. sg. proto. (in sense 'was born')
·ructha I.1a.7; III.2.1; *ro*-pret. pass. pl. proto.
berthair v.3.12; pres. subj. pass. sg. abs.
brith XVIII.20.6; vn. f.

berna f.; gap, breach;
mbernai XIII.13.10; dat. sg. nasalized by preceding prep. *in*

bert x.10.12; see *berid*

bertaigidir shakes, brandishes;
no-mbertaigedar VI.4.1; pres. ind. 3 sg. conj. w. infixed pron. 3 sg. m. w. reflexive force = he exults
nos-mbertaigedar xv.15.4; pres. ind. 3 sg. conj. w. infixed pron. 3 sg. f.
rond-mbertaigestar xv.15.1; *ro*-pret. 3 sg. conj. w. infixed nasalization (rel.) and infixed pron. 3 sg. m. reflexive

bértait VI.4.6; VI.4.11; see *berid*

berthair v.3.12; see *berid*

bés m.; custom; x.9.6; x.Gl.15; in phrase *is*

bés dúib-si = it is customary among you; see VIII.G.37.a

betha XIX.P.4.3; see *bith*

bethid IX.Gl.10; see *bethu*

bethu m.; life;
bethid IX.Gl.10; acc. sg.
bethid IX.Gl.10; dat. sg.

beus XI.11.1; XII.12.1; XII.12.7; XIII.13.1; XIV.14.1; still, yet; *in comram beus* = on with the contest

bfiad xx.P.6.8; see *fíad*

bfirteititt xx.P.6.8; see *fírteitt*

biad nt.; food; III.2.1; IV.3.3; VI.4.6; nom. sg.; IV.3.1; acc. sg.;
mbiad III.2.1; VIII.6.1; nasalized by poss. pron. 3 pl.
biada x.Gl.13; acc. pl.

biada x.Gl.13; see *biad*

biaid III.2.4; see *a·tá*

biáil m.; axe;
béla XI.Gl.18; gen. sg.

bíathad VII.5.13; see *biathaid*

bíathaid (·**bíatha**) feeds, nourishes, supports;
no·bíata VII.5.14; impf. pass. sg.
bíathad VII.5.13; vn. m. dat. sg.

bic XIII.13.5; see *bec(c)*

bid v.3.11; XI.Gl.16; xv.15.12; see *is*

biit XII.Gl.20; see *a·tá*

Bile a place in Co. West Meath; see also *robilib* XIX.P.3.15;
Biliu XVIII.20.2; dat. sg.

Biliu XVIII.20.2; see *Bile*

binn xx.P.9.4; sweet, melodious

bith m.; world;
betha XIX.P.4.3; gen. sg.

bith IV.3.8; see *a·tá*

biuc x.9.5; see *bec(c)*

blái XIX.P.4.3; f.; field, plain

blíadain f.; year;
blíadna XVIII.20.8; gen. sg.
bliadna III.2.3; gen. sg.
bliadan VII.5.11; gen. pl.
mbliadan VII.5.13; gen. pl. nasalized by preceding num. *secht*
bliadan VII.5.11; see *blíadain*

blíadna III.2.3; XVIII.20.8; see *blíadain*

bó f.; cow;
bó XI.11.7; gen. pl.

búaib v.3.12; dat. pl.

boc x.Gl.15; billy goat

boc xx.P.9.4; soft, tender

boccóit f.; small shield, buckler;
    boccótib xvi.17.3; dat. pl.

boccótib xvi.17.3; see *boccóit*

boí i.1a.1; i.1a.2; see *a·tá*

boíthi iv.3.7; see *a·tá*

bráen xx.P.8.3; m.; drop, rain, shower

brágae m.; neck, throat;
    brágit xiv.14.9; acc. sg.
    brágat xiv.14.9; gen. sg.
    brágit xvii.18.1; dat. sg.

brágat xiv.14.9; see *brágae*

brágit xiv.14.9; xvii.18.1; see *brágae*

bráth doom, judgment;
    brátha xii.Gl.20; gen. sg. in phrase *lá brátha* = Doomsday

brátha xii.Gl.20; see *bráth*

bráthair ix.7.2; m.; brother

brecca xix.P.3.4; nom. pl. of adj. *brecc* 'speckled, dappled, freckled'

Bréfne a district in the northwest of the country, roughly the modern counties of Cavan and Leitrim
    Bréfni ii.1b.8; dat. sg.

Bréfni ii.1b.8; see *Bréfne*

Bricne mac Carbaid viii.6.8; more usually Bricriu mac Carbaid; a nobleman of Ulster, nicknamed *Nemthenga* (Poison-tongue) since he made a pastime of causing strife and dissension among friends. In this tale it is he who suggests that the warriors fight for the privilege of carving the pig. In another tale *Fled Bricrend* 'The Feast of Bricriu' he appears, like Mac Dathó, to represent the lord of the otherworld feast.

brith xviii.20.6; see *berid*

broind xix.P.3.4; see *brú*

brónaig xix.P.4.4; nom. pl. *brónach* (adj.); sad, sorrowful

brot m.; goad, particularly for driving cattle;
    mbrot xv.15.12; gen. pl. nasalized by preceding gen. pl.

brú f.; belly;
    broind xix.P.3.4; dat. sg.
    a broind lit. out of the belly

bruden f.; hostel, large banqueting hall;
ii.1b.8;

mbrudin i.1a.7; acc. sg. nasalizing by preceding acc. sg. art.

mbruidin vii.5.7; acc. sg.

bruidne vii.5.3; gen. sg.

bruidin ii.1b.9; dat. sg.

bruidin ii.1b.9; see *bruden*

bruidne vii.5.3; see *bruden*

bruinne f.; breast;
    bruinni xvi.16.9; acc. sg.

bruinni xvi.16.9; see *bruinne*

búaib v.3.12; see *bó*

búaid ix.Gl.12; nt.; victory

buide xx.P.9.1; f.; good will, satisfaction, favor, thanks;
    ní buide frit xiv.14.5; probably a shortened version of *ní-tuilli buide frit* = I do not court your favor, I have no respect for you

buidech adj.; satisfied, content;
    buidig vi.4.7; m. nom. pl.

buidig vi.4.7; see *buidech*

buille f.; stroke, blow; xvii.18.4;
    builli viii.6.9; acc. sg.

builli viii.6.9; see *buille*

buith xiv.Gl.28; see *a·tá*

C

cach (cech) adj.; every, each;
    cach oín every single
    cech vii.5.8; x.9.6; xvi.16.5; xix.P.3.2
    cach ii.1b.10; xvi.16.5; xix.P.4.4
    gach xix.P.4.4
    cecha xviii.20.6; gen. sg. f.

cách m.; everyone; viii.6.9; viii.Gl.9; x.10.3; x.10.9; xi.11.4; xii.12.10; xiii.13.4; xiii.13.8; xiv.14.4; xvii.18.3; xvii.18.5

caill f.; wood, forest;
    caille xx.P.7.4; gen. sg.; xx.P.10.4; dat. sg.

caín adj.; fine, beautiful, good; xv.15.11; often prefixed to nouns to form compd.; see *caínmessa*

caínmessa xix.P.3.14; gen. sg. of *caínmess*; compd. of *caín* 'fine, good, beautiful' + *mess* 'tree-fruit, acorns'

cairm (cia + airm) i^n = where; xi.11.6;
    cairm indom·acca where did you see me? xi.11.6

cáit xx.P.9.2; see *a·tá*

cani XV.Gl.29; interrog. ptc. expecting an affirm. answer; see Thurneysen G.292

cara m.; friend;
  charait III.2.4; dat. sg. (lenited by prep. *do = di*)
  carat VII.5.9; gen. pl.

carat VII.5.9; see *cara*

carnáil f.; heap (of corpses); XVII.18.4

carpat m.; chariot; III.2.3; x.9.9; XVIII.20.3;
  charpait XVII.19.3; XVII.19.4; gen. sg.
  charput XVIII.20.2; dat. sg.

cath m.; battle, contention;
  chath v.3.11; nom. sg. (lenited by poss. pron. 3 sg. m.)
  cath XVII.18.8; nom. sg.

cath buadach adj.; victorious in battle;
  cath buadaig XV.15.9; gen. sg. m.

cath buadaig XV.15.9; see *cath buadach*

cathir nt.; city;
  cathraig XII.Gl.21; dat. sg.

cathraig XII.Gl.21; see *cathir*

cech VII.5.8; x.9.6; XVI.16.5; XIX.P.3.2; see *cach*

cecha XVIII.20.6; see *cach*

ceilid hides, conceals;
  chél XX.P.8.2; 1 sg. fut. conj.

céiliu IV.3.8; see *céle*

céle (céile) m.; companion, fellow, mate, spouse, the other of two;
  ché(i)li VIII.6.9; XVII.18.5; gen. sg. (obj. of a vn.) lenited by preceding poss. pron. 3 sg. m.
  céiliu IV.3.8; dat. sg.

Cell Dara Kildare;
  Cill nDara XVIII.20.1; acc. sg. after prep. *sech*; hence nasalization of *Dara* (after acc. sg. *Cill*)

Celtchair (mac Uithechair) a champion of Ulster, renowned for his great size; IX.7.4; XIII.13.4;
  a Cheltchair XIII.13.5; XIII.13.6; voc. sg.

cen prep. + acc. leniting; without; see Thurneysen G.273, 501; functions as neg. marker when governs a vn.; see Thurneysen G.545; IV.3.1; IV.3.8; XVI.16.5; XX.P.8.3; XX.P.8.4;
  nad·raba cen guin XVI.16.5; lit. that I was not without killing . . . = that I killed . . .
  cena XVIII.20.7 + pron. 3 sg. nt.; lit. without it = otherwise; *ní·laimtis cena*

XVIII.20.7 = they did not dare (do) otherwise; see *ro·laimethar*

cén XX.P.8.4; myself; see *fadéin*

cena XVIII.20.7; see *cen*

cenco^n conjunction; though . . . not; for older *ceni*; IV.3.3; IV.3.7

cendach XX.P.6.4; see *luind cendach*

cenél X.Gl.13; race, people, tribe

cenmothá prep. + acc.; besides; III.2.3; VIII.6.1; in origin a combination form of the prep. *cen* 'without' prefixed to the subst. vb. *a·ta*; the verbal element was originally inflected for tense and num.

cenn nt.; head, end; VII.5.4; VII.5.13; x.9.6; X.Gl.15; XVI.17.5; XVIII.20.2;
  chenn VI.4.6; VI.4.10; IX.7.4; XI.11.11; XII.12.5; XIII.13.10; XIV.14.9; XVI.16.5; XVII.19.4; XVIII.20.3
  chinn XVI.16.9; gen. sg. (lenited by preceding vn. in dat. sg.)
  chiunn XI.11.11; dat. sg. (lenited by poss pron.)
  chinn XI.11.13; XV.15.4; dat. sg. (lenited by poss. pron.)
  cinn III.2.3; dat. sg. of time = at the end of . . .
  ar chenn VI.4.6; VI.4.10; acc. sg. after prep. *ar* used idiomatically;
    téit ar chenn + gen. (or poss. pron. if obj. is pronominal) = goes to meet, goes to fetch
  ara cenn VII.5.4 = to meet them (w. poss. pron. 3 pl. *a*)
  armo chenn-sa XIII.13.10 = to meet me (w. poss. pron. 1 sg. *mo*)
  fort chenn XIV.14.9; lit. on your head; probably = on your behalf; prep. *for* + *t* (poss. pron. 2 sg. leniting) + *cenn*

cennaige m.; merchant; XIV.Gl.28; gen. sg.

cennaigi XIV.Gl.28; see *cennaige*

cennide f.; headgear, helmet;
  cennidi XV.15.4; acc. sg.

cennidi XV.15.4; see *cennide*

cepóc f.; some type of choral song, possibly erotic;
  chepóce XVIII.20.6; gen. sg. (obj. of a vn.)

cerba XX.P.7.5; conj. of *cerbaid* 'cut, diminish'

cét (1) hundred; III.2.3; VII.5.11

cét (2) prefixed to nouns in compounds 'first';

   cétgabáil II.1b.11; see *gabaid*

   céttadall II.1b.12; see *do·aidlea*

   cét-meic XII.12.5; see *mac*

   cét-gaisciud XIV.14.7; see *gaisced*

   fo chét-oír XIII.13.5; see *úar*

   hi cét-oír III.2.3; see *úar*

Cet (mac Mágach) IX.8.1; X.9.4; X.9.6; X.10.1; X.10.2; X.10.4; X.10.6; XI.11.1; XI.11.3; XI.11.5; XII.12.1; XII.12.3; XII.12.4; XII.12.7; XII.12.9; XII.12.11; XIII.13.1; XIII.13.3; XIII.13.5; XIV.14.1; XIV.14.3; XIV.14.6; XV.15.7; XV.15.9; XV.15.11; XVI.16.2; XVI.16.3; XVI.16.6;

   mac Mágach V.3.13

   Chet XVI.16.9; dat. sg. lenited by prep. *do*

   a Cheit XV.15.8; XVI.16.4; voc. sg.

céta first; adverbial, prefixed to verbs;

   céta-tudchad-so XIV.14.7 = you came first; see *do·tét*

céta-tudchad-so XIV.14.7; see *do·tét* and *céta*

cétgabáil II.1b.11; see *cét* (2) and *gaibid*

cethorca forty; VIII.6.1

cétna adj.; same; III.2.4; X.10.12; XI.11.1;

   chétna I.1a.6; gen. sg. m. (lenited by preceding gen. sg. m.)

cét-oír III.2.3; see *úar* and *cét*

cétomus adv.; first; XI.11.2

charait III.2.4; see *cara*

charpait XVII.19.3; XVII.19.4; see *carpat*

charput XVIII.20.2; see *carpat*

chath V.3.11; see *cath*

Cheit XV.15.8; XVI.16.4; see *Cet mac Mágach*

chél XX.P.8.2; see *ceilid*

ché(i)li VIII.6.9; XVII.18.5; see *céle*

chenn VI.4.6; VI.4.10; IX.7.4; XI.11.11; XII.12.5; XIII.13.10; XIV.14.9; XVI.16.5; XVII.19.4; XVIII.20.3; see *cenn*

chepóce XVIII.20.6; see *cepóc*

Chet XVI.16.9; see *Cet mac Mágach*

chétgaisciud XIV.14.7; see *cét* (2) and *gaisced*

chétmeic XII.12.5; see *cét* (2) and *mac(c)*

chétna I.1a.6; see *cétna*

chét-óir XIII.13.5; see *úar* and *cét*

chéttadall II.1b.12; see *cét* (2) and *do·aidlea*

chinad XX.P.8.2; see *cin*

chinn XI.11.3; XV.15.4; XVI.16.9; see *cenn*

chiunn XI.11.11; see *cenn*

chloíndíbircthib XVI.17.3; dat. pl. (after prep. *do*) of a compd. of *cloín* 'slanting, evil' and *díburcud* 'shooting, darting'; vn. of *do·bidci* 'pelts, shoots' = evil pelting

chlúasaib IX.Gl.11; see *clúas*

chnámchomaig XIX.P.4.8; compd. of *cnám*: m.; bone; and *comach*: vn.; breaking, pounding

chocrích XIV.14.8; see *cocrích*

choíced II.1b.8; see *coíced*

choimded XIV.Gl.28; see *coimdiu*

chois XVII.18.1; see *cos*

cholainn XVII.19.4; see *colainn*

chomairle V.3.15; see *comairle*

chomalnad IX.Gl.12; see *comalnaithir*

chommaín III.2.3; see *commaín*

chomméit III.2.4; see *comméit*

chomram X.10.13; XII.12.11; XVI.17.1; see *comram*

chomramaib VIII.6.8; see *comram*

chomrame XVI.16.3; see *comram*

chon I.1a.4; I.1a.5; I.1a.6; III.2.3; VI.4.6; XVII.19.5; XVIII.20.2; see *cú*

Chonchobair XVIII.20.4; see *Conchobar*

Chonchobor V.3.12; see *Conchobar*

Chonchobuir VIII.6.7; IX.7.1; see *Conchobar*

Chonchobur III.2.4; VI.4.9; see *Conchobar*

chotlud IV.3.8; see *con·tuili*

chotulta IV.3.7; see *con·tuili*

chriss XVI.16.9; see *criss*

Chríst VII.5.11; XV.Gl.31; see *Críst*

Chrísst XV.Gl.31; see *Críst*

chrú XVII.18.4; see *crú*

chúairt XVI.17.3; see *cúairt*

chungid I.1a.5; I.1a.6; III.2.3; III.2.4; XVI.16.3; see *con·dieg*

chuntabairt VI.4.9; see *cuntabart*

cía (1) interrog. pron.; who?, what?; V.3.14; V.3.15; XI.11.3; XII.12.9; XIII.13.3; XV.15.6; XVII.19.1; nom. sg. m. and f.; who?;

   cía lassa XIX.P.1.2; with whom

   cid IV.3.4; VIII.Gl.9; X.10.5; X.10.13; XII.12.11; XII.12.13; XIII.13.14; XVI.16.2; nt. nom. acc.; what?

   cid·dia X.10.4; XIII.Gl.22; see *di*; lit. from what is? = whence? why?

cía indas VIII.6.8; what manner of . . . ? how?; see *indas*

cindas VIII.6.7; IX.7.4; = *cía indas*

coich X.10.2; originally gen. sg. of *cía* = whose?, but by the time of SMMD gen. force probably lost = who?

cuich XIV.14.3; *coich*

See *VII.G.32 and Thurneysen G.286*

cía (2) conjunction; though, although; XI.Gl.17;

cid v.3.10; = *cía* + past subj. 3 sg. enclitic form of *is* = though it would be . . . ; see *is*

cid XII.Gl.19; XIX.P.2.2; = *cía* + pres. subj. 3 sg. enclitic form of *is* = though it be; see *is*

See *IX.G.41.2 and Thurneysen G.561-62*

cích f.; breast; XV.15.9

cid (1) IV.3.4; VIII.Gl.9; X.10.4; X.10.5; X.10.13; XII.12.11; XII.12.13; XIII.13.14; XIII.Gl.22; XVI.16.2; see *cía* (1)

cid (2) v.3.10; XII.Gl.19; XIX.P.2.2; see *cía* (2)

Cill nDara XVIII.20.1; see *Cell Dara*

cimbid m.; captive, prisoner; VII.Gl.5

cin m.; fault, sin;

chinad XX.P.8.2; pl.

cindas VIII.6.7; IX.7.4; see *cía* (1) and *indas*

cinn III.2.3; see *cenn*

claideb m. *o*-stem; sword;

claidiub XII.12.12; dat. sg.

claidiub XII.12.12; see *claideb*

clinn XX.P.9.3; see *clinnid*

clinnid rings, sounds;

clinn XX.P.9.3; 3 sg. pres. conj.

clithach sheltering, protective;

clithaige XX.P.7.4; gen. sg.

clithar XX.P.10.4; sheltering, protective

cloc XX.P.9.3; m.; bell

clúas f.; ear;

chluasaib IX.Gl.11; dat. pl. lenited by preceding prep. *huá (ó)*

cluinit XX.P.6.5; see *ro·cluinethar*

clúm XX.P.7.4; f.; down, feathers, hair

cnoí XIX.P.3.14; nom. pl. *cnó* 'nut'

co (1) prep. w. acc.; to, as far as, till; IV.3.1; VI.4.8; VII.5.13; XIII.13.6; XVIII.20.6;

coa IV.3.7; + poss. pron. 3 sg. m.

cucum XII.12.11; + pron. 1 sg.

cucum-sa XII.12.13; XIII.13.14; + pron.

1 sg. + emph. suffix 1 sg.

cuccum-sa XVI.16.3; + pron. 1 sg. + emph. suffix 1 sg.

cucut-su XIII.13.12; + pron. 2 sg. + emph. suffix 2 sg.

cuci-sium I.1a.7; III.2.1; + pron. 3 sg. + emph. suffix 3 sg.

cucce XVI.16.2; + pron. 3 sg. f.

cucainni X.9.6; XIV.14.7; + pron. 1 pl. + emph. suffix 1 pl.

See *Thurneysen G.501-02*

co (2) prefixed to adjectives to form adverbs;

co sochruid VI.4.6

co h-uallach VI.4.6

See *Thurneysen G.239-40*

co^n (3) prep. + dat. nasalizing; with; IV.3.8; X.Gl.15; XI.11.12; XII.12.12; XIII.13.13; XVIII.20.8;

cusna XII.12.11 + art. pl.

See *Thurneysen G.502-04*

co^n (4) conjunction;

(a) w. the ind. = so that, until; often simply = 'and'; IV.3.1; VI.4.5; IX.8.1; X.10.12; XI.11.11; XII.12.12; XIII.13.12; XIV.14.9; XIV.14.10; XV.15.1; XVI.16.9; XVI.17.5; XVI.17.6; XVII.18.3; XVII.18.4; XVII.18.5; XVII.19.4; XVIII.20.3;

(b) w. *ro*-subj. = in order that; VII.5.14; X.9.5; XVII.19.1; XVIII.20.6;

conna· XII.12.12; XIV.14.9; + neg. preverb

cona· XVI.17.6; + neg. preverb

corro· XVII.19.4; + perf. ptc. *ro*

corot· X.9.5; + perf. ptc. *ro* + infixed pron. 2 sg.

conid XIV.14.10; + pres. ind. 3 sg. enclitic form of *is* = so that it is . . .

combo XVII.18.4; + pret. 3 sg. *is*

See *IX.G.41.4 and Thurneysen G.554-55*

'co IV.3.1; see *oc*

co-a IV.3.7; see *co* (1)

cocad m.; war; VII.5.11

cocrích f.; boundary, borderland, no man's land; VIII.6.11; X.9.7;

chocrích XIV.14.8; dat. sg. lenited by art. dat. sg.

coíca m.; fifty; VII.5.8

coíced (a) adj.; fifth, one of five;

choíced II.1b.8; lenited by art. f. nom.

sg.; *in choiced bruden* = one of the five
hostels
(b) nt.; province, one of the five provinces of Ireland; VII.5.3; XIV.14.11
coich X.10.2; see *cía* (1)
coimdiu m.; Lord;
choimded XIV.Gl.28; gen. sg. (obj. of vn.)
lenited by preceding gen. sg. m. of art.
coin VI.4.5; VI.4.9; XIX.P.4.8; see *cú*
coiri II.1b.10; II.1b.11; see *core*
colainn f.; body;
cholainn XVII.19.4; lenited by poss. pron.
3 sg. m.
coll m.; hazel;
cuill XIX.P.3.14; XIX.P.3.15; gen. sg.
co·lluid XI.11.11; see *téit*
comairle f.; counsel, advice;
chomairle V.3.15; lenited by art. nom.
sg. f.; see *con·airlethar*
comalnaithir fulfills;
comalnad vn.
chomalnad IX.Gl.12; vn. lenited by preceding poss. pron. 3 sg., obj. of the vn.
comard adj.; equally high; XVII.18.4; compd.
of *com* (equative prefix) + *ard* (high);
comard ra as high as
co·mbátar VII.5.3; XVII.18.4; see *a·tá*
co·mbert X.10.12; XI.11.11; see *co^n* and
berid
combo XVII.18.4; see *is*
co·mboi X.10.12; see *a·tá*
commaín f.; equivalent;
chommaín III.2.3; lenited by poss. pron.
3 sg.
comméit f.; equal amount; *com* (equative
prefix) + *méit* = size, amount;
a chomméit cétna an equal amount;
III.2.4
commus m.; comparison, judgment as equal;
comsa XV.15.10; gen. sg.; predicative gen.
at comsa frim you are of comparison
with me = you are a match for me
comram m.; fight, contest, combat; XI.11.1;
XII.12.1; XII.12.7; XIII.13.1; XIV.14.1;
XVI.16.7;
chomrame XVI.16.3; gen. sg.
comrama IX.8.3; gen. sg.
chomram X.10.13; XII.12.11; XVI.17.1;

dat. sg.
chomramaib VIII.6.8; dat. pl.
oínchomram XVI.16.4; single combat; see
oín
comrama IX.8.3; see *comram*
comsa XV.15.10; see *commus*
con XVII.19.1; see *cú*
cona XVI.17.6; see *co^n* (4)
co-n-accatar XV.15.1; see *ad·cí*
con·airlethar takes counsel, deliberates;
no-chomairled IV.3.7; past subj. 3 sg. rel.
comairle V.3.15; vn.; counsel, advice
Conall (Cernach mac Findchoíme) XV.15.1;
XV.15.3; XV.15.5; XV.15.8; XV.15.9;
XV.15.11; XV.15.12; XVI.16.1; XVI.16.3;
XVI.16.4; XVI.16.9; XVI.16.10; XVI.17.1;
XVI.17.4; one of the most prominent of the
warriors of Ulster; his name is thought to be
linked with that of the Gaulish god *Cernunnos*—a horned god associated with fertility
and herding;
mac Findchoíme XV.15.10
con·ceil hides, conceals;
con·celar IV.3.9; pres. ind. pass. sg.
con·celar IV.3.9; see *con·ceil*
Conchobair I.1a.6; XVIII.20.3; XVIII.20.8;
see *Conchobar*
Conchobar legendary king of Ulster; III.2.4;
VIII.6.5; VIII.6.11; X.9.3; XV.15.4; XV.15.7;
XVIII.20.5; XVIII.20.7;
Conchobair I.1a.6; XVIII.20.3; XVIII.20.8;
gen. sg.
Chonchobur III.2.4; VI.4.9; dat. sg. lenited by preceding prep.
Chonchobor V.3.12; dat. sg. lenited by
preceding prep. *do*
Chonchobuir VIII.6.7; IX.7.1; voc. sg.
Chonchobair XVIII.20.4; voc. sg.
co·ndechaid XIII.13.12; see *téit*
con·dieg (·cuindig) asks for, requests;
cungid vn.
chungid I.1a.5; I.1a.6; III.2.3; III.2.4;
XVI.16.3; vn. lenited in I.1a.5, I.1a.6, and
III.2.4 by poss. pron. 3 sg. obj. of the vn.;
lenited in III.2.3 and XVI.16.3 by preceding prep. *do*
co·n-epred XII.Gl.19; see *as·beir*
co·n-érbrat XVIII.20.6; see *as·beir*

Conganchness mac Dedad IX.7.4; a warrior of the West Munster tribe of the Érainn, also known as *Cland Dedad* (*cland* = family, children);

    Congan-chness = horn-skin

conid XIV.14.10; see *co^n* (4) and *is*

conna XII.12.12; XIV.14.9; see *co^n* (4)

Connacht III.2.3; VI.4.4; XVII.19.2; see *Connachta*

Connachta III.2.3; VII.5.7; XVI.17.2; XVII.18.2; XVII.19.2; always pl.;

    (a) the men of Connaught

    (b) Connaught

    Connacht III.2.3; VI.4.4; XVII.19.2; gen.

    Connachtaib IX.8.1; XVI.16.5; XVII.18.1; dat.

Connachtach m.; a man of Connaught

    Connachtaig XVI.16.5; gen. sg.

Connachtaib IX.8.1; XVI.16.5; XVII.18.1; see *Connachta*

Connachtaig XVI.16.5; see *Connachtach*

conna·ētai XIV.14.9; see *co^n* (4), *ad·cota*

conna·ruc XII.12.12; see *conna* and *ruc*

con·tuili (·cotlai) sleeps;

    ·*ro-chotlus* XVI.16.5; *ro*-pret. 1 sg.

    cotlud vn.

    chotlud IV.3.8; acc. sg. lenited by prep. *cen*

    chotulta IV.3.7; gen. sg. lenited by preceding nom. sg. f. noun

córae abstract noun fr. adj. *coir*; proper;

    córai XIV.14.9; dat. sg. in phrase *i córai* = properly

córai XIV.14.9; see *córae*

co·ralta VII.5.14; see *fo·ceird*

core m.; cauldron;

    coiri II.1b.11; acc. sg.

    coiri II.1b.10; dat. sg.

    cori II.1b.9; nom. pl.

cori II.1b.9; see *core*

corot·aicciller X.9.5; see *ad·gládathar* and *co^n* (4)

corr XX.P.6.4; f.; crane, heron

co·rrabae XI.11.10; see *a·tá*

corro XVII.19.4; see *co^n* (4)

cos f.; leg, foot;

    chois XVII.18.1; du. acc.

    oin-chois XII.12.12; acc. sg.; a single foot;

    see *oin*

cosmaili XV.Gl.31; adj.; like, similar

co·tarat IX.8.1; see *do·beir*

créchtach adj.; covered in wounds or scars, bloodied;

    créchtaig XV.15.9; gen. sg.

créchtaig XV.15.9; see *créchtach*

Cremthann nía Náir IV.3.9; legendary king of Ireland

crích border, territory; II.1b.8; dat. sg.

cride nt.; heart; XV.15.9; XV.15.11

criss m.; belt;

    chriss XVI.16.9; dat. sg. lenited by poss. pron. 3 sg. m.

Críst Christ; XIII.Gl.22; XIX.P.2.4;

    Chríst XV.Gl.31

    Chríst VII.5.11; XV.Gl.31

crú nt.; blood;

    chrú XVII.18.4; dat. sg. lenited by art. dat. sg.

Crúachain Con-Alad always pl.; a place of the *Araid* in West Munster (lit. Crúachain of the Speckled Dogs);

    Crúachnaib Con-Alad IX.7.1; IX.7.2; dat.

Crúachnaib Con-Alad IX.7.1; IX.7.2; see *Crúachain Con-Alad*

crúadéigme XX.P.6.4; hard, harsh + f.; a cry, scream

Crúaichniu mac Ruadluim IX.7.2; a champion of the West Munster tribe of the *Araid*, brother of *Senláech*

cú m.; dog, hound; I.1a.2; I.1a.3; V.3.11; XVII.19.1; XVII.19.2; XVII.19.3;

    coin VI.4.5; VI.4.9; acc. sg.

    coin XIX.P.4.8; nom. pl.

    con XVII.19.1; gen. sg.

    chon I.1a.4; I.1a.5; I.1a.6; III.2.3; VI.4.6; XVII.19.5; XVIII.20.2; gen. sg. lenited by art. gen. sg.

cúairt f.; circuit; in phrase *imma chúairt* (XVI.17.3) = round about him; prep. *imm* + *a* (poss. pron. 3 sg. leniting) + *cúairt*

Cúalann II.1b.8; see *Cúalu*

Cúalu a district of what is now called Co. Wicklow

cúana XX.P.6.5; f.; wolf pack, hound pack

cucainni X.9.6; XIV.14.7; see *co* (1)

cucce XVI.16.2; see *co* (1)

cuccum-sa XVI.16.3; see *co* (1)

cuci-sium I.1a.7; III.2.1; see *co* (1)

cucum XII.12.11; see *co* (1)

cucum-sa XII.12.13; XIII.13.14; see *co* (1)

cucut-su XIII.13.12; see *co* (1)

cuich XIV.14.3; see *cía* (1)

cuill XIX.P.3.14; XIX.P.3.15; gen. sg. *coll* = hazel

cuirid put;
  cuirthir XIX.P.4.9; pres. ind. pass. sg.

cuirthir XIX.P.4.9; see *cuirid*

cuit f.; share, portion; XV.15.5; XVII.18.2

cúl m.; back; XVIII.20.3

cumachtae power; XV.Gl.32

cumma adj.; equal, indifferent, immaterial; V.3.14; *cumma* + subordinate clause = it does not matter (that) . . .

cundubairt XIII.Gl.22; see *cuntabart*

cuntabairt VI.4.5; see *cuntabart*

cuntabart f.; doubt, uncertainty;
  cundubairt XIII.Gl.22; acc. sg.
  chuntabairt VI.4.9; dat. sg. lenited by poss. pron. 1 sg. *mo*
  cuntabairt VI.4.5; dat. sg.

cur m.; hero, champion;
  curad XV.15.9; XV.15.11; gen. sg.

curad XV.15.9; XV.15.11; see *cur*

Cúscraid (Mend Macha mac Conchobair) XIV.14.2; XIV.14.4; XIV.14.10; Cúscraid, the stammerer, of Emain Macha, son of Conchobar, a warrior of Ulster

cusna XII.12.11; see *co*ⁿ (3)

cutal adj.; empty, weak, humble; V.3.15

D

d' IX.7.1; see *do* (2)

dá two; III.2.3; VII.5.3; VII.5.8; X.Gl.15; XII.Gl.21; XV.15.12; XVII.18.1;
  dí XVIII.20.8; nom. f.
  dib V.3.14; m. dat.; in phrase *dib línaib* = both (see *lín*)
  See VI.G.28

dabar VIII.6.4; see *di*

Da-Choca II.1b.8; master of a hostel in Co. West Meath

Da Derg II.1b.8; master of a hostel near present-day Dublin

d-a-gniú-sa VI.Gl.3; see *do·gní*

daig f.; fire, flame;
  daigid XVI.16.5; acc. sg.

daigid XVI.16.5; see *daig*

daim XIX.P.3.6; XX.P.6.5; see *dam* (1)

daimid (·daim) suffers, concedes;
  ro·ddét XV.15.7; *ro*-pret. pass. sg.

dálaid (·dála) makes an appointment, makes a tryst, arranges a meeting;
  ro·dálsat-som VII.5.1; *ro*-pret. 3 pl.

dam (1) m.; ox, beef, stag; II.1b.10; VIII.6.1;
  daim XIX.P.3.6; XX.P.6.5; nom. pl.

dam (2) IX.8.3; XX.P.8.1; see *do* (2)

damdabach f.; a great vat, a great enclosing shelter; XVI.17.3

damgaire f.; (a) a herd of deer, (b) bellowing of a stag; XIX.P.3.7

dam-sa IX.7.4; see *do* (2)

dano I.1a.6; III.2.4; VI.4.7; VII.5.2; VII.5.7; VII.5.8; VII.5.12; X.9.7; X.9.11; X.10.10; XI.11.14; XII.12.6; XII.12.14; XII.Gl.20; XIII.13.9; XIII.13.15; XVI.16.2; XVI.17.5; XVII.18.2; XVII.18.3; XVII.18.5; XVII.18.7; XVII.19.5; then, indeed, moreover

dar VIII.6.9; XV.15.12; XVII.18.4; XVIII.20.8; see *tar*

dar hési X.Gl.14; see *tar*

dara XVI.16.9; XVIII.20.3; see *tar*

Da-Rēo see *Mac Da-Réo*

darsin V.3.13; see *tar*

Dathó see *Mac Dathó*

Dauíd XIII.Gl.23; David

daur XVII.18.6; nt.; oak

de III.2.4; IX.7.4; X.10.12; XI.11.2; XII.12.12; XVI.17.6; XVII.19.5; see *di*

deacht XV.Gl.32; divinity

dead f.; end;
  fo-déoid IX.8.1; XII.12.4; at last, finally
  i ndiaid XIX.P.3.4; following, behind

dech III.2.3; adj.; best

dechuid XIII.Gl.24; see *téit*

degcaratrad III.2.4; fine friendship, compd. of *deg* 'good, fine' and *caratrad* 'friendship'

déicsin XIV.Gl.27; see *do·écci*

deilb XIV.14.4; see *delb*

delb f.; shape, appearance;
  deilb XIV.14.4; dat. sg.

delgnacha XIX.P.3.11; gen. pl. f. *delgnach* 'thorny, prickly'

demin adj.; certain;
>   *demniu* IX.Gl.11; comp.
demniu IX.Gl.11; see *demin*
déntar VIII.6.10; see *do·gni*
dénti XIV.Gl.27; see *do·gni*
dênum XV.Gl.31; see *do·gni*
dér XX.P.8.4; acc. sg.; a tear
>   *ndér* XX.P.8.1; gen. pl.
derb adj.; clear, certain, sure; V.3.12;
dercain XIX.P.3.8; see *dercu*
dercu nt.; acorn;
>   *dercain* XIX.P.3.8; nom. pl.
·derglé see *diglé*
deróil XX.P.10.2; mean, small
dertan XX.P.10.2; m. and f.; storm, weather
de-sin VIII.6.4; see *di*
dessid IX.8.2; X.9.11; XI.11.14; XII.12.6;
XII.12.14; XIII.13.15; XVI.16.10; see *saidid*
dethaite XIX.P.4.7; smoky, dusky, sooty
deug f.; drink;
>   *dig* IV.3.1; acc. sg.
d'fácbáil IX.7.1; see *fo·ácaib*
Dhé XX.P.8.1; see *Dia*
di prep. + dat. leniting; of, off, from, in consequence of, as; X.10.3; X.10.3; XIII.13.2;
XIV.Gl.26; XV.Gl.31
>   *de* XI.11.2
>   *do* III.2.4; V.3.12; V.3.12; X.10.11;
>   XVI.16.5; XVI.16.6; XIX.P.3.13; XIX.P.3.15
>   *dim* XIII.Gl.24; w. suffixed pron. 1 sg.
>   *de* III.2.4; IX.7.4; X.10.12; XII.12.12;
>   XVI.17.6; XVII.19.5; w. suffixed pron. 3
>   sg.
>   *is de ata X* XVII.19.5; = it is as a conse-
>   quence of it that X is = this is why X is
>   (so called)
>   *de-sin* VIII.6.4; *di* w. suffixed pron. 3 sg.
>   + dem. ptc. = from that
>   *díb* VII.5.10; VIII.6.9; IX.7.1; XVII.19.1; w.
>   suffixed pron. 3 pl. = of them
>   *diib* IX.Gl.12; w. suffixed pron. 3 pl.; of
>   them
>   *dia* I.1a.4; XV.15.4; *di* w. poss. pron. 3 sg.
>   m.; of his, from his
>   *dabar* VIII.6.4; *di* w. poss. pron. 2 pl.; as
>   a consequence of your
>   *ni dabar samail riss sin* not as a conse-
>   quence of your equality with that

dia X.10.4; XIII.Gl.22; *di* w. rel. ptc. = as
a consequence of which . . . ; *cid dia* = as
a consequence of what? = why?
din II.1b.11; II.1b.12; XVII.18.4; *di* w.
art. dat. sg.; of the
>   *dona* XVI.17.3; *di* w. art. pl.; of the
>   See VIII.G.38.a and Thurneysen G.504-06
dí XVIII.20.8; see *dá*
Día m.; God; V.3.15; XIV.Gl.27;
>   *a Dhé* XX.P.8.1; voc.
dia III.2.4; IV.3.8; XII.Gl.21; see *do* (2)
dia I.1a.4; X.10.4; XIII.Gl.22; XV.15.4; see *di*
dia XVIII.20.8; on the day of; old gen. sg. of
word for 'day'; (cf. Lat. *dies*); *dia bliadna* a
year from that day
diaid XIX.P.3.4; see *dead*
dianit XIX.P.3.5; prep. *do* + rel. ptc. *a* + nasalization + 3 sg. pres. ind. of cop. *it* = to
which is; see *is* and *do* (2)
dia·ta X.10.4; see *di* and *a·ta*
díb VII.5.10; VIII.6.9; IX.7.1; XVII.19.1; see
di
dib V.3.14; see *dá* and *lín*
didiu IV.3.1; X.Gl.15; XV.15.1; XV.Gl.32;
XVI.16.1; then, therefore, hence; from *de* +
suidiu = as a consequence of that; see *suide*
dig IV.3.1; see *deug*
digen XII.Gl.19; see *do·gni*
di·glé becomes clear, is illuminated;
>   *·derglé* VI.4.5; *ro*-pret. 3 sg. proto. (*di-
>   ro-glé*)
diib IX.Gl.12; see *di*
díl XX.P.8.2; m.; payment
dím XIII.Gl.24; see *di*
din II.1b.11; II.1b.12; XVII.18.4; see *di*
díthrebach m.; hermit, recluse;
>   *díthrebaig* XX.P.9.3; voc.
díthrub X.Gl.15; m. or f.; desert;
>   *ndíthrebaib* XX.P.6.5; dat. pl.
dítin XII.Gl.21; see *dítiu*
dítiu f.; protection, shelter;
>   *dítin* XII.Gl.21; dat. sg.
dítnit XIX.P.3.5; pres. ind. 3 pl.; *dítnid*;
shelters, protects, affords a shelter
díumassaig XIX.P.4.8; dat. sg.;
>   *díummsach* proud, arrogant, vicious,
>   insolent
dixit IV.3.2; IV.3.6; XV.15.11; (Lat.) said

do (1) poss. pron. 2 sg. leniting; iv.3.9;
v.3.10; ix.7.1; x.Gl.13; xi.11.7; xi.11.11;
xii.12.5; xiii.13.6; xiii.13.12; xiv.14.7;
xiv.14.9;
   t' xviii.20.5
*For forms following a prep., see individual
prepositions.*

do (2) prep. w. dat. leniting; to, for; used to
support a vn.; used to express the sub. of a
vn. or the agent of a pass. or impers. vb.;
  (a) = to
  do iv.3.7; iv.3.8; iv.3.9; v.3.13; vi.4.5;
   vi.4.9; ix.8.3; xvi.16.9; xvii.18.1;
   xviii.20.1
  dam xx.P.8.1; + pron. 1 sg.
  dom vii.Gl.6 + pron. 1 sg.
  duit xiii.13.13; xvi.16.4; xvi.16.7;
   xx.P.9.1; + pron. 2 sg.
  duit-siu xi.11.11 + pron. 2 sg. + emph.
   suffix 2 sg.
  ṅduit viii.Gl.7; + pron. 2 sg. nasalized by
   preceding nt. adj.
  dó x.10.12; xiii.Gl.23; + pron. 3 sg.
  dún vi.4.2; xiii.Gl.23; + pron. 1 pl.
  dún-ni xv.Gl.31; + pron. 1 pl. + emph.
   suffix 1 pl.
  dúib vii.5.5; viii.6.3; + pron. 2 pl.
  dóib iii.2.1; vi.4.6; viii.6.1; xvii.18.6; +
   pron. 3 pl.
  dóib-sium v.3.14; + pron. 3 pl. + emph.
   suffix
  dond xv.15.7; + art. dat. sg.
  don xvi.17.1; + art. dat. sg.
  dun xii.Gl.21; + art. dat. sg.
  dona vi.4.2; + art. pl.
  atát … dún viii.6.11; there are to us = we
   have; + pron. 1 pl.
  dia viii.6.1; + poss. pron. 3 sg. f.
  (b) = for
  dianit xix.P.3.5; *do* + rel. ptc. *a* + nasalization + 3 sg. pres. ind. of cop. *it* = to
   which is; see *is*
  dó v.3.11; + pron. 3 sg.
  dúib viii.6.4; xv.15.6; + pron. 2 pl.
  dúib-si ix.Gl.10; x.9.6; xiv.Gl.27; + pron.
   2 pl. + emph. suffix
  dún xvi.16.8; + pron. 1 pl.
  dóib iii.2.1; vii.5.12; + pron. 3 pl.

  (c) supporting a verbal noun
  do i.1a.5; iii.2.1; ix.7.4; ix.8.3; x.9.4;
   x.10.1; x.10.13; xi.11.1; xii.12.11;
   xiv.Gl.28; xiv.Gl.28; xv.15.5; xv.15.8;
   xvi.16.3; xvi.17.3; xvi.17.4; xvi.17.5;
   xviii.20.6; xx.P.8.2
  du xii.Gl.21; xv.Gl.31
  d' (before a vowel of lenited /f/) ix.7.1
  dom xiii.13.5; + poss. pron. 1 sg. (obj. of
   the vn.)
  dia iii.2.4; xiii.Gl.22; + poss. pron. 3 sg.
   (obj. of the vn.)
  dubar xiv.Gl.27; + poss. pron. 2 pl. (obj.
   of the vn.)
  (d) expresses subject of a verbal noun, or
   the agent of a passive or impersonal verb
  dam + pron. 1 sg.; ix.8.3
  dam-sa ix.7.4; + pron. 1 sg. + emph. suffix 1 sg.
  duit-siu xi.11.2; + pron. 2 sg. + emph.
   suffix 2 sg.
  dún x.9.8; xiv.14.8; + pron. 1 pl.
  dóib ix.8.1; + pron. 3 pl.
  *See iii.G.11.2; viii.G.37.a; viii.G.38.b;
  and Thurneysen G.506*

do (3) iii.2.4; v.3.12; x.10.11; xvi.16.5;
xvi.16.6; xix.P.3.13; xix.P.3.15; see *di*
dó v.3.11; x.10.12; xiii.Gl.23; see *do* (2)
do·aidlea visits, hits;
  do·n-áraill xvii.19.4; *ro*-pret. 3 sg. w. infixed pron. 3 sg.
  tadall vn.; in phrase *cét-tadall* (ii.1b.12);
   dat. sg.; first go, first attempt; see *cét*
do·áirci effects, causes; ix.Gl.10
do·airic (·**tairic**) comes to an end;
  ·tairnic xvi.17.5; pret. 3 sg. proto.
  tairec vn.; obtaining, getting
  thairiuc xv.15.5; dat. sg. lenited by preceding prep. *do*
do·airling (to-ar-ling-) leaps down;
  ·tarblaing xv.15.2; *ro*-pret. 3 sg.
do·airret meets;
  ·tarraid x.9.8; xiv.14.8; *ro*-pret. 3 sg. impersonally w. sub. indicated by *dún*–see
   do (2)–w. prefix *imma* = mutually; lit. it
   was met mutually to us = we met one
   another
do·alla (·**talla**) takes off;

thall xi.11.13; xii.12.12; pret. 3 sg. rel.
do·beir (·tabair) gives, brings, takes;
do-s·beir iv.3.8; pres. ind. 3 sg. w. infixed pron. 3 sg. f.
do·berar xvii.18.8; pres. ind. pass. sg.
do·bered ii.1b.11; impf. 3 sg. deut.
·taibred ii.1b.11; impf. 3 sg. proto.
·tucad ii.1b.12; impf. 3 sg. proto.
do·bertis x.Gl.15; impf. 3 pl. deut.
do·bér xvi.16.4; fut. 1 sg. deut.
do-don·béra v.3.13; fut. 3 sg. deut. w. infixed pron. 1 pl.
do·bértar iii.2.3; fut. pass. 3 pl. deut.
do·bērthar iii.2.4; fut. pass. 3 sg.
do·bérad x.10.13; xii.12.13; xvi.16.7; condit. 3 sg. deut.
do·t·bérad xiii.13.14; xvi.16.2; condit. 3 sg. deut. w. infixed pron. 2 sg.
Perf. forms are supplied by do·rat (·tarat) *for the meaning 'give' and by* do·uc (·tuc) *when the meaning is 'bring' or 'take'*
do·ratus vi.4.5; perf. 1 sg. deut.; I have given
do·rat viii.6.9; xiv.14.11; perf. 3 sg. deut.
·tarat ix.8.1; xvii.18.1; perf. 3 sg. proto.
do·ratad xiv.Gl.26; xvi.17.3; perf. pass. sg. deut.
·tardda iv.3.9; perf. subj. 2 sg. proto.
tuc xx.P.8.1; 2 sg. impv.
tucus xii.12.5; perf. 1 sg. proto.; I have brought
tucad iv.3.7; v.3.15; viii.6.1; perf. pass. sg.
·tucad ii.1b.12; 3 sg. impf.
tabair v.3.14; impv. 2 sg.
do·berthae iii.2.1; past. subj. pass.
tabairt iii.2.4; xi.11.7; xvi.16.9; f.; vn.
do·bér xvi.16.4; see *do·beir*
do·bérad x.10.13; xii.12.13; xvi.16.7; see *do·beir*
do·berar xvii.18.8; see *do·beir*
do·bered ii.1b.11; see *do·beir*
do·bértar iii.2.3; see *do·beir*
do·berthae iii.2.1; see *do·beir*
do·bērthar iii.2.4; see *do·beir*
do·bertis x.Gl.15; see *do·beir*

dochum x.Gl.15; nominal prep. w. gen.; to
do·coí xii.Gl.20; see *téit*
do·cúadaiss xiv.14.9; see *téit*
do·cúadais·siu x.9.7; see *téit*
do·cūadus·sa x.10.7; see *téit*
do·cuirethar puts, places;
·tarlae ro-pret. 3 sg. (ix.8.1); impers.; usual meaning 'it happened'; here prefixed by *imma* (= mutually); perhaps 'came together, came to blows'; sub. expressed by *doíb–do* (2) + pron. 3 pl.; therefore *imma·tarlae doíb* = they came together
do·dechaid x.10.1; see *do·tét*
do·dechammar-ni iii.2.3; iii.2.4; see *do·tét*
dodon·áncatar vi.4.2; see *do·ic(c)*
dodon·béra v.3.13; see *do·beir*
do·écci (·décci) sees;
ńdéicsin xiv.Gl.27; dat. sg. of vn. *déicsiu* (after prep. *do*) nasalized by preceding poss. pron. 2 pl.
do·eclainn searches out;
du-n-eclannar xiv.Gl.28; pres. ind. pass. sg. deut. infixed nasalization caused by conjunction *amal*
du·érglas xiv.Gl.28; ro-pret. pass.
do·fíuschi wakes
dúscit xx.P.6.7; 3 pl. pres. of *dúscid*; late form
do·foeth v.3.11; see *do·fuit*
do·foídi sends;
do-rofoíd v.3.15; ro-pret. 3 sg. + infixed pron. 3 sg. m.
do·fúargaib ix.8.2; see *do·ocaib*
do·fuit (·tuit) falls; (later *do·tuit*);
do·foeth v.3.11; fut. 3 sg. deut.
·thōetsat v.3.14; fut. 3 pl. proto.
·tuittit xix.P.3.14; pres. ind. 3 pl. proto.
do·tuittit xix.P.3.14; pres. ind. 3 pl. deut.
do·gní (·déni) makes, does;
d-a-gniú-sa vi.Gl.3; pres. ind. 1 sg. deut. w. infixed pron. 3 sg. nt. and emph. suffix
ní-m·déni v.3.15; pres. ind. 3 sg. deut. neg. w. infixed pron. 1 sg. = it does not make me . . .
do·n-gniat viii.Gl.8; pres. ind. 3 pl. deut. w. infixed nasalization (rel.)

déntar VIII.6.10; impv. pass. sg.

du-nda-rigni xv.Gl.31; *ro*-pres. 3 sg. deut. w. infixed pron. 3 pl. and infixed nasalization (indirect speech)

du-gén XII.Gl.19; fut. 1 sg. deut.

·digen XII.Gl.19; fut. 1 sg. proto.

dénti XIV.Gl.27; verbal of necessity; *ní-·dénti dúib-si* = you should not do

dénum xv.Gl.31

do·goa chooses;
do-ngegad XVII.19.1; condit. 3 sg. infixed nasalization because in rel. clause
do·rraíga XVII.19.2; *ro*-pret. 3 sg.

dóib III.2.1; VI.4.6; VII.5.12; VIII.6.1; IX.8.1; XVII.18.6; see *do* (2)

doib-sium v.3.14; see *do* (2)

do·ic (·tic) comes; sometimes w. direct obj.;
tecat VI.4.6; XVI.17.1; 3 pl. impv.
tánacais-siu XI.11.9; XIII.13.9; pret. 2 sg. w. emph. suffix 2 sg.
·tánic XIII.13.8; pret. 3 pl. proto.
táncatar I.1a.6; VII.5.3; pret. 3 pl. proto.
dodon·áncatar VI.4.2; pret. 3 pl. deut. w. infixed pron. 1 pl. = who have come to us

doirsiu XVII.18.4; XVII.18.5; see *dorus*

do·léici (·teilci) throws, hurls;
do·llécim-se XI.11.11; pres. ind. 1 sg. deut. w. infixed pron. 3 sg. f. + emph. suffix
dos·léicim-se x.10.12; pres. ind. 1 sg. deut. w. meaningless infixed pron. + emph. suffix
do·léici XVI.16.9; pres. ind. 3 sg. deut. w. infixed pron. 3 sg. nt.
do·reilgis XIII.13.23; *ro*-pret. 2 sg. deut.
do·n-arlaic XVIII.20.3; *ro*-pret. 3 sg. deut. w. infixed pron. 3 sg. refl. = he threw himself
tarlaic x.10.11; *ro*-pret. 3 sg. proto.
teilciud XI.Gl.18; vn.

do·llécim-se XI.11.11; see *do·léici*

do·lluid XVIII.20.1; see *do·tét*

do·luid VII.5.4; see *do·tét*

do·luigi forgives;
do·rolgida XIII.Gl.23; *ro*-pret. pass. pl.
du·luigter XIII.Gl.23; pres. ind. pass. pl.

dom VII.Gl.6; XIII.13.5; see *do* (2)

do·meil consumes, enjoys;
tomil x.Gl.13; impv. 2 sg.
do·m-meil x.Gl.13; pres. ind. 3 sg.

do·m-meil x.Gl.13; see *do·meil*

domuin XIX.P.3.10; see *domun*

domun m.; world, earth, country;
domuin XIX.P.3.10; gen. sg.

don XVI.17.1; see *do* (2)

dona (1) VI.4.2; see *do* (2)

dona (2) XVI.17.3; see *di*

do·n-áraill XVII.19.4; see *do·aidlea*

do·n-arlaic XVIII.20.3; see *do·léici*

dond xv.15.7; see *do* (2)

do·ngegad XVII.19.1; see *do·goa*

do·n-gniát VIII.Gl.8; see *do·gní*

donn adj.; brown;
duinn XIX.P.3.10; gen. sg.

do·ocaib (·tocaib) raises, hangs up;
do·fúargaib IX.8.2; *ro*-pret. 3 sg.
túargabar XIX.P.4.2; *ro*-pres. pass. pl.

do·rat VIII.6.9; XIV.14.11; see *do·beir*

do·ratad XIV.Gl.26; XVI.17.3; see *do·beir*

dorcha XIX.P.4.7; XIX.P.4.10; adj.; dark, gloomy

dordán m.; buzzing, humming, droning, intoning; XIX.P.3.7; xx.P.10.3

do·reilgis XIII.13.11; see *do·léici*

do·rofoíd v.3.15; see *do·foidi*

do·roich comes to, attains;
do·roich x.10.9; x.10.10; pres. ind. 3 sg. deut.
nís·toirchi x.9.10; pres. ind. 2 sg. proto. w. infixed pron. 3 sg. f. (anticipating the obj. *-in muicc*)

do·rolgida XIII.Gl.23; see *do·luigi*

do·róscai (·derscaigi) surpasses, excels;
nderscaigthe XIV.Gl.28; past participle pass.; distinguished, excellent; nasalized by preceding nt. noun

do·rraíga XVII.19.2; see *do·goa*

dorus nt.; later m.; door;
dorus XIII.13.6; acc. sg.
dorus VII.5.8; acc. du.
ndoruss VII.5.3; dat. sg. nasalized by prep. i^n
ndorus XI.11.7; XVII.18.8; dat. sg. nasalized by prep. i^n

ndoruis II.1b.9; nom. pl. nasalized by
secht^n
ndoruiss VII.5.8; nom. pl. nasalized by
secht^n
doirsiu XVII.18.4; XVII.18.5; acc. pl.
i ndorus + gen. = in front of (a building)
dos·léicim-se X.10.12; see *do·léici*
do·soí IV.3.8; turns;
soaid XX.P.7.5
doss-eillti XIX.P.3.4; does of the thicket (?)
dot·bérad XIII.13.14; XVI.16.2; see *do·beir*
do·tét (·taét) comes, goes to;
tait VII.5.6; impv. 2 pl.
do·lluid XVIII.20.1; pret. 3 sg.
do·luid VII.5.4; pret. 3 sg.
dot·luid XIII.13.10; pret. 3 sg. used impersonally w. infixed pron. 2 sg. = you (sg.)
came; a relatively uncommon construction
do·eth I.1a.5; pret. pass. sg. used impersonally; it was come = messengers came
·tudchad-so XIV.14.7; perf. pret. 2 sg.
proto. w. emph. suffix; in phrase *cucainni
ceta·tudchad-so* = (it was) to us that you
came first
do·dechaid X.10.1; perf. pret. 3 sg.
do·dechammar-ni III.2.3; III.2.4; perf.
pret. 1 pl. + emph. suffix 1 pl.
See also the entry téit *and Thurneysen
G.472–73*
dot·luid XIII.13.10; see *do·tét*
do·tuittit XIX.P.3.14; see *do·fuit*
draigin XIX.P.3.11; blackthorn, sloe
drécht portion; XIII.Gl.22
drissi XIX.P.3.11; gen. pl. of *dris* (f.);
bramble, briar, thornbush
drochcostud XVI.17.3; evil custom; *droch* =
adjectival prefix; bad, evil; *costud* = custom
drochdaíni XVI.17.3; evil people; *droch* =
adjectival prefix; bad, evil; *daíni* = nom. pl.
duine 'person'
Drochet Coirpri XVIII.20.1; the bridge of
Coirbre in Co. Kildare
Druim-Dá-Maige XVIII.20.1; the hill of the
two plains in Co. Kildare
du XII.Gl.21; XV.Gl.31; see *do* (2)
duai XIX.P.3.12; gen. sg. of *dóe* (m.); rampart

dub adj.; black; XIX.P.2.2; XIX.P.4.7;
XIX.P.4.10;
dubaib XIX.P.4.1; dat. pl.
dubaib XIX.P.4.1; see *dub*
dubar XIV.Gl.27; see *do* (2)
du·érglas XIV.Gl.28; see *do·eclainn*
du·gén XII.Gl.19; see *do·gní*
dúib VII.5.5; VIII.6.3; VIII.6.4; XV.15.6; see
do (2)
dúib-si IX.Gl.10; X.9.6; XIV.Gl.27; see
do (2)
dúil f.; element;
dúlib XIV.Gl.28; dat. pl.
duine m.; man, person;
oenduine XIX.P.3.2
duini XVI.16.5; gen. sg.
daini XVI.17.3; gen. pl.
duini XVI.16.5; see *duine*
duinn XIX.P.3.10; see *donn*
duit XIII.13.13; XVI.16.4; XVI.16.7;
XX.P.9.1; see *do* (2)
duit-siu XI.11.2; XI.11.11; see *do* (2)
dúlib XIV.Gl.28; see *dúil*
du-luigter XIII.Gl.23; see *do·luigi*
dumachaib XIX.P.3.6; dat. pl. of *dumach*
(f.); bank, mound
dun XII.Gl.21; see *do* (2)
dún VI.4.2; VIII.6.11; X.9.8; XIII.Gl.23;
XIV.14.8; XVI.16.8; see *do* (2)
du·nda-rigni XV.Gl.31; see *do·gní*
du-n-eclannar XIV.Gl.28; see *do·eclainn*
dún-ni XV.Gl.31; see *do* (2)
dús XVII.19.1; to see if . . . , in order to
know; in origin *do* + *fhius* (dat. sg. of *fius* =
knowledge) = for knowledge . . .
dúsacht XX.P.6.6; m.; awaking, arousing
dúscit XX.P.6.7; see *do·fíuschi*

E

é independent stressed pron. 3 sg. m.; he, it;
é so XII.12.3; *é* + dem. ptc. 'this'
hé VIII.Gl.7
eblait XV.15.12; see *agid*
écen f.; necessity;
ba écen ón XVIII.20.7; it was necessary
ech m.; horse, steed; XIX.P.3.2;
(da) ech III.2.3; nom. du.
na heocho X.9.9; acc. pl.

Echbél mac Dedad a champion of the West Munster tribe of the *Érainn* (*Cland Dedad*); *Echbél* horse-lip, horse-mouth

   Echbél mac nDedad IX.7.3; acc. sg. after prep. *la*, hence nasalization of *Dedad* after acc. sg. *mac*

écht XV.15.12; XV.15.12; m.; deed of violence

ed independent pron. 3 sg. nt.; it; II.1b.11; XV.Gl.31; XV.Gl.32;

   is ed no-ithed that is (what) he would eat

ega XV.15.9; XV.15.11; see *aig*

égid (·*égi*) screams, raises the alarm;

   égthir X.10.8; pres. ind. pass. sg. (impers.)

   ro·éged XI.11.8; *ro*-pret. pass. sg. (impers.)

   ro·héged XIII.13.7; *ro*-pret. pass. sg. (impers.)

   égim XI.11.9; vn.

égim XI.11.9; see *égid*

égthir X.10.8; see *égid*

eirg XVI.16.1; see *téit*

éirge m.; rising, arising; *fri h-éirge* XX.P.6.6

éiss f.; track; in phrase *dar hési* (X.Gl.14) = after; see *tar*

ela f.; swan;

   n-ela XV.15.11; gen. sg. nasalized by preceding nt. noun

Emain Macha Navan Fort, Co. Armagh; "capital" of Ulster, royal residence of *Conchobar*; XVIII.20.6

emde isolated impv.; beware!; XVIII.20.4

én m.; bird; XIX.P.4.4;

   eóin XIX.P.4.4; nom. pl.

   eónu XX.P.6.7; acc. pl. (later also nom. pl.)

Éogan (mac Durthacht) XI.11.4; XI.11.6; king of *Fernmag*

eóin XIX.P.4.4; see *én*

eónu XX.P.6.7; see *én*

·eper XII.Gl.19; see *as·beir*

·eperr XIII.Gl.23; see *as·beir*

·epir XV.Gl.29; see *as·beir*

·epled V.3.10; see *at·bail*

·epred XII.Gl.19; see *as·beir*

·epur VI.Gl.2; see *as·beir*

éra V.3.13; nt.; refusal; vn. of *eraid*

·érbrat XVIII.20.6; see *as·beir*

ere nt.; burden, load; XVI.17.6

Érenn VII.5.14; VIII.6.8; see *Ériu*

Ériu f.; Ireland;

   Hériu I.1a.4; nom. sg.

   (h)Érenn VII.5.3; IX.8.3; XI.11.12; gen. sg.

   n-Érenn VII.5.14; VIII.6.8; gen. sg.; nasalized by preceding gen. pl.

   (h)Érinn II.1b.8; dat. sg.

ernigde XIII.Gl.24; f.; prayer

eroímer XV.Gl.32; see *ar·foím*

err XV.15.11; m.; chariot fighter, warrior;

   err XV.15.12; du. nom.

errach XX.P.6.1; m.; springtime

·essara IV.3.3; see *ithid*

et Lat. 'and'; XV.15.11

étach nt.; garment; XIV.Gl.28

·étai XIV.14.9; see *ad·cota*

Etan Bán XIX.P.1.3; proper name; Fair Etan

etha XIX.P.3.9; gen. sg. *ith* (nt.); corn, grain; see *ith*

etha V.3.11; see *téit*

ethre nt.; end, tail; XV.15.11; Thurneysen, following Pokorny, suggests translating 'plumage'

etir . . . ocus VII.5.1; both . . . and; see *itir*

étiuth X.Gl.14; clothing

etorro VII.5.11; XVII.19.1; see *itir*

F

f-a-dam XI.Gl.17; see *fo·daim*

fadéin refl. pron. 2 sg.; yourself; IX.7.2; see *cén* and *féin*

   do brathair fadéin your own brother

faicébat V.3.12; see *fo·ácaib*

fáilid adj.; joyous; XI.Gl.16

fáilte f.; joy, welcome; I.1a.7 acc. sg.; VI.4.11 nom. sg.;

   failti VII.5.4.; XV.15.3; acc. sg. abstract noun fr. *failid* = joyous

fáilti VII.5.4; XV.15.3; see *fáilte*

Fálmag V.3.13; a literary name for Ireland; 'the plain of the stone of Fál'; the Stone of Fál was a phallic stone that stood on the hill of Tara; it played an important part in the *Feis Temhra* (Feast of Tara), the principal kingship ritual of pagan Ireland

far^{n} poss. pron. 2 pl.; your; nasalizing; used idiomatically in X.9.6;

far-n-Ultaib *far* + dat. of apposition = you Ulstermen

dabar VIII.6.4; prep. *di* + *far^n*; see *di*

·*farcaib* XVI.17.6; see *fo-ácaib*

féchem m.; debtor; VII.Gl.6

fecht nt.; time, occasion;

 a fecht-sa XVI.17.1; art. nt. + *fecht* + dem. ptc. = this time, then

 fecht and X.10.7; *fecht* + *and* (prep. *i^n* + suffixed pron. 3 sg.); lit. a time in it = once upon a time

fecht-sa XVI.17.1; see *fecht*

fégaid XIX.P.5.1; 2 pl. impv. *féchaid*; looks, watches, keeps a lookout

feidm nt.; load, stress, effort; XIX.P.3.2

féin refl. pron. 2 sg.; yourself; X.9.9; see *fadéin*

féith f.; sinew, vein;

 féthi XIV.14.9; acc. pl.

féne IV.3.8; see *fían* and *ferg*

féor XX.P.6.9; nt.; grass

fer m. *o*-stem; man; II.1b.11; IV.3.9; V.3.11; V.3.15; XV.15.12 nom. sg.; XV.15.12; XV.15.12; XV.15.12 acc. sg.;

 fir IX.7.4; gen. sg.

 fiur XV.15.7; dat. sg. (lenited by dat. sg. of art.)

 fir XI.11.12; nom. pl.

 firu IX.8.1; acc. pl.

 fer V.3.11; VII.5.14; VIII.6.8; gen. pl.

 feraib IX.8.3; dat. pl.

feraib IX.8.3; see *fer*

feraid (·fera) VII.5.4; XX.P.10.2; 3 sg. pres.; pours, showers, sheds; w. noun *failti* (joy, welcome); *feraid failti fri X* = he welcomes X;

 ferait XV.15.3; pres. ind. 3 pl. abs.

 ro·ferad I.1a.7; *ro*-pret. pass. sg.

ferait XV.15.3; see *feraid*

ferann nt.; land, field;

 ferunn XII.12.5

ferg f.; anger;

 ferge XV.15.9; gen. sg.

 ferg féne IV.3.8; lit. anger of a warrior band; kenning for 'warrior'; see *fían*

Fergus (mac Roích) XVII.18.6; a gigantic warrior prince of Ulster; his name means 'manly vigor, son of stallion' (see *fer* and *guss*)

Fer Loga XVII.19.4; XVIII.20.3; XVIII.20.6; XVIII.20.8; charioteer of Ailill and Medb

Fernmag an ancient kingdom; part of present-day Monaghan;

 Fernmaige XI.11.4; gen. sg.

Fernmaige XI.11.4; see *Fernmag*

ferr IX.7.3; X.10.3; XVI.16.6; better, best; comparative of *maith*

fertais XVII.19.3; XVII.19.4; see *fertas*

fertas f.; chariot shaft;

 fertais XVII.19.3; acc. sg.

 fertais XVII.19.4; dat. sg.

ferthigsecht f.; stewardship;

 ḟerthigsecht VIII.6.2; dat. sg. lenited by preceding art. dat. sg.

ferunn XII.12.5; dat. sg.; see *ferann*

·fes V.3.15; see *ro·fitir*

fessin refl. pron. 3 sg. m. and nt.; himself, itself; VII.5.4; VIII.6.2

fet XX.P.7.3; XX.P.9.4; f.; whistle

·fetar XIX.P.1.1; see *ro·fitir*

fethi XIV.14.9; see *feith*

fhífea XIX.P.1.4; see *foaid*

fíach raven; XIX.P.4.5

fíad XX.P.6.8; m.; wild animal, deer, stag

fíadnaise nt.; eyewitness testimony; XV.15.12; based on prep. *fíad* = in the presence of

fían f.; band of warriors;

 féne IV.3.8; gen. sg. w. *ferg*

fiche m.; twenty; VI.G.28

 fichit III.2.3; VII.5.13; nom. pl.

fichit III.2.3; VII.5.13; see *fiche*

fid XX.P.6.9; XX.P.7.2; m.; a tree, a wood

Fid n-Gaible XVIII.20.1; a wood in Co. Kildare

fífea XIX.P.1.2; see *foaid*

find X.10.1; XI.11.2; adj.; fair; V.3.11; gen. pl.;

 finn XIX.P.2.2

Findchoím proper name; mother of *Conall Cernach* = fair and shapely;

 Findchoíme XV.15.10; gen. sg.

 mac Findchoíme XV.15.10 = *Conall Cernach*

Findchoíme XV.15.10; see *Findchoím*

finn XIX.P.2.2; see *find*

fir IX.7.4; XI.11.12; see *fer*

fír adj.; true, real, just; x.9.4; x.10.1; xi.11.2; xv.15.8; xvi.16.3; xvi.16.6

firteititt xx.P.6.8; *fír* 'true' + 3 pl. pres. *teichet* or *teithet* 'flees, runs away'

firu ix.8.1; see *fer*

fitir viii.Gl.9; see *ro·fitir*

fiur xv.15.7; see *fer*

flann xv.15.9; adj.; red

fled f.; banquet, feast;

fleid vii.5.9; acc. sg. lenited by prep. *im*

fleid vii.5.9; see *fled*

fo prep. + dat. leniting; under, along, according to; xiii.13.5; xv.15.9; xvii.19.3; xix.P.5.2;

fon x.9.10; x.Gl.15; xi.11.9; xiv.14.11; + art. dat. sg.

fom xvi.16.5; + poss. pron. 1 sg.

foa xvii.18.1; + poss. pron. 3 sg.

foa ix.7.1; + poss. pron. 3 pl.

sair fo thuaid xix.P.5.2; to the northeast; see Thurneysen G.511-13

fó adj.; good; xix.P.3.1; xx.P.7.1; xx.P.7.6

foa ix.7.1; xvii.18.1; see *fo*

fo-ácaib (**·fácaib**) leaves [behind] (*fo-ad-gab-*);

·faicébat v.3.12; fut. 3 pl. proto.

fo-rácbais x.9.9; xiv.14.9; *ro*-pret. 2 sg.

fo-rácbais-siu ix.7.2; *ro*-pret. 2 sg. + emph. ptc. 2 sg.

·farcaib xvi.17.6; *ro*-pret. 3 sg.

fo·rácbad ix.7.3; *ro*-pret. pass. sg.

fácbal vn.; f.

d'fácbáil ix.7.1; dat. sg. preceded and lenited by prep. *do* (*o* elided before lenited *f*- which is phonetically zero)

foaid sleeps, spends the night;

fífea xix.P.1.2; fut. 3 sg.

fhifea xix.P.1.4; fut. 3 sg. (lenited by *nícon*)

fo·ceird puts, throws, performs, falls; supplied by *cuirethar* and *ro·la*;

ro·lá iv.3.1; xv.15.4; xviii.20.2; *ro*-pret. 3 sg. deut.; in iv.3.1 used impersonally; in xviii.20.2 used intransitively 'it fell'

ros·lá x.9.2; pret. 3 sg. deut. w. infixed pron. 3 pl. anticipating pl. obj. *na h-ulto*; used impersonally = it threw them, the Ulstermen

·rrala xvii.19.4; *ro*-pret. 3 sg. proto. used

intransitively = it fell; nasalized by preceding conj. *co*^{n}

·rralsat xvii.18.5; *ro*-pret. 3 pl. proto. nasalized by preceding conj. *co*^{n}

·ralta vii.5.14; past subj. pass. sg. = might be brought about

fochen stressed on 2 syllable; welcome; xv.15.9; xv.15.11;

is fochen dóib vi.4.6 (cop. + *fochen* + prep. *do* + suffixed pron. 3 pl. = they are welcome)

fo·ciallathar provides for;

nib-farchelsam vii.5.5; *ro*-pret. 1 pl. neg. w. infixed pron. 2 pl. (-*b*) = we have not provided for you

fochricc f. nom. sg.; reward; x.Gl.14

focul nt.; word, phrase; xiv.14.9

fo-daim suffers;

f-a-dam xi.Gl.17; pres. subj. 1 sg. w. infixed pron. 3 sg. nt.

fo-déoid at last, finally; ix.8.1; xii.12.4; see *dead*

fogabar ix.8.3; see *fo·gaib*

fo·gaib finds, gets;

fogabar ix.8.3; impv. pass. sg.;

pret. supplied by *fo·fri-* (which loses *fo*- if any other prefix is present);

·fríth x.9.1; xvi.17.2; pret. pass. sg.

fogamar xix.P.3.1; m.; autumn

fogur m.; *o*-stem; sound; viii.Gl.9

foir x.Gl.15; xiv.Gl.26; see *for*

foiss xix.P.3.1; gen. sg. *foss* m.; remaining in a place, state of rest

fola xvi.16.9; xix.P.4.5; see *fuil*

follaigidir neglects;

ni-ro-follaiged vii.5.2; *ro*-pret. pass. sg. w. neg. preverb

fom xvi.16.5; see *fo*

fon x.9.10; x.Gl.15; xi.11.9; xiv.14.11; see *fo*

for prep. w. dat. and acc.; on, upon, over; often confused w. prep. *ar*; i.1a.1; vi.4.4; viii.Gl.8; ix.8.1; x.10.12; xiii.Gl.22; xv.15.2; xvii.18.4; xvii.18.5; xvii.18.6; xvii.19.2; xvii.19.4; xviii.20.1; xix.P.3.2;

forsin xiv.14.11 + sg. art.

forna xvii.18.4; xvii.18.5; + pl. art.

fort xiv.14.9; + poss. pron. 2 sg. leniting

fora x.10.4; xii.12.12; xvi.16.9; xvii.18.4; + poss. pron. 3 sg.

form x.10.11; xi.11.10; xiii.13.11; + suffixed pron. 1 sg.

foir x.Gl.15; xiv. Gl.26; + suffixed pron. 3 sg. m.

forru xii.Gl.20; + suffixed pron. 3 pl. *See viii.G.38.c and Thurneysen G.513-14*

fora x.10.4; xii.12.12; xvi.16.9; xvii.18.4; see *for*

fo·rácbad ix.7.3; see *fo-ácaib*

fo·rácbais x.9.9; xiv.14.9; see *fo·ácaib*

fo-rácbais-siu ix.7.2; see *fo·ácaib*

forard xx.P.7.2; *for*- 'intensive' + *ard* 'high, tall'

fordeirge xix.P.4.5; gen. sg. of *forderg*; compd. of *for* (intensifying prefix) and *derg* (adj.) 'red' = dark red

Forgaill Manaich ii.1b.8; see *Forgall Manach*

Forgall Manach master of a hostel at a site in present-day Co. Dublin; *Forgaill Manaich* ii.1b.8; gen. sg.

forglide xx.P.7.2; participle of *for-gella* 'proven, chosen, choice'

forgránda adj.; hideous; xiii.13.2; compd. of *for* (intensive prefix) and *gránda* 'ugly'

format nt.; envy; vn. of *fo·moinethar* = envies; *formut* vi.Gl.1; dat. sg.

formna pl.; bands, troops; vi.4.10

form-sa x.10.11; xi.11.10; xiii.13.11; see *for* and viii.G.38.c and viii.G.38.d

formut vi.Gl.1; see *format*

forna xvii.18.4; xvii.18.5; see *for*

forru xii.Gl.20; see *for*

forsin xiv.14.11; see *for*

fort xiv.14.9; see *for*

fota adj.; long; iv.3.2

fraích m.; heath; xviii.20.3

fraíchrad nt.; heath *fraíchrud* xviii.20.3; dat. sg.

fraíchrud xviii.20.3; see *fraíchrad*

fraig f.; wall; iv.3.8

frecndairc xv.Gl.31; see *hi frecndairc*

frén f.; root; *frénaib* xvii.18.6; dat. pl.

frénaib xvii.18.6; see *frén*

fri prep. + acc.; toward, against, to, for, with; iv.3.7; v.3.10; v.3.14; vii.5.10; xii.Gl.20; xiii.Gl.23; xv.15.3; xvi.16.5; xix.P.2.3; xix.P.3.3; xix.P.3.7; xix.P.3.12; xix.P.4.6; xx.P.6.6;
fria v.3.11; + poss. pron. 3 sg.
frimm xix.P.2.4; + suffixed pron. 1 sg.
frim xv.15.10; + suffixed pron. 1 sg.
frim-sa ix.8.3; x.10.13; + suffixed pron. 1 sg. + emph. ptc.
frit xiv.14.5; + suffixed pron. 2 sg.
fris v.3.14; + suffixed pron. 3 sg. nt.
frin-ni xiii.Gl.23; + suffixed pron. 1 pl. + emph. ptc. 1 pl.
frib-si vi.Gl.1; + suffixed pron. 2 pl. + emph. ptc. 2 pl.
friu i.1a.7; vii.5.4; xviii.20.8; + suffixed pron. 3 pl.; later often *ri(re)*
ra xvii.18.4; + poss. pron. 3 sg. (anticipating following gen. *tige*)
riss viii.6.4; + pron. 3 sg. nt. (*riss sin*)
See Thurneysen G.514-15

fria v.3.11; see *fri*

frib-si vi.Gl.1; see *fri*

frim xv.15.10; see *fri*

frimm xix.P.2.4; see *fri*

frim-sa ix.8.3; x.10.13; see *fri*

frin-ni xiii.Gl.23; see *fri*

fris v.3.14; see *fri*

fris-áli attends to, carries on; *frithálid* xii.12.1; impv. 2 pl.

frit xiv.14.5; see *fri*

·fríth x.9.1; xvi.17.2; see *fo·gaib*

frithálid xii.12.1; see *fris·áli*

fri tóeb xix.P.3.3; xix.P.3.12; see *toíb*

friu i.1a.7; vii.5.4; xviii.20.8; see *fri*

fúachtnaigid trespasses, injures, hurts; *ro·fuachtnaig* vii.5.10; ro-pret. 3 sg. lenited because in leniting rel. clause

fúaim nt.; sound, noise; xix.P.4.6

fúal m.; urine; *fúail* xiii.13.13; gen. sg. (lenited by preceding dat. sg.)

fúail xiii.13.13; see *fúal*

fuil f.; blood; *fola* xvi.16.9; xix.P.4.5; gen. sg.

fuil xx.P.9.2; see *a·tá*

fuilet xii.12.5; see *a·tá*

G

gabar m. and f.; horse;
  gabair XVIII.20.8; du. nom. f.
gabair XVIII.20.8; see *gabar*
gabáil XVIII.20.6; see *gaibid*
gabais XVII.18.6; see *gaibid*
gach XIX.P.4.4; see *cach*
gaeth XX.P.10.3; f.; wind;
  gaíth XX.P.6.2; dat. sg.
  gaithe XX.P.7.3; gen. sg.
gai m.; spear;
  gai X.9.9; XIV.14.9; XIV.14.9; nom. sg.
  gai XI.11.10; XIII.13.11; XIII.13.12;
    XVI.16.5; acc. sg.
  ngai X.10.12; XI.11.11; acc. sg. nasalized
    by preceding acc. sg. art.
  gai X.10.11; dat. sg.
  goo XII.12.4; acc. pl.
gaibes IX.Gl.12; x.9.6; see *gaibid*
gaibid (·gaib) takes, obtains, gets, seizes, accepts, sings;
  gebid XVI.17.5; pres. ind. 3 sg.
  gaibes IX.Gl.12; x.9.6; pres. ind. 3 sg. rel.
  gabais XVII.18.6; pret. 3 sg.
  ro·gabus XVI.16.5; *ro*-pret. 1 sg. deut.
  ro·gab IX.8.2; XVI.16.10; XVII.19.3;
    XIX.P.5.7; *ro*-pret. 3 sg. deut.
  co·rragab XVIII.20.3; *ro*-pret. 3 sg.
    proto.
  gabáil XVIII.20.6; vn.; dat. sg.
  cet-gabail II.1b.11; at the first taking;
    dat. sg.
  ru-n-d-gab XII.Gl.21; 3 sg. perf.; w. nt.
    infixed pron. used in sense of 'there is,
    there exists' after a conjunction that takes
    a rel. clause or in indirect speech
  ru-n-d gabsat XII.Gl.21; 3 pl. perf.
gaile VIII.6.8; see *gal*
gaim XIX.P.4.7; winter; see *geimred*
gainithir is born;
  ro·ngénair-som XIV.Gl.26; *ro*-pret. 3 sg.
    + emph. ptc. 3 sg.
  ro·ṅgenad-som XIV.Gl.26; *ro*-past subj.
    3 sg. + emph. ptc.
  gignither XX.P.6.2; 3 sg. fut.
gairg XIX.P.4.6; adj.; rough, blunt, fierce
gaisced nt.; arms, armor, exploit, venture;

IX.8.2; X.9.6; acc. sg.;
  gaiscedaib IX.8.2; dat. pl.
  gaisciud XIV.14.7; dat. sg.
  chét-gaisciud XIV.14.7; dat. sg. prefixed
    by *cét* 'first' lenited by poss. pron. 2 sg.
    do (1)
  gaibid gaisced X.9.6; takes arms, becomes
    a warrior
gaiscedaib IX.8.2; see *gaisced*
gaisciud XIV.14.7; see *gaisced*
gaíth XX.P.6.2; see *gaeth*
gaithe XX.P.7.3; see *gaeth*
gal f.; fight, exploit, valor, warlike deed;
  gaile VIII.6.8; gen. sg.; in phrase *laith*
    gaile; see *laith*
  gail IV.3.8; dat. sg.; in compd. *londgal*;
    see *lond*
galar nt.; disease
  ngalur XIII.13.13; dat. sg. nasalized by
    preceding prep. *co^n* (4)
gamnach f. gen. pl.; milch-cow; VII.5.13
garb adj.; rough, coarse, harsh, rude;
    XIX.P.4.7
gáu XV.Gl.31; falsehood, false judgment;
  is gáu dún-ni it is a lie for us; VIII.G.37.a
gebid XVI.17.5; see *gaibid*
geimred nt., *o*-stem; winter;
  geimrid XIX.P.4.6; gen. sg.
  rogeimred XIX.P.4.1; nom. sg. preceded
    by intensifying prefix *ro*-
geimrid XIX.P.4.6; see *geimred*
gein nt.; birth;
  ngein VII.5.11; dat. sg.
geissid XX.P.10.4; cries out, shrieks, roars
gignither XX.P.6.2; see *gainithir*
gilla m.; young man, lad; XIV.14.5; nom. sg.;
  a gillai XIV.14.7; voc. sg.
  gillai VIII.6.11; nom. pl.
  gille IX.7.1; gen. pl.
gillai VIII.6.11; XIV.14.7; see *gilla*
gille IX.7.1; see *gilla*
glaedit XX.P.6.3; 3 pl. pres.; cry out; also,
stick fast;
  glaidsit XX.P.6.3; 3 pl. pret.
glaidsit XX.P.6.3; see *glaedit*
glan XX.P.10.3; adj.; clean, pure, clear
glanaid cleans
  ro·glan XII.12.4; *ro*-pret. 3 sg.

glass adj.; green, blue, gray; fresh, raw, sharp (weather); xx.P.6.1; xx.P.6.9; xx.P.7.4

glé adj.; clear; xiii.Gl.22

glúaiseba xx.P.7.3; see *glúasid*

glúaiss xx.P.7.3; see *glúasid*

glúasid stir, set in motion;
  glúaiseba xx.P.7.3; 3 sg. fut.
  glúaiss xx.P.7.3; 3 sg. pres. conj.

glúin xvi.16.5; see *glún*

glún nt.; knee;
  glúin xvi.16.5; dat. sg.

gním m.; deed, action; v.3.12;
  gnímu xv.Gl.31; acc. pl.

gnímu xv.Gl.31; see *gním*

gonaid (·**goin**) slays, kills;
  guin xvi.16.5; vn.; acc. sg.

goo xii.12.4; see *gai*

grád xii.Gl.20; grade, order

guin xvi.16.5; see *gonaid*

guth xi.Gl.18; m.; voice, sound

guss m.; vigor, strength; xv.15.9

H

hé viii.Gl.7; see *é*

heocho x.9.9; see *ech*

Hérenn ii.1b.8; vii.5.3; ix.8.3; xi.11.12; see *Ériu*

heretic xv.Gl.32; heretic

Hériu i.1a.4; see *Ériu*

hési x.Gl.14; see *éiss*

hi iii.2.3; ix.7.3; xiv.Gl.28; xv.Gl.31; xviii.20.1; see *i^n*

hi frecndairc xv.Gl.31; at present

hinnsénaib xx.P.6.7; see *innsénaib*

hó xiii.Gl.22; xv.Gl.32; see *ó* (1)

hó viii.Gl.8; see *ó* (2)

hóegedaib vi.4.2; see *óegi*

hoenurán xix.P.1.4; see *oenurán*

hominum Lat. 'of men'; xiii.Gl.22

hóre^n conj.; because; related to *uair*; vii.Gl.5

húa ix.Gl.11; see *ó* (1)

húachtar xiii.13.12; see *úachtar*

húaim xiii.Gl.24; see *ó* (1)

húait xi.11.7; see *ó* (1)

húallach vi.4.6; see *úallach*

húare xv.Gl.31; see *úar*

huili i.1a.3; i.1a.7; ix.Gl.12; see *uile*

h-Ulto x.9.2; see *Ulaid*

I

í deictic ptc., always stressed, suffixed to def. art.; see *int·i*

i^n prep. w. dat. (= in, at) and w. acc. (= into, to) nasalizing; ii.1b.8; ii.1b.8; ii.1b.8; ii.1b.8; v.3.13; vi.Gl.3; vii.5.1; vii.5.3; vii.5.3; viii.6.4; x.9.2; xi.11.7; xiii.13.10; xiv.14.9; xvii.18.4; xvii.18.8; xvii.19.3; xvii.19.4; xviii.20.1; xviii.20.2; xx.P.7.6;
  hi iii.2.3; ix.7.3; xiv.Gl.28; xv.Gl.31; xviii.20.1
  in ii.1b.10

i^n before verbs = in which;
  i-tai iv.3.2; in which you are; see *a-tá*
  i-taat viii.6.8; in which are; see *a-tá*

issin vii.5.6; + art. acc. m. and f.

isin i.1a.7; ii.1b.11; vii.5.7; x.9.7; xviii.20.3; xviii.20.3; + art. acc. m. and f.

isind ii.1b.8; xiv.Gl.26; + art. dat. sg.

isin ii.1b.9; vii.5.9; viii.Gl.8; xi.11.8; xviii.20.3; + art. dat. sg.

issin xiv.14.8; + art. dat. sg.

im xvi.16.5; + poss. pron. 1 sg.

inna ix.8.2; ix.Gl.12; xv.15.1; xvii.19.1; + poss. pron. 3 sg.

ina iii.2.1; x.10.14; xvi.17.5; xx.P.6.2; also *inna*

innar xv.15.12; + poss. pron. 1 pl.

inar xv.15.12; + poss. pron. 1 pl.

indiut-su xi.Gl.16; + suffixed pron. 2 sg. + emph. ptc. 2 sg.

ind vii.5.8; + suffixed pron. 3 sg. m.

and + suffixed pron. 3 sg. nt.;
  (a) = in it
  (b) = there, then; frequently in phrase *is and* ... 'it is there (then) that ... ';
  iv.3.2; iv.3.6; x.Gl.15; xv.15.2; xv.15.4; xv.15.9; xvii.18.6; xvii.19.1; xvii.19.4; xviii.20.2; xviii.20.3; *fecht and* x.10.7 = one time
  (c) in existential sentences, e.g., *a-tá fer and* = there is a man; xii.12.5; xii.Gl.20; xix.P.3.2; w. dem. ptc.;
    cia and-so? = who is this?; xi.11.3
    coich and-so? = who(se) is this?; x.10.2

indi II.1b.9; v.3.14; x.9.8; + suffixed
pron. 3 sg. f. dat.
is VIII.6.11; XV.15.1; XV.15.12; XVI.16.7;
XVI.16.8; XVI.17.3; shortened variant of
isin 'in(to) the' before *tech* acc. or *taig*
dat.; see *tech*
'sa XX.P.9.2; + art. before cons.
See *VIII.G.38.c and Thurneysen G.518–
22*
·*íada* XIX.P.2.4; see *íadaid*
íadaid (·*íada*) closes, shuts;
　íadfaider XIX.P.2.3; fut. pass. sg.
　nár-íada XIX.P.2.4; pres. subj. 3 sg. pre-
　ceded by *ná* + *ro*
íadfaider XIX.P.2.3; see *íadaid*
íar^n prep. w. dat. nasalizing; after, along,
according to; XVIII.20.3; XIX.P.4.3;
XIX.P.4.10;
　íar sin VI.4.1; VI.4.8; + dem. ptc.; after
　that
　íarsint II.1b.11; + art. dat. sg.
　íarum VII.5.7; VIII.6.1; XII.Gl.20;
　XVI.17.4; + suffixed pron. 3 sg. nt.; after
　is; used in sense of 'afterwards, then'
　See *Thurneysen G.515–16; IX.G.45*
íarmairt v.3.14; acc. sg.; sequence, consequence
íarnlestar XIX.P.4.9; compd. *íarn* 'iron' +
lestar (nt.) 'a vessel'
íarsint II.1b.11; see *íar^n*
íarthar nt.; the west, western part;
　n-íarthur II.1b.8; dat. sg. nasalized by
　prep. *i^n*
íarum VII.5.7; VIII.6.1; XII.Gl.20; XVI.17.4;
see *íar^n*
íath nt.; land, country; XIX.P.3.10;
　íathmaige XIX.P.4.4
im XVI.16.5; see *i^n*
im prep. w. acc. leniting; about, around,
concerning; VII.5.9; XII.12.5; *imm*
XIX.P.3.9;
　immin XIV.Gl.28; + art. acc. sg.
　immum X.10.8; XIII.13.7; XVIII.20.6; +
　suffixed pron. 1 sg.
　immum-sa XI.11.8; + suffixed pron. 1 sg.
　+ emph. ptc. 1 sg.
　imbi v.3.14; + suffixed pron. 3 sg. m.
　immi XVI.17.3; + suffixed pron. 3 sg. m.

impe VII.5.14; + suffixed pron. 3 sg. f.
imma XVI.17.3; + poss. pron. 3 sg. m.
imma + rel. ptc.; this form used before
verbs, most often in impers. constructions
to mean 'mutually';
　imma·tarlae dóib IX.8.1; they came
　together; see *do·cuirethar*
　imma·tarraid dún X.9.8; XIV.14.8;
　they met one another; see *do·airret*
　immu-n-cúalammar XIV.Gl.25; we
　heard one another; see *ro·cluinethar*
　nímu-n-accamar XIV.Gl.25; we did not
　see one another; see *ad·cí*
imma^n prefixed to prepositions, turns
them into adverbs;
　imma + *la* > *immalle* I.1a.6; together,
　at the same time, simultaneously
　See *Thurneysen G.516–18*
i mbárach VIII.6.4; tomorrow
imbi v.3.14; see *im*
imchomrac nt.; meeting, combat;
　n-imchomruc-ni XV.15.12; dat. sg. nasal-
　ized by poss. pron. 1 pl. followed by
　emph. suffix 1 pl. referring back to *ar^n*
imchomruc-ni XV.15.12; see *imchomrac*
imda adj.; many; XX.P.6.8
imda f.; couch, cubicle, throne;
　imdai III.2.1; acc. sg.
　imdai VIII.6.8; x.10.1; dat. sg.
　imdad VII.5.8; gen. pl.
imdad VII.5.8; see *imda*; noun
imdai III.2.1; VIII.6.8; x.10.1; see *imda*
im·dích (imm-di-fich-) protects;
　im·díched I.1a.3; impf. 3 sg.
im·díched I.1a.3; see *im·dích*
imma XVI.17.3; see *im*
immach XVII.18.7; XVII.19.1; out; prep. *i^n*
+ acc. sg.; see *mag*
immalle I.1a.6; together, at the same time;
see *im*
imma·tarlae IX.8.1; see *do·cuirethar* and *im*
imma·tarraid X.9.8; XIV.14.8; see *do·airret*
and *im*
immi XVI.17.3; see *im*
immin XIV.Gl.28; see *im*
immorchor m.; moving around, turning
around; IV.3.1
immum X.10.8; XIII.13.7; XVIII.20.6; see *im*

immum-sa xi.11.8; see *im*

immu-n-accamar xiv.Gl.25; see *ad·cí* and
im

immu-n-cúalammar xiv.Gl.25; see *im* and
ro·cluinethar

immurga ix.8.2; see *immurgu*

immurgu however, but, indeed; ii.1b.12;
vii.5.1; vii.5.9; vii.5.14; viii.6.6; ix.8.2;
xiii.Gl.23; xvi.16.9; xvi.16.10; xvi.17.3;
xvii.18.1

impe vii.5.14; see *im*

im-rullatar viii.6.11; see *im·tét*

imscarad m.; (mutual) separation;
n-imscarad xv.15.12; nasalized by preceding poss. pron. 1 pl.

imsním m.; worry, anxiety;
n-imsním vi.4.5; dat. sg. nasalized by
preceding prep. *i^n*

im·tét goes around, goes about;
im-rullatar (im-ro-lodatar) viii.6.11; ro-
pret. 3 pl. irregular form, perf. forms of
téit (·tét) usually supplied by *do·coid*

imthimchiul xiv.Gl.28; surrounding; vn. of
im·timchella goes around, surrounds

in def. art.; the;
in nom. sg. m.; i.1a.3; ii.1b.11; iii.2.3;
iv.3.2; iv.3.9; v.3.11; v.3.12; v.3.15;
vii.Gl.5; x.9.9; xi.11.1; xii.12.1;
xii.12.7; xiii.13.1; xiii.Gl.22; xiv.14.1;
xiv.14.5; xiv.14.9; xiv.Gl.28; xv.15.4;
xvii.18.4; xvii.18.5; xvii.18.8; xvii.19.1;
xvii.19.2; xvii.19.3
int nom. sg. m.; ix.8.1
ind nom. sg. m.; x.Gl.15; xv.Gl.32
in nom. sg. f. leniting; ii.1b.8; iv.3.6;
iv.3.8; v.3.10; v.3.14; vii.5.12; viii.6.1;
viii.6.5; viii.6.7; xi.11.13; xvii.18.4
ind nom. sg. f. leniting; xiv.Gl.28
a^n nom. sg. nt. nasalizing; ii.1b.12;
ix.7.2; ix.Gl.10; xii.Gl.19; xvi.17.1
in^n nom. sg. nt. nasalizing; vii.5.8;
xix.P.5.3
in^n acc. sg. m. and f. nasalizing; ii.1b.11;
vi.4.5; vi.4.6; vi.4.9; viii.6.11; viii.Gl.9;
x.9.10; x.10.12; xi.11.11; xvi.17.5;
xvi.17.6; xix.P.5.3
in gen. sg. m. and nt. leniting; i.1a.4;
i.1a.5; i.1a.6; vi.4.6; vii.5.7; x.Gl.15;

xi.Gl.18; xv.15.2; xviii.20.2; xix.P.3.12
ind gen. sg. m. leniting; xii.12.12;
xii.12.13; xvi.17.6; xvii.18.5; xvii.18.6;
xvii.18.8
int gen. sg. m. leniting; ix.8.2
na gen. sg. f.; ix.8.3; x.9.4; x.10.1;
xv.15.8; xvi.17.4; xvi.17.5; xvii.18.1
na nom. pl.; iii.2.1; x.9.2; x.9.9;
xvii.18.4
na nom. du.; xv.15.12
inna acc. pl.; x.Gl.13
na gen. pl. nasalizing; xii.12.11; xix.P.3.3;
xix.P.3.7
art. + dem. ptc. *so* = this; see *so*
art. + dem. ptc. *sin* = that, see *sin*
art. + deictic ptc. *í*; see *intí*
See v.G.23.1 and Thurneysen G.293-99

in xv.15.8; see *inn* and *is*

in ii.1b.10; see *i^n*

ina iii.2.1; x.10.14; xvi.17.5; xx.P.6.2; see
i^n

inar xv.15.12; see *i^n*

ind x.Gl.15; xii.12.12; xii.12.13; xiv.Gl.28;
xv.Gl.32; xvi.17.6; xvii.18.5; xvii.18.6;
xvii.18.8; see *in*

ind vii.5.8; see *i^n*

indaas than (is); xv.Gl.32; in origin a subordinate clause; the vb. is inflected in 1 and 2
persons;
indaí-siu x.10.3; 'than you (are)' followed by emph. ptc. 2 sg.
indó-sa xvi.16.6; 'than I (am)' followed
by emph. ptc. 1 sg.
'na v.3.12

indaí-siu x.10.3; see *indaas*

indala x.Gl.15; second, one of two

indas nt.; manner, way, sort, condition;
fon n-indas-sin x.9.10; xiv.14.11; in
that way
cía indas? viii.6.8; how? what manner
of?; see *cía* (1)
cindas? viii.6.7; ix.7.4; = *cía indas*
indas n- xv.Gl.31; w. following clause =
how, as

indi ii.1b.9; v.3.14; x.9.8; see *i^n*

indile f.; cattle; iii.2.4

indiut-su xi.Gl.16; see *i^n*

indom-acca xi.11.6; see *ad·cí*

indó-sa xvi.16.6; see *indaas*

indossa stressed on 2 syllable; now; xii.12.2

ingen f.; daughter; xiii.13.13;
n-ingena xviii.20.6; nom. pl.; nasalized
by preceding poss. pron. 3 pl.

Inloth Mór (mac Fergusa meic Léti) a warrior of Ulster; ix.7.3

in·medónach adj.; inward, internal;
n-inmedónach-ni xii.Gl.21; functioning as
a noun; innards, entrails; gen. pl. obj. of a
vn., nasalized by preceding poss. pron. 1
pl. followed by an emph. ptc. 1 pl.

inn xii.12.3; see *is*

inna x.Gl.13; see *in*

inna ix.8.2; ix.Gl.12; xv.15.1;
xvii.19.1; see *iⁿ*

innahí xv.Gl.31; see *inti*

innahí-siu x.Gl.13; see *inti*

innar xv.15.12; see *iⁿ*

inni Mac Dathó iv.3.1; see *inti*

innocht ix.7.1; xv.15.12; tonight

innsénaib xx.P.6.7; dat. pl. collective of *inis*;
f.; island

inse viii.Gl.7; adj.; difficult

int ix.8.1; ix.8.2; see *in*

in tain conjunction; when; xiii.Gl.23;
in tan xv.15.1
art. + dat. sg. of *tan* (f.) = time; lit. at the
time that . . .
See ix.G.41.4 and Thurneysen G.552

in tan xv.15.1; see *in tain*

intí (int-hi) art. + deictic ptc. *í* (which is
always stressed) = the latter, the aforementioned;
(a) w. proper names: *inní Mac Dathó:* iv.3.1
(b) w. dem. suffix: *aní-sin:* xiv.Gl.27
(c) as antecedent for a rel. clause:
innahí-siu x.Gl.13; acc. pl. + emph.
suffix = those things that . . .
innahí xv.Gl.31; acc. pl.; those things
that . . .
inti xv.Gl.32; nom. sg.; he who . . .
See airindí

is(s) is; (cop.) no vn.; no distinction between
pret. and impf.;
at vii.Gl.6; xv.15.10; xvi.16.6; pres. ind.
2 sg.
am vii.Gl.5; pres. ind. 1 sg.

is(s) ii.1b.8; ii.1b.11; iv.3.2; iv.3.2;
iv.3.6; v.3.12; v.3.15; vi.4.6; vi.Gl.3;
vii.Gl.4; vii.Gl.5; viii.6.5; viii.6.6;
viii.6.11; viii.Gl.7; viii.Gl.7; ix.Gl.10;
ix.Gl.11; ix.Gl.12; x.9.6; x.9.6; x.10.3;
xi.Gl.18; xii.12.4; xii.Gl.20; xiv.14.4;
xiv.14.9; xiv.Gl.28; xv.15.2; xv.15.4;
xv.15.5; xv.15.9; xv.Gl.31; xv.Gl.32;
xvi.16.3; xvi.16.6; xvi.16.8; xvii.18.6;
xvii.19.1; xvii.19.3; xvii.19.4; xvii.19.5;
xviii.20.2; xviii.20.3; pres. ind. 3 sg.
as xv.Gl.32; pres. ind. 3 sg. rel. leniting
ní iii.2.4; iv.3.9; v.3.14; vi.Gl.1;
viii.Gl.7; xi.Gl.17; xiv.14.5; xiv.Gl.26;
xiv.Gl.27; xv.Gl.30; xx.P.8.3; pres. ind.
3 sg. neg.
ním xx.P.8.4; I am not
inn xii.12.3; pres. ind. 3 sg. interrog; is it?
in xv.15.8
bad vi.4.2; vi.4.10; impv. pl. 2 or impv.
sg. 3
bid v.3.11; xi.Gl.16; xv.15.12; fut. 3 sg.
níba x.9.4; x.10.1; xi.11.2; xviii.20.6;
fut. 3 sg. neg.
bas iii.2.3; pres. subj. 3 sg. rel.
bas v.3.12; fut. 3 sg. rel.
ba i.1a.4; v.3.11; ix.7.1; ix.7.2; x.Gl.15;
xii.12.12; xvii.18.2; xviii.20.7; past 3 sg.
nibo vii.5.8; ix.7.3; past 3 sg. neg.
níptar vii.5.9; past 3 pl. neg.
masu xiii.Gl.22; 3 sg. pres. ind. suffixed
to *ma* = if
dianit xix.P.3.5; prep. *do* + rel. ptc. + nasalization + cop. 3 sg. ind. 'to which is'
mad v.3.13; x.Gl.14; pres. subj. 3 sg. suffixed to *má* = if; see *má*
manip v.3.12; xiii.13.5; pres. subj. 3 sg.
neg. suffixed to *má* = if
cid v.3.10; past subj. 3 sg. suffixed to
cia = although; see *cia*
mad xvi.16.7; past subj. 3 sg. suffixed
to *má* = if; see *má*
conid xiv.14.10; conj. *co ⁿ* (4) + 3 sg.
pres. ind. enclitic form of *is(s)*
combo xvii.18.4; conj. *co ⁿ* (4) + pret. 3
sg.
*See ii.G.9; iv.G.16; vii.G.33, 34;
viii.G.37, 38.g; and Thurneysen G.483–94*

is· VIII.6.11; XV.15.1; XV.15.12; XVI.16.7; XVI.16.8; XVI.17.3; see i^n and *tech*

isin I.1a.7; II.1b.11; VII.5.7; X.9.7; XVIII.20.3; see i^n

isin II.1b.9; VII.5.9; VIII.Gl.8; XI.11.8; see i^n

isind II.1b.8; XIV.Gl.26; see i^n

issin VII.5.6; see i^n

issin XIV.14.8; see *i*

is·taig VIII.6.11; XVI.16.7; XVI.16.8; XVI.17.3; see *tech*

is·taig-seo XV.15.12; see *tech*

is·tech XV.15.1; see *tech*

i suidiu XVII.18.4; see *suide*

i-taat VIII.6.8; see i^n and *a·tá*

i-tai IV.3.2; see i^n and *a·tá*

ith nt.; corn, grain;

   etha XIX.P.3.9; gen. sg.

ithgurtu XIX.P.3.9; compd. of *ith* 'corn, grain' and *gurtu* acc. pl. of *gort* 'field'

ithid eats;

   no·ithed II.1b.11; impv. 3 sg.

   n·essara IV.3.3; pres. subj. 2 sg. nasalized by conj. *cenco^n*

itir prep. + acc.; between; VII.5.8;

   etir . . . ocus VII.5.1; both . . . and

   etorro VII.5.11; XVII.19.1; + suffixed pron. 3 pl.

L

la prep. + acc.; with, by;

   (a) expresses possession: *a·ta biad latt*; you have food

   (b) expresses judgments: *ba becc . . . la Connachta a cuit*; the Connaught men thought their portion small

   (c) sometimes expresses agent VI.4.4; VII.5.7; VIII.6.4; IX.7.3; XV.15.12; XVI.17.2; XVI.17.3; XVII.18.2; XVIII.20.7;

   lim-sa V.3.14; IX.7.1; + pron. 1 sg. + emph. suffix

   lemm XI.Gl.17; + pron. 1 sg.

   lium XII.Gl.19; + pron. 1 sg.

   latt XVIII.20.6; + pron. 2 sg.

   lat IV.3.3; + pron. 2 sg.

   leis VI.4.3; XVIII.20.8; + pron. 3 sg.

   lenn XV.15.5; + pron. 1 pl.

   liunn IX.Gl.11; + pron. 1 pl.

   lib IX.7.4; XIII.Gl.22; + pron. 2 pl.

leo VI.4.4; + pron. 3 pl.

léo-som VII.5.2; + pron. 3 pl. + emph. suffix

leu-som X.Gl.15; + pron. 3 pl. + emph. suffix

lassa^n XIX.P.1.2; prep. + rel. ptc.; with whom . . . ; *cia lassa^n*

   See VIII.G.38.b, g and Thurneysen G.523

laa (lá) nt.; day; XII.Gl.20; nom. sg.;

   ló XIX.P.4.10; dat. sg.

   laa VI.4.3; acc. pl.

   llá XIX.P.3.3; gen. pl. (nasalized by preceding art. gen. pl.)

   n-oénló VII.5.1; VII.5.3; dat. sg. of *oénlá* compd. of *oén* 'one' and *laa* nasalized by prep. i^n

·labradar IV.3.7; see *labraithir*

labraithir speaks;

   ·labradar IV.3.7; pres. ind. 3 sg. conj.

lachain XX.P.6.3; see *lachu*

lachu f.; duck;

   lachain XX.P.6.3; nom. pl.

láech m.; warrior; X.9.1; X.10.1; X.10.3; XI.11.2; XIII.13.2; XVI.16.6; XVI.17.2

laíchcenn XII.12.5; warriors' heads; pl. of compd. of *laích* 'warrior' and *cenn* 'head'

Laigin always pl. (a) the Leinstermen; (b) Leinster;

   Laigniu I.1a.3; VIII.6.4; acc.

   Laignib I.1a.1; dat.

laigiu XV.Gl.32; less; comp. of *becc* 'small'

Laignib I.1a.1; see *Laigin*

Laigniu I.1a.3; VIII.6.4; see *Laigin*

láim IX.8.2; X.10.12; XV.15.1; XVI.16.5; XVII.19.1; see *lám*

·laimtis XVIII.20.7; see *ro·laimethar*

láir XIX.P.3.12; see *lár*

láith VIII.6.8; pl. of *láth* (m.) warrior; in phrase *láith gaile* = warriors of valor

laithe XIV.Gl.26; day

laithi XVI.16.5; see *lathe*

lám f.; hand;

   láim IX.8.2; X.10.12; XVI.16.5; acc. sg.

   láim XV.15.1; XVII.19.1; dat. sg.

Lám X.10.10; = *Lám Gábuid*

Láme Gábaid X.10.3; see *Lám Gábuid*

Lám Gábuid X.10.4; a warrior of Ulster;

   Láme Gábaid X.10.3; gen. sg.

Glossary

lán i.1a.4; xix.P.3.13; xix.P.5.7; adj.; full;
lán di . . . = full of . . .
Used as intensive prefix, see *lángairit*
lángairit xix.P.3.3; compd. of *lán* 'full, complete' (perhaps intensive) and *gairit* 'short'
lár nt.; floor, ground, surface, middle (of a hall); x.10.12; xv.15.2; xvii.18.4; xvii.18.5; xvii.18.6
lassa xix.P.1.2; see *la*
lat iv.3.3; see *la*
lathe nt.; day; v.3.11;
laithi xvi.16.5; gen. sg.; in phrase *cach óen-laithi* = every single day; see *cach* and *oín*
latt xviii.20.6; see *la*
lecc f.; flagstone;
licce xv.15.9; gen. sg.
lécud ix.8.3; see *léicid*
léic x.Gl.13; see *léicid*
léicid (·léici) lets loose, lets fly, lets go, dismisses; xiii.Gl.22
ro·lécus xiii.13.12; ro-pret. 1 sg. deut.
ro·lécis xi.11.10; ro-pret. 2 sg. deut.
ro·léci xvii.19.2; ro-pret. 3 sg. deut.; he let himself loose = he set upon
ro·léced xviii.20.8; ro-pret. pass. sg. deut.
·rrailced xvii.19.1; ro-subj. past 3 sg. proto. nasalized by preceding conj. *coⁿ* (4)
lécud ix.8.3; m.; vn.
léic x.Gl.13; impv. 2 sg.; *léic uait* 'let go from you'
no leicthe x.Gl.15; perf. pass. sg.
leis vi.4.3; xviii.20.8; see *la*
leithlissi xix.P.3.12; gen. sg. of compd. of *leth* 'half' + *les* 'enclosed space around a house'; perhaps compd. of *leth* + *shlissi* < *slis* = sidewall, edge
lemm xi.Gl.17; see *la*
lenaid follows, sticks to; w. prep. *di*; *lenaid dím* = sticks to me, follows me;
ro·lil xiii.Gl.24; ro-pret. 3 sg.
lenn xv.15.5; see *la*
lennán m.; beloved, sweetheart, darling;
lennán-sa xviii.20.6; nom. sg. + emph. suffix
lennán-sa xviii.20.6; see *lennán*
leo vi.4.4; see *la*
léo-som vii.5.2; see *la*

les m.; need, what is needed;
ro·ic les + gen. = he needs; ix.7.1
lesanmannaib xii.12.11; dat. pl. of *les-ainm* 'nickname'; a compd. of *les* 'need, lack, want' and *ainm* 'name'
less m.; courtyard, enclosed space around a dwelling;
less vii.5.6; acc. sg.
liss xvii.18.5; xvii.18.6; xvii.18.8; gen. sg.
liss xvii.18.7; dat. sg.
leth nt.; side; vi.4.4; vii.5.7; xvii.19.4; see also *leithlissi* xix.P.3.12
leu-som x.Gl.15; see *la*
lía v.3.11; more; comp. of *il* 'much'
líath adj.; gray, gray-haired; xiii.13.2
lib ix.7.4; xiii.Gl.22; see *la*
licce xv.15.9; see *lecc*
lilgach f. gen. pl.; milch-cow; iii.2.3
lim-sa v.3.14; ix.7.1; see *la*
lín m.; number;
línaib v.3.14; dat. du.; in phrase *dib línaib* = both
línad xix.P.5.8; vn. *línaid* 'fills'; of tide = 'flowing, flood'
línaib v.3.14; see *lín*
lind nt.; drink, ale; vi.4.6
lingid (·ling) leaps;
ro·ling xviii.20.3; ro-pret. 3 sg.
linnuisci xx.P.6.3; f. *linn* 'pool, pond' + *uisce* 'water'
liss xvii.18.5; xvii.18.6; xvii.18.7; xvii.18.8; see *less*
lium xii.Gl.19; see *la*
liunn ix.Gl.11; see *la*
llá xix.P.3.3; see *laa*
lluid xi.11.11; see *téit*
ló xix.P.4.10; see *laa*
loég m.; calf;
loíg xix.P.3.4; nom. pl.
Lóegaire (Buadach) x.9.4; one of the foremost champions of Ulster;
buadach victorious
a Lóegairi x.9.3; x.9.5; voc. sg.
Lóegairi x.9.3; x.9.5; see *Lóegaire*
lóg x.Gl.14; price, pay
loga xv.15.9; see *lug*
loíg xix.P.3.4; see *loég*

loim nt.; sip, draught, drop; XVI.16.9

loittid (·**loitti**) wounds, injures, destroys;
  ro·loitt XIV.14.9; *ro*-pret. 3 sg.

lomán XV.15.12; branch or trunk stripped of its bark? (obscure)

lom adj.; bare;
  luim V.3.13; acc. sg. f.

lon m.; blackbird, ousel;
  luin XX.P.9.1; voc.

lond adj.; angry, harsh;
  in compounds:
    lond-bruth XV.15.9; angry heat
    lond-gail IV.3.8; angry valor
    lond-gliaid XV.15.12; acc. sg. of *lond-gléo* 'angry fight'
    luind cendach XX.P.6.4

lond-bruth XV.15.9; see *lond*

lond-gail IV.3.8; see *lond*

lond-gliaid XV.15.12; see *lond*

lotar VII.5.7; see *téit*

Lúachair Dedad a place in West Munster of the *Érainn* (*Cland Dedad*);
  Lúachra Dedad IX.7.1; gen. sg.

Luachra Dedad IX.7.1; see *Lúachair Dedad*

lúaith f.; ashes, dust; V.3.13; acc. sg.

luc XIV.Gl.26; place

luchair XV.15.9; brightness, glitter

lug m.; lynx, hero
  loga gen. sg.; XV.15.9

Lugaid mac Con-Rui IX.7.3; son of Cú Roí mac Dairi, a king of West Munster, who plays a prominent part in the Ulster cycle

luid VI.4.8; XVI.17.4; XVII.19.1; see *téit*

luim V.3.13; see *lom*

luin XX.P.9.1; see *lon*

luind cendach XX.P.6.4; corrupt (see analysis)

M

m' X.Gl.14; XIII.Gl.24; see *mo*

má (ma) conjunction; if;
  mani II.1b.12; + neg. marker
  manid V.3.10; + neg. marker + infixed pron. 3 sg. nt. (meaningless—associated w. vb. *at·bail*)
  masu XIII.Gl.22; + pres. ind. 3 sg. cop.
  mad V.3.13; X.Gl.14; + pres. subj. 3 sg. cop.

manip V.3.12; XIII.13.5; + neg. + pres. subj. 3 sg. cop.

mad XVI.16.7; + past. subj. 3 sg.
  See IX.G.41.3 and Thurneysen G.558

mac(c) m.; son; frequent in proper names;
  e.g., *Inloth Mór mac Fergusa* IX.7.3 = Great Inloth, son of Fergus;
  mac X.9.6; XII.12.13; XIII.13.13; XV.15.10; nom. sg.
  macc XV.Gl.32; nom. sg.
  meic gen. sg.; XII.12.5; XII.12.11; in phrase *cenn do chétmeic* = the head of your first son
  maicc XV.Gl.32; gen. sg.

macdacht adj.; indeclinable; XVIII.20.6; of marriageable age, nubile

Mac Da-Réo master of a hostel in Brefne, in the northwest of the country; roughly the modern counties of Cavan and Leitrim;
  Meic Da-Réo II.1b.8; gen. sg.

Mac Dathó I.1a.1; IV.3.1; VIII.6.2; XVII.19.1; a legendary king of Leinster and master of a hostel; in another tale, his name is explained as meaning 'son (*mac*) of the two (*da*) dumb ones (*tó*).' But it seems more likely that Mac Dathó, like the other masters of hostels—Da Derg, Mac Da-Réo, Da Choca—represents the god of the Otherworld Feast, an extremely common motif in Celtic literature;
  Meic Datho V.3.11; VII.5.3; VII.5.12; XVIII.20.9; gen. sg.

mac Mágach V.3.13; see *Cet mac Mágach*

macraille testicles; XIII.13.12; gen. sg.

mad V.3.13; X.Gl.14; XVI.16.7; see *ma* and *is*

mag nt.; plain, field; frequent in place-names;
  maige XIX.P.4.4; gen. sg.
  maigib XVII.19.3; dat. pl.
  acc. sg. petrified in *immach* = out XVII.18.7; XVII.19.1 after prep. *i^n*; lit. (in)to the plain

magen f.; dwelling place; XV.15.11

Maigib Ailbi XVII.19.3; see *Mag n-Ailbi*

Mag n-Ailbi a plain extending from Carlow and Laoix as far as Kildare;
  Maigib Ailbi XVII.19.3; XVII.19.5; dat.

maicc XV.Gl.32; see *mac(c)*

maidid (·**maid**) breaks, breaks out;

maidith XVII.18.5; pres. ind. 3 sg.
maidit XVII.18.7; pres. ind. 3 pl.
ro·mebaid XVII.19.2; *ro*-pret. 3 sg. deut. used impersonally in phrase *ro-mebaid for Connachta* 'the Connaught men were defeated'
·rroemid XVI.16.9; *ro*-pret. 3 sg. proto. (< **ro·memid*– reduplicated pret.)
maidm vn.; nt.; rout, defeat
mmaidm XVIII.20.1; nasalized by preceding art. (nt.)
ru-maith VIII.Gl.8; *ro*-pres. 3 sg.
maidit XVII.18.7; see *maidid*
maidith XVII.18.5; see *maidid*
maidm XVIII.20.1; see *maidid*
maige XIX.P.4.4; see *mag*
maigib XVII.19.3; see *mag*
maín f.; jewel, treasure; IV.3.9
mairfithir VIII.6.4; see *marbaid*
Maistin XVIII.20.1; a place in Co. Kildare
maith (a) adj.; good, well; IV.3.9; VI.4.2; VIII.6.5; VIII.6.6; VIII.6.11; XIV.14.6; XV.15.5;
  is maith lenn XV.15.5; we like; lit. we judge it good
  (is) maith VIII.6.11; XIV.14.6; agreed, so be it
  (b) as noun (usually pl.); nobles, gentry; *mathe* VI.4.10; gen. pl.
maldacht curse;
  maldachta X.Gl.15; acc. pl.
maldachta X.Gl.15; see *maldacht*
manath XV.15.12; obscure; *fer manath*; Pokorny suggests 'man of the awls,' i.e., 'worker in leather, shoemaker'
maní II.1b.12; see *ma*
manid V.3.10; see *ma* and *is*
manip V.3.12; XIII.13.5; see *ma* and *is*
marb adj.; dead;
  marbaib XIII.Gl.22; dat. pl. used as noun 'the dead'
marbad IX.7.4; see *marbaid*
marbaib XIII.Gl.22; see *marb*
marbaid (·marba) kills;
  marbthair VII.5.12; pres. ind. pass. sg.
  mairfithir VIII.6.4; fut. pass. sg. or pl.
  marbad IX.7.4; vn.; dat. sg.
marbthair VII.5.12; see *marbaid*

masu XIII.Gl.22; see *ma* and *is*
matanraid m.; morning time; XX.P.6.6
mathe VI.4.10; see *maith*
mbachlach XII.12.11; see *bachlach*
mbárach VIII.6.4; see *i mbárach* 'tomorrow'
mbas IX.Gl.10; see *bás*
mbélaib-ni X.9.4; X.10.1; see *bél*
mbernai XIII.13.10; see *berna*
mbert X.10.12; XI.11.11; see *berid*
mbiad III.2.1; VIII.6.1; see *biad*
mbliadan VII.5.13; see *bliadain*
mbrot XV.15.12; see *brot*
mbrudin I.1a.7; see *bruden*
mbruidin VII.5.7; see *bruden*
mé XII.12.4; independent stressed pron. 1 sg.; I
mebul XI.Gl.17; f.; shame;
  ní mebul lemm I do not judge it shameful; XI.Gl.17
  See VIII.G.38.g
Medb legendary queen of Connaught, wife of *Ailill*;
  Medba XVII.19.4; gen. sg.
  Meidb I.1a.5; III.2.3; VI.4.5; XVII.19.3; dat. sg. Her name means 'the intoxicating one.' She is thought to be associated with the goddess of kingship, to whom the king was ritually married at his initiation— this to insure her favor in producing good crops. She thus represents one aspect of the mother-earth goddess. One of the features of the initiation ceremony was a ritual drink.
Medba XVII.19.4; see *Medb*
medraid XX.P.6.7; is merry, excites, intoxicates
meic XII.12.5; XII.12.11; see *mac*
Meic Da-Réo II.1b.8; see *Mac Da-Réo*
Meic Datho V.3.11; VII.5.3; VII.5.12; XVIII.20.9; see *Mac Dathó*
Meidb I.1a.5; III.2.3; VI.4.5; XVII.19.3; see *Medb*
méith adj.; fat; IX.7.1;
  méithiu IX.7.2; comp.
méithiu IX.7.2; see *méith*
Mend (mac Sálchada) XII.12.8; XII.12.10; a warrior of Ulster
menic IX.7.1; often

menma m.; mind, wit; v.3.10;
menma-so v.3.10; + emph. suffix 2 sg.
(after poss. pron. 2 sg.)
menma-so v.3.10; see *menma*
menn xv.15.12; clear, distinct
m'ernigde xiii.Gl.24; see *ernigde*
mese xii.12.12; see *messe*
Mes Roída an alternative name for Mac
Dathó meaning 'fosterling (*mes*) of the great
wood (*ro-fida*)';
Mes Roída meic Dathó v.3.11; gen. sg.
mess xix.P.3.13; m.; tree fruit, acorns;
messa xix.P.3.14; gen. sg.
messa iii.2.4; worse; comp. of *olc* 'bad'
messe xi.11.13; xii.12.12; independent
stressed pron. 1 sg.; I;
mese xii.12.12
Mide Meath, one of the five provinces of
ancient Ireland;
Midi ii.1b.8; xviii.20.3; gen. sg.
Midi ii.1b.8; xviii.20.3; see *Mide*
mílach xix.P.5.4; adj. based on noun *míl*
'animal';
mílach abounding in animals
milis adj.; sweet;
milsi x.Gl.13; acc. pl.
milsi x.Gl.13; see *milis*
mmaidm xviii.20.1; see *maidid*
mmucce ix.8.3; xvi.17.4; xvi.17.5;
xvii.18.1; see *mucc*
mmuicce xv.15.8; see *mucc*
mná iv.3.9; xviii.20.6; see *ben*
mnaí v.3.10; see *ben*
mnáib iv.3.9; see *ben*
mo poss. pron. 1 sg. leniting; my; xii.12.4;
xvi.16.5; xviii.20.6; xix.P.2.2; xx.P.8.2
m' (before vowels) x.Gl.14; xiii.Gl.24
For forms when suffixed to prepositions,
see individual prepositions
mó v.3.12; see *mór*
moch xx.P.6.6; early
mochen stressed on 2 syllable; welcome;
vii.5.5; viii.6.3; = *fochen*
mod iv.3.8; action, manner; (special usage)
attention
mogda adj.; churlish, mean; v.3.12
móin xx.P.10.1;f.; bog, peat moss, turf, peat
móir vi.4.5; xv.15.3; xx.P.10.1; see *mór*

mór (a) as an adj.; great, large, huge; ix.7.3;
x.10.1; xi.11.2; xiii.13.2; xvii.18.6;
mór vi.4.5; dat. sg. m.
móir vi.4.5; xv.15.3; xx.P.10.1; dat. sg.
f.
mó v.3.12; comp.; more, bigger
(b) as a noun; a great deal, a large number; v.3.11; xviii.20.6; xx.P.6.8
múaid xix.P.5.3; adj. of uncertain meaning;
noble?
mucc f.; pig; vii.5.12; viii.6.1; viii.6.5;
viii.6.7; xi.11.1;
muicc x.9.10; acc. sg.
mucce x.9.4; x.10.1; gen. sg.
mmucce ix.8.3; xvi.17.4; xvi.17.5;
xvii.18.1; gen. sg.
muice xviii.20.9; gen. sg.
mmuicce xv.15.8; gen. sg.
muicc ix.8.2; xv.15.1; xvi.16.1;
xvi.16.10; dat. sg.
mucca viii.6.4; nom. pl.
mucca viii.6.4; see *mucc*
mucce x.9.4; x.10.1; see *mucc*
mug m.; slave, servant; iv.3.9
muicc ix.8.2; x.9.10; xv.15.1; xvi.16.1;
xvi.16.10; see *mucc*
muice xviii.20.9; see *mucc*
muine xx.P.9.2; m.; brake, thicket, bush
Muinremor xii.12.2; xii.12.3; see *Muinremur mac Ger(r)ginn*
Muinremuir xii.12.4; see *Muinremur*
Muinremur (mac Ger(r)ginn) ix.7.2; a champion of Ulster;
a Muinremuir xii.12.4; voc. sg.
Muinremor xii.12.2; xii.12.3
muinter f.; people, household, retinue;
muintire xiv.14.9; gen. sg.
muintire xiv.14.9; see *muinter*
muir nt.; sea; xix.P.5.3

N

na (1) nor; v.3.12; xiii.13.13; see *no* (2)
na (2) iii.2.1; ix.8.3; x.9.2; x.9.4; x.9.9;
x.10.1; xii.12.11; xv.15.8; xv.15.12;
xvi.17.4; xvi.17.5; xvii.18.4; xix.P.3.3;
xix.P.3.7; see *in*
na (3) xvi.16.5; see *a^n* 'that which'
na (4) v.3.12; see *indaas*

n-acat xv.Gl.31; see *ad·cí*

nach adj.; any; xi.Gl.16; xv.Gl.30;
  nach oín xi.Gl.16; anyone

nád xv.Gl.31; xx.P.9.3; neg. ptc. used in
subordinate clauses

n-ad-chiam ix.Gl.11; see *ad·cí*

nad·fil xvi.16.8; see *a·tá*

nad·raba xvi.16.5; see *a·tá*

na⟨d⟩·tét v.3.10; see *téit*

n-aél ii.1b.11; see *aél*

naem xx.P.8.4; late form; see *noíb*

n-aergarthe xii.Gl.19; see *ar·gair*

n-ag ix.7.2; see *ag*

n-ái x.Gl.15; see *ái*; see Thurneysen G.280

n-aili xi.11.13; see *aile*

n-aill ii.1b.12; xiii.13.12; see *aile*

náimtea viii.Gl.8; see *namae*

n-allaib xviii.20.8; see *all*

namae m.; dental stem; enemy;
  náimtea viii.Gl.8; acc. pl.

na-mmucce ix.8.3; xvi.17.4; xvi.17.5; see
mucc

nár-iada xix.P.2.4; see *íadaid*

n-árlastar iv.3.5; see *ad·gládathar*

náte xv.Gl.29; no; (*nád* + *é*)

n-athesca iii.2.2; see *athesc*

ṅdá xii.Gl.21; see *dá*

-ndechaid xiii.13.12; see *téit*

ṅdéicsin xiv.Gl.27; see *do·écci*

ndér xx.P.8.1; see *dér*

nderglé vi.4.5; see *di-glé*

ṅderscaigthe xiv.Gl.28; see *do-róscai*

ndithrebaib xx.P.6.5; see *dithrub*

ndoruis ii.1b.9; see *dorus*

ndoruiss vii.5.8; see *dorus*

ndorus xi.11.7; xvii.18.8; see *dorus*

ndoruss vii.5.3; see *dorus*

ṅduit viii.Gl.7; see *do*

nech someone, anyone; iv.3.7; xiv.Gl.27;
dat. sg.; xix.P.2.3;
  neich v.3.10; gen. sg.
  ní ii.1b.12; iv.3.7; nt. acc. sg. = anything,
  something
  ní v.3.10; nt. nom. sg.

n-ega xv.15.9; xv.15.11; see *aig*

neich v.3.10; see *nech*

neim nt.; venom, malice; vii.5.14

n-ela xv.15.11; see *ela*

n-epred xii.Gl.19; see *as·beir*

n·érbrat xviii.20.6; see *as·beir*

n-Érenn vii.5.14; viii.6.8; see *Ériu*

n-eróimer xv.Gl.32; see *ar-fóim*

n·essara iv.3.3; see *ithid*

net xx.P.9.2; m.; nest

ngaí x.10.12; xi.11.11; see *gaí*

ngalur xiii.13.13; see *galar*

ngein vii.5.11; see *gein*

ní (1) neg. marker prefixed to verbs;
ii.1b.12; iv.3.9; vi.Gl.2; vii.5.2; x.9.1;
xii.Gl.19; xiii.Gl.23; xiv.14.5; xiv.Gl.25;
xvi.17.2; xvii.18.1; xviii.20.7; xix.P.1.1;
xx.P.8.2

ní (2) iii.2.4; iv.3.9; v.3.14; vi.Gl.1;
viii.Gl.7; xi.Gl.17; xii.Gl.19; xiv.Gl.26;
xiv.Gl.27; xv.Gl.30; xx.P.8.3; see *is*

ní (3) ii.1b.12; iv.3.7; v.3.10; see *nech*

n-íarthur ii.1b.8; see *íarthar*

níba x.9.4; x.10.1; xi.11.2; xviii.20.6; see
is(s)

nib·farchelsam vii.5.5; see *fo·ciallathar*

nibo vii.5.8; ix.7.3; see *is(s)*

nícon not; v.3.12; v.3.15; viii.Gl.9;
xiii.13.13; xix.P.1.4; xix.P.2.3;
  nícos^n iv.3.5; *nícon* + infixed pron. 3 sg.
  f. nasalizing
  See Thurneysen G.538

nícos iv.3.5; see *nícon*

ni·fuilet xii.12.5; see *a·ta*

ním xx.P.8.4; see *is*

ni-m bia x.Gl.14; see *a·tá*

n-imchomruc-ni xv.15.12; see *imchomrac*

ní-m·déni v.3.15; see *do·gní*

n-imscarad xv.15.12; see *imscarad*

n-imsním vi.4.5; see *imsním*

nīmu-n-accamar xiv.Gl.25; see *im, ad·cí, ní*

n-indas-sin x.9.10; xiv.14.11; see *indas,
sin*

n-indi v.3.14; see *indi* and *i^n*

n-ingena xviii.20.6; see *ingen*

n-inmedónach-ni xii.Gl.21; see *in-medónach*

niptar vii.5.9; see *is(s)*

niro·chotlus xvi.16.5; see *con·tuili*

niro·follaiged vii.5.2; see *follaigidir*

nis·rainnfe xii.12.2; see *rannaid*

nis·toirchi x.9.10; see *do-roich*

no (1) verbal prefix w. various functions:

(a) prefixed to the impf. ind. and to the pret. subj.

(b) supports infixed pronouns before simple verbs

(c) marks a vb. as rel. in certain contexts; i.e., in those persons where there is no distinctive rel. ending

Discussed under individual verbs

no, nó (2) or; IX.8.3; XIX.P.2.2

no·beth XVI.16.7; see *a·tá*

no·bíata VII.5.14; see *biathaid*

no-chomairled IV.3.7; see *con·airlethar*

no-d n-ail VIII.Gl.7; see *ailid*

no-d-ranna XV.15.7; see *rannaid*

n-oénaidchi XVI.16.5; see *oénaidchi*

n-oénló VII.5.1; VII.5.3; see *laa*

n-oénsúil XI.11.12; see *súil*

noíb (a) noun; a saint

(b) adj.; holy; see *naem*

a nnoíb-sa XII.Gl.19; nt. art. + *noíb* + emph. ptc. = the holy thing

nóin f.; the ninth canonical hour;

cecha nóna XVIII.20.6; gen. sg.; every evening

n-oínsúil XI.11.12; see *súil*

no-ithed II.1b.11; see *ithid*

no·léicthe X.Gl.15; see *léicid*

no-mbertaigedar VI.4.1; see *bertaigidir*

nóna XVIII.20.6; see *nóin*

nónbair XVI.17.6; see *nónbar*

nónbar m.; nine men;

nónbair XVI.17.6; gen. sg.

no·oircthe X.Gl.15; see *orgid*

nos-mbertaigedar XV.15.4; see *bertaigidir*

no-taí IV.3.4; see *a·tá*

no-t ail VIII.Gl.7; see *ailid*

no-théged II.1b.11; see *téit*

núall VIII.Gl.8; nt.; cry

n-uile XIV.14.11; see *uile*

n-Ultaib X.9.6; see *Ulaid*

O

ó (1) prep. w. dat. leniting; from; I.1a.5; III.2.3; III.2.4; X.Gl.15;

hó XIII.Gl.22; XV.Gl.32

húa IX.Gl.11

oⁿ V.3.15; + rel. ptc.; by whom . . . + nasalizing rel. clause

hóⁿ XV.Gl.32; + rel. ptc.; from whom . . . + nasalizing rel. clause

ónd XIII.13.13; XIV.14.10; + art. dat. sg.

ón IV.3.1; XVI.16.1; XVI.16.10; + art. dat. sg.

úaim IV.3.8; XII.12.12; + pron. 1 sg.

húaim XIII.Gl.24; + pron. 1 sg.

úait X.Gl.13; XII.12.5; + pron. 2 pl.

húait XI.11.7; + pron. 2 sg.

uaib XIII.Gl.22; XIX.P.5.1; + pron. 2 pl.

See VIII.G.38.a and Thurneysen G.524

ó (2) conj. leniting usually followed by a perf. tense; since, after; XII.12.5; XVI.16.5;

hó VIII.Gl.8;

See IX.G.41.4 and Thurneysen G.553

óc m.; young warrior, young nobleman;

a ócu VII.5.5; voc. pl.

oc prep. w. dat.; at, near, by; frequently w. a vn., in combination w. which it forms a progressive aspect, e.g., *oc techt*: XVIII.20.3, going; VII.Gl.4; XI.11.7; XII.12.12; XVI.16.9; XVII.18.5; XVIII.20.2; XVIII.20.3;

ocond VIII.6.2; + art. dat. sg.

ocon IX.8.2; XV.15.1; + art. dat. sg.

oca VII.5.13; + poss. pron. 3 sg. f. (obj. of following vn.)

'co IV.3.1; + poss. pron. 3 sg. m.

acum-sa IX.7.1; + pron. 1 sg. + emph. suffix

occo I.1a.2; + pron. 3 sg.

boí cú occo there was a dog at him = he had a dog

acci XVI.16.10; + pron. 3 sg. f.

ocainni IX.7.2; + pron. 1 pl. emph. suffix 1 pl.

acaib X.9.6; + pron. 2 pl.

See VIII.G.38.a and Thurneysen G.524–25

oca VII.5.13; see *oc*

ocainni IX.7.2; see *oc*

occo I.1a.2; see *oc*

ocon IX.8.2; XV.15.1; see *oc*

ocond VIII.6.2; see *oc*

ócu VII.5.5; see *óc*

ocus and; I.1a.4; I.1a.5; I.1a.6; I.1a.7; II.1b.8; II.1b.9; II.1b.10; II.1b.11; III.2.3; III.2.4; VI.4.1; VI.4.2; VI.4.3; VI.4.4; VI.4.5; VI.4.6; VI.4.10; VI.4.11; VII.5.1; VII.5.4;

vii.5.7; vii.5.8; viii.6.1; viii.6.4; viii.6.9;
ix.7.4; ix.8.2; x.9.9; xi.11.11; xiii.13.12;
xiv.14.9; xv.15.1; xv.15.4; xv.15.12;
xvi.16.5; xvi.16.9; xvi.16.10; xvi.17.5;
xvii.19.1; xvii.19.2; xvii.19.3; xvii.19.4;
xviii.20.3; xviii.20.6; xviii.20.8
See Thurneysen G.548-49
oégi m.; guest;
  hoégedaib vi.4.2; dat. pl.
oén see *oín*
oénaidchi xvi.16.5; see *adaig* and *oín*
oénduine xix.P.3.2; see *duine*
Óengus (mac Láme Gábaid) x.10.3; x.10.14;
a warrior of Ulster, son of Lám Gábuid
óenlaithi xvi.16.5; see *lathe* and *oín*
oénló vii.5.1; vii.5.3; see *laa* and *oín*
oénsúil xi.11.12; see *súil* and *oín*
oéntama xviii.20.6;
  mná oéntama lone women, women without husbands
oenurán dim. of *oénar* (= *oínfer*); one person, a single person;
  a hoenurán xix.P.1.4; dat. sg. of apposition preceded by poss. pron. 3 sg. f.; gem.;
  alone (*h* is pronounced)
ógríar xviii.20.5; compd. of *óg* (intact, complete, whole) + *ríar* (wish)
oíb xix.P.3.3; appearance, beauty, favor;
(Greene suggests 'harvest')
oín (oén) adj. num.; one;
  cach oén every single; xvi.16.5
  nach oín xi.Gl.16; anyone
  Frequently in compounds prefixed to
  nouns; see vi.G.27.1 and Thurneysen
  G.242-43
oín-chois xii.12.12; see *oín* and *cos*
oínchoisseda xii.12.13; see *oínchoissid*
oínchoissid one-legged;
  oínchoisseda xii.12.13; gen. sg.
oínchomram xvi.16.4; see *oín* and *comram*
oínfer ix.8.1; ix.8.3; ix.Gl.12; one man; see
oín and *fer*
óir xviii.20.8; see *ór*
oisseillti xix.P.3.4; a compd. of *oss* (m.)
'deer' + *elit* (f.) 'doe, hind'; in gen. pl. = deer
herd? (Meyer) or hinds? (Jackson)
ol says; iii.2.3; iii.2.4; viii.6.5; viii.6.6;
viii.6.7; viii.6.8; viii.6.10; viii.6.11; ix.7.1;

ix.7.2; ix.7.3; ix.7.4; x.9.3; x.9.4; x.9.6;
x.10.1; x.10.2; x.10.3; x.10.4; x.10.6;
xi.11.1; xi.11.2; xi.11.3; xi.11.4; xi.11.5;
xi.11.6; xii.12.1; xii.12.2; xii.12.3;
xii.12.4; xii.12.7; xii.12.8; xii.12.9;
xii.12.10; xii.12.11; xiii.13.1; xiii.13.2;
xiii.13.3; xiii.13.4; xiii.13.5; xiv.14.1;
xiv.14.2; xiv.14.3; xiv.14.4; xiv.14.5;
xiv.14.6; xv.15.5; xv.15.7; xv.15.8;
xv.15.12; xvi.16.1; xvi.16.2; xvi.16.3;
xvi.16.4; xvi.16.6; xvi.16.9; xvi.17.1;
xviii.20.5; xviii.20.6;
  olse vi.4.2; vi.4.5; vi.4.9; vii.5.5; viii.6.3;
  ix.8.3; xviii.20.4; said he
  See Thurneysen G.255
olc evil; v.3.11; v.3.14
oldás than (is); ix.7.3; ix.Gl.11; in origin a
subordinate clause, consisting of *ol* (prep.)
'beyond' + abs. rel. 3 sg. pres. of *a·tá* 'is'
See Thurneysen G.477-78
olse vi.4.2; vi.4.5; vi.4.9; vii.5.5; viii.6.3;
ix.8.3; xviii.20.4; see *ol*
ón xv.15.12; xvi.17.2; xviii.20.7; see *suide*
ón iv.3.1; xvi.16.1; xvi.16.10; see *ó* (1)
ond xiii.13.13; xiv.14.10; see *ó* (1)
ór nt.; gold;
  óir xviii.20.8; gen. sg.
orcain xvi.16.5; see *orgid*
orgid (·oirg) slays, pillages;
  no oircthe x.Gl.15; impf. pass. pl.
  orcain xvi.16.5; vn. acc. sg.
ós xix.P.3.10; xx.P.10.4; prep. + dat.; over,
above;
  úas ix.8.2
  See Thurneysen G.527
ō·tucad v.3.15; see *do·beir*

P

pecad m.; sin; x.Gl.15;
  pecthae x.Gl.15; gen. pl.
  pecthe xii.Gl.20; nom. pl.
  pecthi xiii.Gl.23; nom. pl.
pecthae x.Gl.15; see *pecad*
pecthe xii.Gl.20; see *pecad*
pecthi xiii.Gl.23; see *pecad*
persin vi.Gl.3; f.; person
popuil x.Gl.15; see *popul*
popul m.; people; x.Gl.15;

popuil x.Gl.15; gen. sg.

precept VII.Gl.4; x.Gl.14; XIII.Gl.22; see *pridchid*

pridcha-sa x.Gl.14; see *pridchid*

pridchid preaches;
no pridchim VII.Gl.5; pres. ind. 1 sg. rel. force marked by preverb *no* (see Thurneysen G.348)
pridcha-sa x.Gl.14; pres. subj. 1 sg. w. suffixed emph. ptc. 1 sg.
ro-pridchus-sa XIII.Gl.22; *ro-*pres. 1 sg. w. suffixed emph. ptc. 1 sg.
precept VII.Gl.4; x.Gl.14; XIII.Gl.22; vn.

prius VI.4.4; first; (Lat.)

R

ra XVII.18.4; see *fri*

rab(a)e IV.3.1; XI.11.10; see *a·tá*

raidid (·raidi) talks, says;
ro·raidset III.2.2; *ro-*pret. 3 pl.

rainn IX.8.3; x.9.4; x.10.1; XI.11.1; xv.15.8; XVI.17.4; see *rannaid*

rainnfe XII.12.2; see *rannaid*

rainnfither VIII.6.7; see *rannaid*

raithe f.; period of 3 months, season; XIX.P.3.1;
raithib XIX.P.4.1; dat. pl.

raithib XIX.P.4.1; see *raithe*

Ráith Imgain XVIII.20.1; a place in Co. Kildare

raithnigi XIX.P.3.5; gen. sg. *raithnech*; heather

·ralta VII.5.14; see *fo·ceird*

rán adj.; noble, illustrious; XIX.P.5.6

rann VIII.6.8; XI.11.2; XVI.17.5; see *rannaid*

·ranna xv.15.7; see *rannaid*

rannaid (·ranna) divides, carves;
no-d·ranna xv.15.7; pres. ind. 3 sg. conj. w. infixed pron. 3 sg. nt. supported by *nó*
rannas xv.15.6; pres. ind. 3 sg. rel.
rainnfe XII.12.2; fut. 2 sg.
rainnfither VIII.6.7; fut. pass. sg. rel.
rann f. vn. nom. sg.; VIII.6.8; XI.11.2; XVI.17.5
rainn IX.8.3; x.9.4; x.10.1; XI.11.1; xv.15.8; XVI.17.4; dat. sg.

rannas xv.15.6; see *rannaid*

rath nt.; grace, in origin vn. of *ernaid* 'bestows' = what is bestowed;
fri rath + gen. = on account of
fria rath (v.3.11) on account of it; *fri* + poss. pron. 3 sg. f. + *rath*

ráth m. and f.; rampart, fort; XIX.P.3.15

re^n prep. w. dat., nasalizing; before; (later *ria^n*); xx.P.6.8;
ria VII.5.11
remib VIII.Gl.8; + pron. 2 pl.
riam VIII.6.9; XI.11.5; XVI.16.5; + pron. 3 sg. nt. functions as adv. = before
riasu xx.P.6.8 + rel.

rebach adj.; athletic, nimble, playful, skilled in feats of strength; XIX.P.5.6

regaid xv.15.12; see *téit*

reithit XIX.P.3.6; see *rethid*

remib VIII.Gl.8; see *re^n*

resíu conjunction; before; followed by a perf. subj. and a clause w. no mark of subordination; XI.Gl.18; XII.Gl.20;
ríasíu III.2.1; a later form
In origin prep. *re^n* + *síu* (anaphoric pron. nt. dat. sg.), i.e., 'before it that . . . '; see *suide*

resurrectione Lat.; resurrection; XIII.Gl.22

rethid runs;
rethit IX.Gl.12; pres. ind. 3 pl. abs.
reithit XIX.P.3.6; pres. ind. 3 pl. abs.

rethit IX.Gl.12; see *rethid*

rí m.; king; I.1a.1; XI.11.4;
ríg XIV.14.4; gen. sg.
ríg XIV.Gl.28; acc. sg.
a rí XIX.P.2.1; voc. sg.

ría VII.5.11; see *re^n*

ríam VIII.6.9; XI.11.5; XVI.16.5; see *re^n*

ríasíu III.2.1; see *resíu*

riasu xx.P.6.8; see *re^n*

ricfaither IX.7.1; see *ro·ic*

ríg XIV.Gl.28; see *rí*

ríg XIV.14.4; see *rí*

rinn nt. and m.; star, constellation; XIX.P.2.1; gen. pl.

riss VIII.6.4; see *fri*

ro verbal ptc., infixed when possible;
(a) in OIr. formed a perf. aspect fr. any tense; later (e.g., in SMMD) associated w. any vb. in the pret.

(b) used to infix dat. pronouns before subst. vb. *a·tá*;

    rot·bia són XII.12.8; that will be to you = you will have that

(c) expresses possibility or ability;

    as·ro-bair he can say (fr. *as·beir* 'says')

See individual verbs; also Thurneysen G.339–43

robarta m.; full tide, flood tide, impetuous course; XIX.P.4.2

ro-bá-sa VI.4.5; see *a·tá*

robilib XIX.P.3.15; dat. pl. of *robile*; compd. of *ro* (intensifying prefix) + *bile* (a large, old tree; a sacred tree)

ro-boí II.1b.8; VII.5.11; XVI.17.3; XVII.18.4; XVII.18.6; see *a·tá*

ro·chluinemmar IX.Gl.11; see *ro·cluinethar*

ro-chotlus XVI.16.5; see *con-tuili*

ro·cloammar XI.Gl.18; see *ro·cluinethar*

ro·cluinethar (·cluinethar) hears; VIII.Gl.9; pres. ind. 3 sg. deut.;

    ro·chluinemmar IX.Gl.11; pres. ind. 1 pl. deut. lenited after *a^n*

    ro·cloammar XI.Gl.18; pres. subj. 1 deut.

    immu-n-cūalammar XIV.Gl.25; perf. 1 pl. proto. preceded by preverb *im* w. rel. ptc. (to indicate mutuality) and an infixed pron. 1 pl.; we have heard one another; see *im*

    cluinit XX.P.6.5; 3 pl. pres.

ro·dálsat-som VII.5.1; see *dálaid*

ro·ddét XV.15.7; see *daimid*

ro-éged XI.11.8; see *égid*

ro-ferad I.1a.7; see *feraid*

ro·fetar XIX.P.1.3; see *ro·fitir*

ro·fetar-sa X.10.6; see *ro·fitir*

ro·finnadar finds out;

    ro·finnatar XII.Gl.20; pass. pres.

ro·finnatar XII.Gl.20; see *ro·finnadar*

ro·fitir (*ro-* disappears when any other preverb is present); knows;

    ro·fetar XIX.P.1.3; pres. ind. 1 sg. deut.

    ro·fetar-sa X.10.6; pres. ind. 1 sg. deut. + emph. ptc.

    ·fetar XIX.P.1.1; pres. ind. 1 sg. proto.

    ·fitir VIII.Gl.9; pres. ind. 3 sg. proto.

    ·fes V.3.15; pret. pass. sg.

ro·fúachtnaig VII.5.10; see *fúachtnaigid*

ro-gab IX.8.2; XVI.16.10; XVII.19.3; XIX.P.5.7; see *gaibid*

ro-gabus XVI.16.5; see *gaibid*

rogeimred XIX.P.4.1; see *geimred*; *geimred* (nt.; winter) preceded by intensifying prefix *ro-*

ro·glan XII.12.4; see *glanaid*

ro-héged XIII.13.7; see *égid*

ro·ic reaches, attains

    ricfaither IX.7.1; fut. pass.

    rotânac pret. 1 sg. (*ro·ānac*); XIII.13.6

ro-lá IV.3.1; XV.15.4; XVIII.20.2; see *fo·ceird*

ro·laimethar dares; *ro* disappears if any other prefix is present;

    ·laimtis XVIII.20.7; impf. 3 pl.

ro-léced XVIII.20.8; see *léicid*

ro·leci XVII.19.2; see *léicid*

ro-lécis XI.11.10; see *léicid*

ro-lécus XIII.13.12; see *léicid*

ro·lil XIII.Gl.24; see *lenaid*

ro·ling XVIII.20.3; see *lingid*

ro·loitt XIV.14.9; see *loittid*

ro·mebaid XVII.19.2; see *maidid*

rón m.; seal; XIX.P.5.5; gen. pl.

rond·mbertaigestar XV.15.1; see *bertaigidir*

ro·ṅgenad-som XIV.Gl.26; see *gainithir*

ro·ngénair-som XIV.Gl.26; see *gainithir*

ro·pridchus-sa XIII.Gl.22; see *pridchid*

ro·raidset III.2.2; see *raidid*

ro·saig (·roich) attains, reaches, hits;

    ·rroacht XVII.18.3; pret. 3 sg. (*t*-pret.) nasalized by preceding conj. *co^n*

ros-bia VI.4.6; VI.4.11; see *a·tá*

ros-lá X.9.2; see *fo·ceird*

ro·súig XVI.17.6; see *súgid*

rota brackish, muddy water; IX.7.1

rotânac XIII.13.6; see *ro·ic*

rot·bia XII.12.8; XIII.13.2; XIV.14.2; see *a·tá*

roth m.; wheel; X.9.9; acc. sg.

rrabae XI.11.10; see *a·tá*

rrabe IV.3.1; see *a·tá*

·rragab XVIII.20.3; see *gaibid*

·rrailced XVII.19.1; see *léicid*

·rrala XVII.19.4; see *fo·ceird*

·rralsat XVII.18.5; see *fo·ceird*

·rroacht XVII.18.3; see *ro·saig*

·rroemid XVI.16.9; see *maidid*

rúadgaiss XIX.P.3.5; compd. of *ruad* (red) +
gas (nt.; twig, sprig, shoot)
·ruc XII.12.12; see *berid*
·rucad XIII.13.13; see *berid*
·ructha I.1a.7; III.2.1; see *berid*
rúin IV.3.9; VII.Gl.5; see *rún*
ru maith VIII.Gl.8; see *maidid*
rún f.; secret, mystery; IV.3.9;
   rúin IV.3.9; VII.Gl.5; acc. sg.
ru-n-d gab XII.Gl.21; see *gaibid*
ru-n-d gabsat XII.Gl.21; see *gaibid*
rús m.; great knowledge, instinct;
XVII.19.1

S

-sa XVI.17.1; see *so*
'sa XX.P.9.2; see *i* + art.
sacart m.; priest; XII.12.12
saebuisci XX.P.7.5; *saeb* 'crooked, askew' +
uisce 'water'
saidid (·said) sits down; perf. forms of this
vb. formed not w. *ro* but w. the double preverb *di-en-*; hence:
   dessid (< *di-en-sad) IX.8.2; X.9.11;
   XI.11.14; XII.12.6; XII.12.14; XIII.13.15;
   XVI.16.10; *ro*-pret. 3 sg.; see Thurneysen
   G.345
   suide vn.; sitting
   téit Ōengus ina suide X.10.14; Ōengus sits
   down; lit. Ōengus goes into his sitting
sáil XII.12.12; see *sál*
sainriud XIV.Gl.28; in particular; dat. sg. of
sainred (nt.; specialty)
sair eastward; X.10.7; XIX.P.5.2;
   sair fo thuaid XIX.P.5.2; toward the
   northeast; see IX.G.45
sál f.; heel;
   sáil XII.12.12; acc. sg.
sám XX.P.7.2; peaceful, calm
samail f.; equality, likeness; VIII.6.4; dat. sg.;
see under *di: (ni) dabar samail riss sin*
samdal XX.P.7.2; peaceful, calm
samlaid like that, thus; XIV.14.9; XIV.Gl.28
samrad XX.P.7.1; m.; summer
scél nt.; story; (in pl.) news, tidings;
   scéla XVIII.20.9; nom. pl.
scéla XVIII.20.9; see *scél*
scían f.; knife; XV.15.1;

scín IX.8.2; acc. sg.
scín IX.8.2; see *scían*
scíath m. dat. sg.; shield; XI.11.10
sech prep. w. acc.; past, by; XVIII.20.1
secht*ⁿ* seven; nasalized; II.1b.9; VII.5.8;
VII.5.13
sén XX.P.7.6; sign, good sign, blessing
Senláech IX.7.1; a champion of the *Araid*;
= old warrior
-seo XV.15.12; see *so*
sét m.; jewel, wealth, anything of value;
   sét III.2.4; gen. pl. (obj. of a vn.)
sí independent pron. 3 sg. f.; she; II.1b.8;
V.3.15
síar westward, to the west; XVIII.20.3;
XVIII.20.8; see IX.G.45 and Thurneysen
G.305
sic thus; (Lat.); XII.Gl.21
side VII.5.13; IX.7.3; IX.8.2; X.9.11;
XI.11.14; XII.12.6; XII.12.14; XIII.13.15;
XVI.16.10; see *suide*
sidi VI.4.3; VI.4.7; XI.Gl.18; XVII.18.3; see
suide
silis V.3.13; see *sligid*
sin dem. suffix; that;
  (a) stressed:
    (i) following a stressed pron.: *sí sin*
    II.1b.8
    (ii) as sub. or obj. of a sentence:
    VI.Gl.3; X.10.3; XI.11.4; XIII.13.4;
    XIV.Gl.26
    (iii) after a prep.: III.2.3; VI.4.1;
    VI.4.8; VIII.6.4
    (iv) after the def. art.: XII.Gl.19;
    XIV.Gl.26; XVIII.20.9
  (b) enclitic:
    after a noun preceded by the def. art.;
    this is the equivalent of a dem. adj.
    construction: VII.Gl.5; *isind aimser sin*
    II.1b.8; at that time; see V.G.23.2 and
    Thurneysen G.299–301
sín XX.P.7.1; f.; storm, season, weather
Sión XII.Gl.21; Zion
sithaister XX.P.7.1; peaceful (or long?)
síthamail XX.P.9.4; peaceful, tranquil
sithchailltib XIX.P.3.8; compd. of *sith*
(long) + *cailltib* (dat. pl. of *caill*: f.; wood,
forest)

slatta XIX.P.3.9; nom. pl. of *slat* (f.; rod, lath, twig, branch)

slíab mountain; XII.Gl.21

slíasat f.; thigh;
slíasait XIII.13.12; acc. sg. (lenited by preceding poss. pron. 2 sg.)

slige f.; road, way;
sligi II.1b.11; dat. sg.
sligeda II.1b.9; nom. pl.

sligeda II.1b.9; see *slige*

sligid (·slig) cuts down;
silis V.3.13; fut. 3 sg.

sliss m.; side, sidewall; XVII.18.4; *leithlissi* (?) XIX.P.3.12

slúag m.; troop, host, band; XVII.18.5;
slúaig IX.8.2; gen. sg.
slúaig V.3.12; nom. pl. lenited by preceding poss. pron. 3 sg. m. *a*

so dem. suffix; this;
(a) stressed:
(i) after stressed pron. *é so*: XII.12.3; XIV.14.3
(ii) sub. of sentence *cïa so?*: XII.12.9; XIII.13.3
(iii) after a prep. *and-so*: XI.11.3
(iv) after def. art. *in-so*: VI.Gl.1
(b) enclitic:
after a noun preceded by the def. art. *-so*, *-sa*, *-seo*;
a fecht-sa: XVI.17.1; this time
is·taig-seo: XV.15.12; in this house;
see V.G.23.2 and Thurneysen G.299–301

soaid XX.P.7.5; see *do·soí*

sochaide f.; a crowd, number, multitude; VII.5.10; XI.Gl.16

sochruid adj.; fine, magnificent, splendid; VI.4.6

socht m.; silence; IV.3.1; X.9.2

soilse f.; light; XIV.Gl.28

soimól nt.; XVII.18.5; a good drinking round; *so* (good) + *im* (about) + *ól* (drinking)

són XII.12.8; XIII.13.2; XIV.14.2; see *suide*

soscéli VII.Gl.4; gen. sg. of *soscél* (nt.; gospel); compd. of the prefix *so* (good) + *scél*

sróin VIII.6.9; see *srón*

srón f.; nose;
sróin VIII.6.9; acc. sg.

srotha XVII.18.4; XX.P.7.5; see *sruth*

sruth m.; river, stream;
srotha XVII.18.4; XX.P.7.5; nom. pl.

súas VI.4.1; upward, up; see Thurneysen G.305; IX.G.45

subai XIX.P.3.8; nom. pl. of *sub* (f.; berry, strawberry)

súgid sucks, soaks in;
ro·súig XVI.17.6; *ro*-pret. 3 sg.

suide (1) anaphoric pron.; this, that, he, the last-mentioned, the latter;
(a) forms when stressed: *suide* (nt. *sodain*); *i suidiu* (dat. sg. nt.) after prep. *iⁿ =* thereby, then; XVII.18.4
(b) forms when enclitic: *side* (nt. *són*, *ón*);
side IX.7.3; IX.8.2; X.9.11; XI.11.14; XII.12.6; XII.12.14; XIII.13.15; XVI.16.10; nom. sg. as sub. of a vb.
sidi VI.4.3; VI.4.7; XVII.18.3; nom. pl. as sub. of a vb.
són XII.12.8; XIII.13.2; XIV.14.2; nom. sg. nt. as sub. of a vb. (*a·tá*)
ón XV.15.12; XVI.17.2; XVIII.20.7; nt. nom. and acc. sg. (originally derived fr. *són* by lenition)
side VII.5.13; gen. sg. attached typically to a noun preceded by a poss. pron.
sidi XI.Gl.18; gen. sg.
See Thurneysen G.301–02

suide (2) X.10.14; see *saidid*

suidiu XVII.18.4; see *suide*

súil f.; eye;
súil XI.11.11; XI.11.13; acc. sg.
n-oénsúil XI.11.12; dat. sg. of compd. of *oín* (one) and *súil* nasalized by prep. *coⁿ* (3); see *oín*
sūlib dat. pl.; IX.Gl.11

sūlib IX.Gl.11; see *súil*

sund adv.; here; VI.Gl.2; VIII.6.8

sút nt. pron.; that; X.9.3

T

t' XVIII.20.5; see *do* (1)

tabair V.3.14; see *do·beir*

tabairt III.2.4; XI.11.7; XVI.16.9; see *do·beir*

táib IV.3.1; see *tóib*

taibred II.1b.11; see *do·beir*

taig VII.5.9; see *tech*

tain XIII.Gl.23; see *in tain*

tairisem m.; standing, sustaining; vn. of *do-ar-sissedar*;

  tairisme IX.8.3; gen. sg.

  thairisme X.9.1; XVI.17.2; gen. sg. lenited by preceding poss. pron. 3 sg. m. *a*

  thairisem XI.11.1; dat. sg. lenited by prep. *do*

tairisme IX.8.3; see *tairisem*

tairiuc XV.15.5; see *do·airic*

·tairnic XVI.17.5; see *do·airic*

tairnith XIX.P.3.13; fr. *do·airndim* 'I let down'?

tairr belly;

  tairr XVI.17.6; acc. sg.

  tarra XVI.17.5; gen. sg.

·taít VII.5.6; see *do·tét*

talam XX.P.8.3; m.; earth, ground

tán f.; driving along, driving off; vn. of *do·aig*; *tán bó* cattle raid

  tánae XI.11.7; gen. sg.

tan XV.15.1; see *in tain*

tánacais-siu XI.11.9; XIII.13.9; see *do·ic*

tanae XI.11.7; see *tán*

táncatar I.1a.6; VII.5.3; see *do·ic*

tánic XIII.13.8; see *do·ic*

tár shame, disgrace; XIV.14.11

tar prep. + acc.; across, over, beyond; X.Gl.15

  dar VIII.6.9; XV.15.12; XVII.18.4; XVIII.20.8

  darsin V.3.13; + art. acc. sg.

  dara XVI.16.9; XVIII.20.3; *tar* + poss. pron. 3 sg.;

    dara aiss XVIII.20.3; over his back = from behind; see *aiss*

  dar hési X.Gl.14; + gen. = after; lit. over (the) track of . . . ; see *éiss*

  See Thurneysen G.530–31

tar cenn X.Gl.15; instead of; see *tar* and *cenn*

·tarat IX.8.1; XVII.18.1; see *do·beir*

tarb m.; bull; XV.15.11

·tarblaing XV.15.2; see *do·airling*

·tardda IV.3.9; see *do·beir*

·tarlae IX.8.1; see *do·cuirethar* and *im*

tárlaic X.10.11; see *do·léici*

tarra XVI.17.5; see *tairr*

tarsnu VIII.6.1;

  dia tarsnu across her (fr. adj. *tarsna* 'cross, transverse')

táthut V.3.14; see *a·tá*

tecat VI.4.6; XVI.17.1; see *do·ic*

tech nt.; house; VII.5.8;

  thech XIX.P.2.2; nom. sg. lenited by preceding *mo*

  thech IV.3.7; acc. sg. lenited by preceding *a*

  tige VII.5.7; XV.15.2; XVII.18.4; gen. sg.

  thige XI.11.7; XIII.13.6; gen. sg. lenited by preceding poss. pron. 2 sg. *do*

  taig VII.5.9; dat. sg.

  tig XIV.Gl.28; dat. sg.

  is·taig VIII.6.11; XVI.16.7; XVI.16.8; XVI.17.3; (in the house, inside)

  is·taig-seo XV.15.12; in this house

  is·tech XV.15.1; similarly fr. *isin tech* (acc. sg.; into the house, inside)

techt XVIII.20.3; see *téit*

techta I.1a.6; III.2.1; III.2.3; III.2.4; pl. nom.; messengers; pl. of *techt* (f.) vn. of *téit*

teilciud XI.Gl.18; see *do·léici*

teinnithir XIX.P.3.13; compd. of *tend* (adj.; firm, hard) and *ithir* (arable land, pasture-land, earth, ground)

téit (·tét) goes, goes to, attains, reaches; supplied by different stems;

  téit VI.4.4; pres. ind. 3 sg. abs.

  ·tét V.3.10; pres. ind. 3 sg. conj. (*na⟨d⟩·tét*)

  téti V.3.10; pres. ind. 3 sg. abs. w. suffixed pron. 3 sg. nt.; attains it

  tiagme-ni IX.Gl.10; rel. pres. ind. 1 pl.

  tiagmi-ni IX.Gl.10; pres. ind. 1 pl.

  no·théged II.1b.11; impf. 3 sg. (lenited to mark rel.)

  eirg XVI.16.1; impv. 2 sg.

  regaid XV.15.12; fut. 3 sg.

  luid VI.4.8; XVI.17.4; XVII.19.1; pret. 3 sg.

  lluid XI.11.11; pret. 3 sg. nasalized by preceding conjunction *co*^{n} (4)

  lotar VII.5.7; pret. 3 pl.

193

etha v.3.11; pret. pass. sg. rel.; it was come

do·cúadus-sa x.10.7; *ro*-perf. 1 sg. deut.

do·cúadais-siu x.9.7; *ro*-perf. 2 sg. w. emph. ptc. deut.

do·cúadaiss xiv.14.9; *ro*-perf. 2 sg. deut. *These last three forms are late hybrid forms made from the Classical OIr. pret.* do·coid *by addition of* s-pret. endings— *generalization of the* s-pret. *is one of the characteristics of later OIr.*

dechuid xiii.Gl.24; perf. 3 sg. proto.

condechaid xiii.13.12; perf. 3 sg. proto., nasalized by preceding conjunction *co*^{n} (4)

tiastar vi.4.10; pres. subj. pass. sg. rel.; it should be come, one should come

techt f.; vn.; *techt* xviii.20.3; dat. sg. after prep. *oc*

do·coí xii.Gl.20; 3 sg. pres. perf. subj. *See also the entry* do·tét *and Thurneysen G.472-73*

tellach nt.; hearth;
    tellaige ii.1b.9; nom. pl.

tellaige ii.1b.9; see *tellach*

Temair Lóchra residence of the kings of the *Érainn* (*Cland Dedad*) (see *Conganchness* and *Echbél*) in West Munster (Co. Kerry); ix.7.3

tempuil x.Gl.15; see *tempul*

tempul m.; temple;
    tempuil x.Gl.15

téora vi.4.3; see *trí* (2)

tes(s) xx.P.7.6; m.; heat, warmth

testa (to-ess-tá-) is lacking; viii.6.4

·tét v.3.10; see *téit*

téti v.3.10; see *téit*

thabairt iii.2.4; see *do·beir*

thairisem xi.11.1; see *tairisem*

thairisme x.9.1; xvi.17.2; see *tairisem*

thairiuc xv.15.5; see *do·airic*

thall xi.11.13; xii.12.12; see *do·alla*

thech iv.3.7; xix.P.2.2; see *tech*

thige xi.11.7; xiii.13.6; see *tech*

thír v.3.12; see *tír*

·thõetsat v.3.14; see *do·fuit*

thóib xii.Gl.21; see *tóib*

thoschith x.Gl.14; see *toschith*

thráth iv.3.1; xii.12.5; see *tráth*

thuaid xix.P.5.2; see *tuaid*

thúarcain xiii.13.5; see *túarcan*

thuath xvi.16.5; see *túath*

thuile iii.2.1; see *tol*

tiagme-ni ix.Gl.10; see *téit*

tiagmi·ni ix.Gl.10; see *téit*

tíastar vi.4.10; see *téit*

tib xx.P.10.3; see *tibid*

tibid touches, laughs at (w. *fri*);
    tib 3 sg. pres. conj.; xx.P.10.3

tig xiv.Gl.28; see *tech*

tige vii.5.7; xv.15.2; xvii.18.4; see *tech*

tinne m.; salted pork; ii.1b.10

tír nt.; land;
    thír v.3.12; dat. sg. (lenited by prep. *di*)
    tír xi.11.8; dat. sg.

tnúthach adj.; jealous, fierce, angry; xv.15.11

tóeb xix.P.3.3; see *tóib*

t'ógriar xviii.20.5; see *do* (1) and *ógriar*

tóib m.; side; xix.P.4.3;
    tóeb xix.P.3.3
    táib iv.3.1; dat. sg.
    thóib xii.Gl.21; nom. du. lenited by preceding *dá*
    fri tóeb xix.P.3.3; xix.P.3.12; + gen. = beside, near, along, in comparison with, in respect to

tóin ix.7.1; see *tón*

·toirchi x.9.10; see *do·roich*

toirthech xx.P.8.3; fruitful, fertile

toísech adj.; first;
    toísigiu xi.Gl.18; comp.; sooner

tóisigiu xi.Gl.18; see *toísech*

tol f.; wish, will;
    thuile iii.2.1; gen. sg. (lenited by preceding dat. sg. noun)

tomil x.Gl.13; see *do·meil*

tón f.; buttock, posterior;
    tóin ix.7.1; acc. pl.

·tongat xvi.16.5; see *tongid*

tongid (·toing) swears;
    tongu xvi.16.5; pres. ind. 1 sg. abs.
    ·tongat xvi.16.5; pres. ind. 3 pl.

tongu xvi.16.5; see *tongid*

tonn f.; wave; xix.P.4.2; gen. pl.

topur xx.P.8.1; m.; well, spring

toschith x.Gl.14; food;

thoschith x.Gl.14; initial lenited by poss. pron. 1 sg. *mo*

trá then, now; III.2.1; VI.4.5; VI.4.9; IX.8.3; XIII.Gl.22; XVII.18.4

tráth nt.; period of 3 days;

thráth IV.3.1; XII.12.5; acc. pl.

tre XIII.13.12; see *tri*

trebar adj.; clever; IV.3.8

trén adj.; strong; XV.15.11

tress m.; combat, fight;

tressa XV.15.11; gen. sg.

tressa XV.15.11; see *tress*

tret XI.11.11; XIII.13.12; see *tri* (1)

trethan XV.15.11; stormy sea

trethe II.1b.9; see *tri* (1)

tri (tre) (later *tria*) (1) prep. w. acc. lenites consonants, prefixes *h*- to vowels; through; VII.5.14;

tre XIII.13.12

tret XI.11.11; XIII.13.12; + poss. pron. 2 sg.

triat XIV.14.9; + poss. pron. 2 sg.

triut X.9.9; + pron. 2 sg.

trethe II.1b.9; + pron. 3 sg. f.

See Thurneysen G.533–34

trí (2) three; III.2.3; IV.3.1; VI.4.3; VII.5.11; VII.5.13; VII.5.14; XII.12.5;

téora VI.4.3; acc. f.

See VI.G.28 and Thurneysen G.242–43

trian nt.; one third; XIV.14.9

triat XIV.14.9; see *tri*

triut X.9.9; see *tri*

tromm adj.; heavy; XIX.P.3.13

troscud m.; fast, fasting; IV.3.2

trúastad m.; hewing, striking; XVII.18.5

tú VIII.Gl.7; independent stressed pron. 2 sg.; you

tuaid the north;

sair fo thuaid XIX.P.5.2; to the northeast

a túaith III.2.4; from the north; prep. *a*ⁿ (from, out of) + *tuaid*

antuaid XII.Gl.21; from the north

See IX.G.45 and Thurneysen G.305

túaith III.2.4; see *tuaid*

túaith V.3.13; see *túath*

túarcan f.; crushing, pounding; vn. of *do·fuairc*

thúarcain XIII.13.5; dat. sg. lenited by

preceding poss. pron. 1 sg. obj. of vn.

túargabar XIX.P.4.2; see *do·ócaib*

túath f.; people;

thuath XVI.16.5; nom. sg. (lenited by poss. pron. 1 sg. *mo*)

túaith V.3.13; acc. sg.

tuc XX.P.8.1; see *do·beir*

·tucad II.1b.12; see *do·beir*

tucad IV.3.7; V.3.15; VIII.6.1; see *do·beir*

tucus XII.12.5; see *do·beir*

·tudchad XIV.14.7; see *do·tét*

tuittit XIX.P.3.14; see *do·fuit*

turbaid f.; prevention, impediment; IV.3.7

turem f.; counting, enumeration;

turim V.3.11; dat. sg. (expressing standard of comp.)

turim V.3.11; see *turem*

tusso independent pron. 2 sg.; you; XV.15.8

U

úacht XX.P.6.2; m.; coldness, chill

úachtar nt.; upper part;

húachtar XIII.13.12; acc. sg.

uaib XIII.Gl.22; XIX.P.5.1; see *ó* (1)

úaim IV.3.8; XII.12.12; see *ó* (1)

úair XIII.13.13; XIV.14.10; see *úar*

úait X.Gl.13; XII.12.5; see *ó* (1)

úallach adj.; proud; VI.4.10

co húallach VI.4.6; adv.; proudly

úar XX.P.6.1; XX.P.10.1; adj.; cold

úar f.; time, hour;

úair XIII.13.13; XIV.14.10; dat. sg.

fo chét·óir XIII.13.5; at once, immediately

hi cét·óir III.2.3; at once

*húare*ⁿ XV.Gl.31; gen. sg. introducing a subordinate clause; because

See Thurneysen G.559

úas IX.8.2; see *ós*

uile all;

uili VI.4.11; VII.5.7; nom. pl.

huili I.1a.3; I.1a.7; acc. pl.

huili IX.Gl.12; nom. pl.

n-uile XIV.14.11; acc. sg. nasalized by preceding acc. sg. noun

Ulad I.1a.6; III.2.4; VI.4.8; VI.4.10; XVIII.20.6; see *Ulaid*

Ulaid xv.15.3; xvii.18.3; always pl.
(a) Ulstermen; (b) Ulster;
 Ulto vii.5.7; x.9.2; xvii.19.2; acc.
 Ulad i.1a.6; iii.2.4; vi.4.10; xviii.20.6;
 gen.
 Ultaib x.10.3; xi.11.2; xiii.13.2; dat.
 n-Ultaib x.9.6; dat. nasalized by preced-

ing poss. pron. 2 pl. *far^n*
 a Ulto xii.12.1; voc.
 Ulad vi.4.8; apparently acc. irregular
Ultaib x.9.6; x.10.3; xi.11.2; xiii.13.2; see
 Ulaid
Ulto vii.5.7; xii.12.1; xvii.19.2; see *Ulaid*
urchor m.; cast, throw; x.10.11

index

Reference is to page numbers. The index lists primarily grammatical categories and inflections. The table of contents may be consulted for references to general topics; the glossary for references to individual words.

Index